anshah

Kashan

Isfahan

Dizful

Shushtär

Yezd

R ... A

Mohammerah
Abadah
Bandar-i-Shahpur

Saidabad

BUBIAN I.
FELEJE I.
KARAGH I.
Kuwait
Bushire

Shiraz

Niris

Firuzabad

Lar

Maghris

BU ALI I.

PERSIAN

Lingeh

KISHM I.

Ras Musa

Qatif
Ras Tannurah
Manama
Ras Beccan

KENN I.

TOMB IS.

Sha'am
Leyrrah

Wab
Djulz
WARDENS
BAHREIN
Meborraa Okai
Hofuf
QATAR
Doha
SATIEM I.
Bedaa

ROMOSA I.

SIER ABOU NEID

GULF

Sharjah

Fajirah

GU

Shaabar
Dhalum

EAST INDIA
COMPANY.
IS.

Abu Debi

Balaimi

Sohar
Sohain

OMAN

Hajar

Katan

TRUCIAL

Senanah

Obri
Nizzawh
Harrara

RUBA' AL KHALI

MW01026897

Hamadan

Syrian
Puimra
Defar
Dumer
Dusa
Tekrit
Serifa
Istabilat
Hit
Qubaisa
Rannadi
Samarra
Khannqin
Kizil Ribat
Baquba
BAGHDAD
Kermanshah
Kom
Kashan
Isfahan

IRAQ
(MESOPOTAMIA)
Karbala
Hillah
Babylon
Twin Rivers
Kut el Imara
Tigris
Euphrates
Dizful
Shushtar
Yezd

Ezrak
EL HAMED
(Stony Plain)
Nejef or Meshed Ali
Al Diwaniya
Lamlum
Samave
Jubellah
Amara
Al Qurna
Daffas
Mohammerah
Abadan
Bandar-i-Shahpur

Jaddat 'Ar'ar
An Nasiriya
Souk eab Shuyukh
Qasr Uthaimie
Sobeir
Basra

Birkat el Jumaimah
Dahman
BUBIAN I.
FELEJE I.
KARAGH I.
Shiraz

lachasiya
Jauf
Bir Assab
Sabukah
Kuwait
Bushire
Niris

KINGDOM
Jobbah
JEBEL
Hail
Hazafah
Maghris
KUWAIT
BU ALI I.
Lar
Lingeh

el Taima
Kefar
SHAMMAR
Kefd
Kowarah
Eyoon
Zulfah
Mejniah
En Nueim
Wabu
Ras Tannurah
Qatif
Manama
Ras Reccan
KENN I.
TOMB IS.
Sh

Modain Salih
Af-Ala
Surah
Rass
Shakra
Hoolah
Djols
BAHREIN
ROMOSA I.

OF
Aneizeh
Sedus
Meborraa
Okai
Hofua
WARDENS
SATIEH I.
Doha
Bedaa
SIER ABOU SEID

Khaibar
Sadiwa
Onman

MEDINA
Ghurab
Ghomeis
Shaarka
Dereyeoyah
Riyadh
Shaabar
EAST INDIA COMPANY IS.
Abu Debis
Balam

Bedr Honem
Kerah
Sarsa
Manfunah
Naam
Dhalum
Hajar
Katan

Suwerikiya
Kurfah
Hauta
TRUCIAL OMAN

Dhool Hatifa
SAUDI
Tropic of Cancer

Kholeis
Ozal
Kobo
Merkab
Laila

Amru
Hararah
Soluomeh L.

MECCA
ARABIA
Zaimeh
Leileh

Taif
Tarabah
Warada L.
Farah
RUBA' AL KHALI
(Great Sandy Desert)

Mekhra
Kaina
Ranelh
Engaia
Mefeleh
Dam

Doga
Roheita
Kalun
Debaba
Letan

Qunfuda
Tenunha
Selayah
Ibi

Halli
Bel Asman

Tabab
Derb Soiman
Wakasha
Thoran

Sanian
Boghasen

Duzan
Abu Arish
Saadeh
Beled Barath

FARASAN IS.
Kaiwan
Oasis of Khab
Majil

SAMUAK I.
Khamir
Amran
Mareb
Marcha
Sawa
Shibam
Tarim
Jaizer
Kamar Bay
Risut

KAMARAN I. (Brit.)
Loheia
Sana
Hotah
Haura
Reidaq
Saihut
Ras Furtak
Kishin

HANISH IS.
Hais
Nissab
Shihair
Misenat

Hodeida
Doran
Surajeh
Biedah
Habban
Hajar
Mukalla

Shuram
Dhamar
Yerim
Reda
Naab
British
Protectorate
Haura

Beit el Fakih
Zebid
Ibb
Raha
Shukra
Sherm Magatim
Sheikh Hurba

Edd
Mocha (Mokha)
Taeizo
Dhala
Birgheg

PERIM I. (Brit.)
ADEN
GULF OF ADEN
Tamridah

FRENCH
Djibouti
Tajura
ARD EL KURI
SOCOTRA (British)

SOMALILAND
Bab el Mandeb
C. Guardaful

OPIA
Las Guri
Meid
ITALIAN

RED SEA
ERITREA
YEMEN
HADRAMAUT

Arabian
KNIGHT

COLONEL BILL EDDY USMC

AND THE RISE OF AMERICAN POWER

IN THE MIDDLE EAST

THOMAS W. LIPPMAN

Selwa Press

Selwa 🌴 Press
www.SelwaPress.com

First Edition
LCCN: 2001012345
ISBN: 9780970115720
Copyright © 2008 by Thomas W. Lippman

Lippman, Thomas W.

    Arabian knight : Colonel Bill Eddy USMC and the rise of American power in the Middle East / Thomas W. Lippman. -- 1st ed. -- Vista, CA : Selwa Press, c2008.

       p. ; cm.
       ISBN: 978-0-9701157-2-0
       Includes bibliographical references and index.

       1. Eddy, William A. (William Alfred), 1896-1962. United States--Foreign relations--Middle East. 3. Middle East--Foreign relations--United States. 4.World War, 1939-1945--Campaigns--Africa, North. 5. Middle East--Politics and government--20th century. I. Title.

DS63.2.U5 L566 2008   2008926323
327.73/056--dc22   0809

Photo of Eddy: Taken by Foto-Venue in Tangier, 1942. Courtesy of
    Leatherneck Magazine
Inset elements: Courtesy of *Leatherneck Magazine*, National Archive,
    and T.C. Barger Collection
Map Element: Courtesy of the American Map Company
Endpaper maps: Courtesy of the American Map Company

Book Design by Charles McStravick

Selwa Press 1101 Portola St. Vista, CA 92084
Printed in the United States of America
10 9 8 7 6 5 4 3 2 1

Contents

MAPS

ACKNOWLEDGMENTS

Writing a biography usually requires reconstructing the life and times of a person one has never met. It cannot be done without the help of many people. I am especially grateful to the Friends of the Princeton University Library, who generously supported my research. I benefited greatly from the enthusiastic assistance provided by Daniel J. Linke, curator of public policy papers at Princeton, and his staff at the Seeley G. Mudd Manuscript Library, who responded with alacrity to all my requests. Staff archivists and historians at the National Archives of the United States rendered indispensable assistance, as did librarians and other colleagues at the Middle East Institute in Washington. I owe debts of gratitude to the relatives and friends of Bill Eddy who gave generously of their time and memories, and to Timothy J. Barger, without whose support this book would not have been written. I thank them all.

A Note on Arabic Words and Names

*T*here is no universally accepted form of transliteration of Arabic words and names into English. I have used the versions commonly found in American newspapers and magazines. No attempt has been made to reproduce the diacritical marks, glottal stops, long vowelings and unique consonants of the original, as is done in academic texts, except where they are part of the standard media transliteration. In Arab countries where France was the primary external power, some names are best known in their French transliterations, such as Camille Chamoun, and those are used here. In quotations of writings by others, I have retained the transliterations of the original. Thus Muhammad may sometimes appear as Mohammed, Muslim as Moslem, Koran as Qur'an, Jeddah as Jidda and Faisal as Feisal or Faysal.

For many years the founding king of modern Saudi Arabia, Abdul Aziz ibn Saud, was known in the West as Ibn Saud, as in the title of Bill Eddy's monograph *F.D.R. Meets Ibn Saud.* In recent times it has become standard practice to refer to him by given name, Abdul Aziz, as is done with other princes of the House of Saud, who are known by given name and patronymic: Fahd ibn Abdul Aziz (Fahd, son of Abdul Aziz), Bandar bin Sultan (Bandar, son of Sultan.) In this book he is King Abdul Aziz, except in quotations from other writers who called him Ibn Saud.

INTRODUCTION

"Bill Eddy was probably the nearest thing
the United States has had to a Lawrence of Arabia."

— PHILIP J. BARAM,
The Department of State in the Middle East

"In the development of America's relations with
the Middle East the early missionaries played a unique role. . . .
In terms of American awareness and knowledge of the area,
the prime source of information has been—until quite recently—
the missionaries who lived and traveled there and who
learned the languages out of professional necessity.
As late as World War II, the U.S. Government drew heavily
on the experience of men of missionary background."

— DAVID H. FINNIE,
Pioneers East: The Early American Experience in the Middle East

Toward the middle of the twentieth century, two countries that were so unlike in history and custom as to be from different stages of civilization forged one of the world's least likely alliances. The United States, beacon of democracy, the richest nation on earth and a military and industrial superpower, joined forces with Saudi Arabia, an impoverished, remote and autocratic kingdom whose people were mostly illiterate, in a mutually beneficial economic and strategic arrangement that has shaped the development of the Arab world for seven decades and endures even now despite deep strains and innumerable challenges.

That alliance did not just happen. It came about because a few visionary individuals recognized its potential benefits. Among these were senior executives of Standard Oil Company of California, who defied the economic gloom of the Great Depression to invest millions in an unfamiliar land; King Abdul Aziz ibn Saud, the founder of modern Saudi Arabia, who recognized that his country would never progress without Western technology and investment and defied the opposition of his own people to acquire them; President Franklin D. Roosevelt, who in the closing months of World War II and of his own life looked beyond the war and into a more promising future for Saudi Arabia and new opportunities there for America; and William Alfred Eddy, Marine Corps officer, war hero, spymaster and diplomat, the catalyst who translated Roosevelt's vision for Saudi Arabia into reality.

To those who value the unique relationship between the United States and the desert kingdom, and to the many citizens of both countries who have profited from it, Eddy is a great unsung hero. He lived among Arabs from Morocco to Yemen. He knew and understood them like few other Americans, and was fluent in multiple dialects of their language. He respected their faith and their culture, and he foresaw with startling prescience many of the trends and ideas that would mark the troubled contemporary history of the Middle East. He was also a prominent member of the inter-agency U.S. government team that created the Central Intelligence Agency, never imagining it would become the reviled source of so much anti-American sentiment around the region.

At the time of William Alfred Eddy's birth in 1896 in Sidon, on the Mediterranean seacoast of what is now Lebanon, only a handful of Americans were living or doing business in the Arab world. Most of them, including Eddy's parents, were Protestant missionaries in Syria and Lebanon, then part of the Ottoman Empire. They made few converts, but their influence was widespread and durable as they brought education to generations of Syrian and Lebanese young people, created the American University of Beirut, and introduced such innovations as the sewing machine and the potato.

The official U.S. government presence in the region was negligible, as was American commercial activity. In 1906 the United States participated with twelve European nations in a conference in Spain designed to shore up French rule in Morocco against competing claims asserted by Germany. And in the aftermath of World War I, in which the United States participated and swung the outcome against Germany and its allies, President Woodrow Wilson personally took part in the negotiations over the remnants of the defeated Ottoman Empire and the disposition of its Arab territories. Aside from those events, Washington mostly kept its hands off the Arab and Muslim worlds.

Yet by the end of Eddy's eventful life in 1962, the United States was the dominant strategic and economic power in the Middle East. The Ottoman Empire had died with World War I and the colonial empires of Britain and France were passing into history. The outside power that mattered most to the Arab world was the United States; its only rival for influence was the Soviet Union. For better or worse, the United States—through intervention in the 1956 Suez war, its support for Israel, its alliance with Saudi Arabia and preeminent role in the oil industry, its Cold War manipulation of regional politics, and its strategic initiatives such as the Eisenhower Doctrine—had come to dominate the landscape.

To understand how and why that transformation came about, it is enlightening to retrace Eddy's career. He was an influential and sometimes crucial participant in many of the events that led the United States into its seemingly permanent entanglement in the Middle East. In others, he was a manipulator behind the scenes and a skillful bureaucratic agitator. Philip Baram's description of him as "probably the nearest thing the United States has had to a Lawrence of Arabia" perhaps romanticizes Eddy's achievements a bit, but it also captures Eddy's life as an American who believed in the Arabs, won their confidence, and forged enduring ties with them to the benefit of his country.

Far from seeing Muslims as hostile and inevitably coming into conflict with "the West," Eddy envisioned a grand rapprochement, a "moral alliance" of the monotheistic peoples of Christianity and Islam, such as he believed Richard Lion-Heart had forged with Saladin in the era of the Crusades.

This vision would never be fulfilled—Cold War politics and the American alliance with Israel intervened—yet even today, when U.S. policies in the Middle East have engendered anger and anti-American sentiment across the Arab world, there remains a deep reservoir of admiration and even affection for Americans and for American ideals. That this is so is attributable at least in part to the legacy of individual Americans who have worked respectfully alongside the Arabs to their mutual benefit for the past 75 years.

It has been unfashionable almost since the creation of Israel in 1948 to look back with admiration on Americans of the twentieth century who cultivated the Arabs and appreciated their way of life and way of thinking. In this age of terrorism, when Muslims in general and Arabs in particular inspire fear among ordinary Americans, esteem for the Arabs and their culture can seem almost unpatriotic. Yet the Americans who sought and nurtured strong ties with the Arabs were justifiably proud of their work, and who is to say how the world might be different today if their views had gained wider currency?

The list of these Americans, who forged relationships with the Arabs that transcended politics, is perhaps not as long as they and their Arab friends would wish, but is nonetheless substantial. It includes prominent Americans as well as those mostly unknown to the public. Not everyone would agree about who should be on this honorable roster, but certainly any such list would name Tom Barger, a pioneer of American oil development in Saudi Arabia and later chief executive of the Arabian American Oil Company, or ARAMCO; Steve Bechtel, the construction magnate; Malcolm Kerr, the scholar who gave his life to the American University of Beirut; the diplomats Parker Hart, Hermann Eilts, and Talcott Seelye; General Richard Lawrence, the first American adviser to the Saudi Arabian National Guard; the academic and historian Bayard Dodge and much of the Dodge family; Mike Ameen, the gregarious oilman who was one of the first Americans to live in Riyadh; the journalist Wilton Wynn; the intelligence operative Ray Close; Karl Twitchell, the engineer whose explorations of the Arabian peninsula laid the foundations for U.S. influence in Saudi Arabia and Yemen; Charles R. Crane, the plumbing fixtures heir whose fascination with the Middle East opened critical pathways of American influence; Dr. Louis Dame, the medical missionary who treated King Abdul Aziz and roamed the Arabian peninsula ministering to the medically desperate; and William Alfred Eddy.

These people led exotic, adventurous lives in far-off, mysterious and often dangerous places. The biography of any one of them would make an interesting story. This is Bill Eddy's.

Chapter One

FRANCE

When William Alfred Eddy began his college studies nearly a century ago, the world was at peace. By the time he graduated, the world was in flames, caught up in the greatest armed conflict in history, and the United States had declared war on Germany. Within a few weeks after commencement he was a participant in the conflagration as a United States Marine. The thrill of leading men in combat and admiration for the Marine Corps would become defining hallmarks of his eventful life, along with his love for his wife, Mary, and his esteem and affection for a people almost unknown to Americans at the time, the Arabs.

In the spring of 1917, Eddy and his fellow graduates of Princeton emerged from their Ivy League cloister into a world vastly different from the one in which they had matriculated four years earlier. While they were peacefully pursuing their studies, the entire global order of the nineteenth century was disintegrating. The appalling carnage of World War I, the Great War, was devastating Europe. Dynasties were collapsing, colonial empires crumbling. Britain and France were spilling the lifeblood of their imperial power in the lethal trenches of Europe's battlefields. The Russian Revolution had begun.

In the Western world, only the United States was on the rise, propelled by its economic might and by German provocation into casting off the preferred neutrality of President Woodrow Wilson and assuming an uncomfortable global prominence. On April 6, 1917, the United States declared war on Germany and committed itself to participate in the great European conflict, by which it was until then almost untouched except by the German torpedoes fired at American ships. American troops would deploy to Europe for the first time, to join Britain, France, Italy and Russia in the epic conflict against Germany, Austria-Hungary, and the Ottoman Turks.

Industrial and agricultural powerhouse though it was, the country was ill prepared for war. Its armed forces were undermanned and lacked weapons, ships, transport facilities, aircraft and even uniforms. As the historian Robert Asprey put it, "Perhaps no world power has ever been so badly prepared for war as was America in 1917." That was soon to change as the country mobilized.

Congress had anticipated the U.S. entry into the war and in the late summer of 1916 passed a bill authorizing substantial increases in the country's military strength. By the following spring that buildup was underway.

At the time that law was passed, the entire United States Marine Corps consisted of 10,265 men—344 officers and 9,921 enlisted men. The law authorized an increase to a total strength of 15,578, and in the event of a national emergency to 18,093. On the day war was declared, the Corps was composed of 462 commissioned officers, 49 warrant officers, and 13,214 enlisted men on active duty, a total of 13,725. By midsummer 1918 the strength of the Corps would rise to 75,101.

In the months before war was declared the Corps expanded slowly, recruiting energetic, patriotic young men who could meet the Marines' rigorous standards of physical ability and combat performance. Then as war neared, America's military ranks swelled with volunteers and, after Congress passed a conscription law in the spring of 1917, with draftees; those drafted could apply to serve in the Marines, but the Corps remained rigorously selective. (The Corps accepted only about one-fourth of those who sought to join between April 1917 and November 1918.) The Marine Corps more than any other service attracted educated and promising young men, and especially student athletes. By some accounts more than half the young men who became Marines during the buildup of 1917-18 were college graduates. Bill Eddy, who had played varsity basketball at Princeton, fit the profile of the ideal young Marine.

In many ways he was an unlikely candidate to become a warrior or military hero. His background and family history were scholarly and religious, as were his professional aspirations. For generations his family had not even lived in the United States, let alone fought in its wars. The Eddys were Presbyterian missionaries in Syria and what is now Lebanon, where Bill Eddy was born.

This cadre of American missionaries was small, and its religious influence was limited because it was difficult, as well as politically ill-advised, to convert Muslims to Christianity. Most of those who accepted their teachings were already Christians, but of other denominations. Nevertheless, the missionaries' historic influence was strong and permanent because of their impact on the education of the local Arabs. The missionaries opened schools for girls as well as boys, wrote and distributed textbooks, and installed Arabic-language printing presses to bring gramatically correct books to a population among whom the language was decaying. As George Antonius wrote in his classic book *The Arab Awakening*, "The educational activities of the American missionaries in that early period [of the mid-1800s] had, among many virtues, one outstanding merit; they gave the pride of place to Arabic and, once they had committed themselves to teaching it, put their shoulders with vigour to the task of providing an adequate literature. In that, they were the pioneers; and because of that, the intellectual effervescence which marked the first stirring of the Arab revival owes most to their labours." They were the first

Americans to influence the thinking and the worldview of any substantial community of Arabs.

Bill Eddy's father, William King Eddy, died while young Bill was still in elementary school, but he left to his children a legacy of esteem and affection for the Arabs who surrounded them, feelings that were reciprocated in the community. E. Alexander Powell, an American consular officer in the Ottoman territories who represented the U.S. government at the elder Eddy's funeral, later wrote that "Though it has been my lot to follow to the grave the remains of many of the great ones of the earth, I have never witnessed so spontaneous an outpouring of grief as was accorded to this simple missionary. It seemed as if all Palestine and Syria had come to do him honor."

Other than that group of missionaries and a team of medical missionaries who created a hospital on the Persian Gulf island of Bahrain early in the twentieth century, Americans were scarce in the Arab world in the years of Eddy's boyhood. What we know today as the Middle East, including the Levant, the Arabian peninsula, Iraq and what is now Israel, was far outside the American sphere of political or economic influence.

Aside from a naval war with the Barbary pirates of North Africa in the early days of the American republic—touched off by raids on American shipping and by President Thomas Jefferson's refusal to continue paying the tribute demanded by the Dey of Algiers and the Pasha of Tripoli—the United States had focused its attentions elsewhere, leaving the Mediterranean, the Levant and the Arabian Peninsula to the Ottoman Turks, the British and the French. Individual adventurers and sometimes small groups of Americans made forays into the region; the most notable was a group of several dozen Civil War military officers from both sides who went to Egypt in the 1870s to serve with the Khedive's army and train his troops. As a government, however, the United States was not much involved.

This American absence was a natural outcome of the Middle East's history before World War II. Geography, commerce, and scholarly contacts forged durable ties between the Arabic speaking peoples of the Middle East and the seafaring powers of Europe that long predated the existence of the United States. And on the U.S. side, Americans were busy elsewhere, beginning with the development of their own country west of the Appalachian Mountains, a process that consumed most of the nineteenth century. By the mid-1800s the United States had commercial treaties with Morocco, Muscat and Ottoman Turkey, but the vast American domestic market limited the need to export. Certainly the United States had no need for Egyptian cotton, or for fruits and vegetables from the Levant. American merchants and industrialists discovered nearby economic prospects in Central America and the Carribbean; there was no urgent reason to take on enterprises in the faraway, unfamiliar Arab world. In most Arab capitals there was no official U.S. government presence or diplomatic mission. The missionaries were on their own.

On the streets of Sidon, Eddy's playmates were mostly Arabic-speaking local children. He and other missionary offspring grew up speaking colloquial Arabic as easily as English. In their generation, Eddy and his contemporaries from the Syria missions became the core of the small cadre of Arabic-speaking regional specialists in the State Department and other U.S. government agencies.

These Americans were comfortable in Damascus, Aleppo, Beirut and Cairo. Most of them spoke a major European language as well as Arabic, and their friends were cosmopolitan Arabs who were citizens of the Mediterranean. They brought with them an understanding of, and sympathy for, the Arabs, and a belief that an era of progress and enlightenment—"The Arab Awakening," as George Antonius called it—was under way in the Arab world. The region they knew as Syria, which included not only today's Lebanon but also parts of Palestine and of what are now Jordan and Iraq, "constituted much more than a home," as Robert Kaplan wrote in *The Arabists*. "It was almost a transplanted version of New England itself: a glorifed tableau of Ivy League brahmins, each with a foothold in the Lebanese mountains, a magical kingdom of Protestant families brimming with a spirit of adventure, rectitude, and religious idealism"—the essence of Bill Eddy's character—"where the twentieth century would not fully arrive until 1948."

The reference to 1948 acknowledges a watershed event in the careers of American Arabists. As Kaplan suggests and as would be expected, their background of life among the Arabs would lead many of these Americans in later years to oppose the 1948 partition of Palestine and the creation of Israel; they lived to see the word "Arabist" become a term of opprobrium in their home country.

Eddy did not come to the United States until it was time for high school. His parents sent him to the College of Wooster, a Presbyterian school in Ohio with its own preparatory academy for teenagers and strong links to the missionary community. The history posted on the college's web site says that Wooster, founded in 1866, "has long emphasized international education. An unusually high percentage of its early graduates went overseas as missionaries, and soon not only their sons and daughters, but also the students from their schools, were enrolling at Wooster as students. There were special houses for these students where every occupant spoke two or three languages and where friendships developed among students from Asia, Africa, and Latin America."

Another bilingual child of missionaries attending Wooster at the time was Mary Emma Garvin, whose parents worked in Chile. She would become Bill Eddy's wife, and would be his closest friend and most faithful traveling companion throughout his adventurous life.

He stayed at Wooster through his sophomore year of college, then transferred to Princeton. This was a logical move because his father, his brother, and many uncles and cousins were Princetonians, and the Princeton Theological seminary, a Presbyterian institution, had extensive ties to the missionary community— Eddy's father had obtained his divinity degree there. Yet the precise reasons for the transfer are not clear from the Eddy family correspondence or from Princeton's records. Before 1920, Princeton did not have a formal admissions process and thus the university's archives contain no documents from Eddy himself explaining why he wanted to move. There is, however, a tantalizing letter dated February 15, 1915, from Eddy's older brother Condit N. Eddy (class of 1912) asking that the university consider admitting Bill Eddy on a scholarship because "Conditions are not satisfactory at Wooster."

JOINING THE CORPS

Nothing in Bill Eddy's entry in the 1917 *Nassau Herald*, Princeton's yearbook, gave any hint of the course his life would take. The yearbook described him as "Presbyterian. Democrat" and recorded his participation on the varsity basketball team, work with local Boy Scouts, and other activities. His "Eating Club," as Princeton's fraternity-like associations of upperclassmen were called, was Dial Lodge. But it is apparent from family correspondence that by the time he was a senior the young scholar had weightier subjects on his mind than college life. He was thinking about the looming war and how he would take part in it. He enlisted as a private in the New Jersey National Guard, and a month after graduation was already in Officer Candidate School at Fort Myer, Virginia. But he and handful of Princeton friends had a higher aspiration: they wanted to be Marines.

The Marine Corps at the time was authorized to give direct commissions to a certain number of young men who had not attended one of the military service academies or had other officer-preparation training. Admission to this group was competitive, and applicants were required to submit letters of recommendation. The most effusive in Eddy's file was from Charles A. Robinson, principal of Peekskill Military Academy in New York.

"For the past three summers Mr. Eddy has been a member of my staff of masters at Camp Pok-O'-Moonshine, teaching German and having complete charge of the department of Manual Training," Robinson wrote. "He filled this position most acceptably and efficiently. Incidentally, he was frequently mentioned as the most popular master on the staff. Mr. Eddy combines in an unusual way the qualities of an all-around man: strong personality, splendid physique, splendid athlete, scholarly, original, interesting and a Christian gentleman."

A letter from Elias Compton, dean of the College of Wooster, described Eddy as "a young man of decided intellectual ability, high scholarship, excellent moral character and unusual qualifications for leadership." This ability to win the approbation of superiors and the loyalty of students and staff members would distinguish Eddy's entire professional career. He was gregarious, witty and principled, qualities that earned the admiration of colleagues both American and Arab.

Eddy wrote directly to Brigadier General John A. Lejeune, then assistant to the commandant of the Corps and later the top Marine himself, asking him to expedite his application. Eddy noted in his letter that he needed proof of his acceptance into the Marine Corps in order to obtain his discharge from the National Guard.

On June 6, 1917, Eddy was notified by Lejeune that he had "successfully passed the examination for appointment as a temporary second lieutenant in the U.S. Marine Corps." On July 4, he reported to the Marine Corps rifle training range at Winthrop, Maryland. According to his military records, he was 21 years old, stood 72.5 inches tall, and weighed 158 pounds.

In handwritten entries in his first "Fitness Report," covering the period from July 4 to July 18, his first two weeks of active duty, he listed his language competence: "As interpreter, Arabic and Egyptian, 3.5. [Egyptians of course speak Arabic, but in a distinctive dialect.] German 2.5. As translator, German 3." He was asked what type of duty he would prefer once commissioned; he listed intelligence officer, military attaché, acquiring foreign languages and "commanding Marine detachment afloat." He specified that if assigned to military attaché duty, he preferred "an Arabic-speaking country."

After rifle instruction at Winthrop, Eddy was transferred to the new base the Marine Corps was developing on the banks of the Potomac River at Quantico, Virginia, where he continued his officer training until October. In the next bunk was a Notre Dame graduate, Francis Patrick Mulcahy, later a Marine aviation hero of both world wars and a lieutenant general, who became a lifelong friend.

Mulcahy was Eddy's kind of man—tough and daring, but also thoughtful and religious. He was a pioneer of combat aviation, flying bombing missions in France during World War I when aircraft were new to warfare. He later commanded aviation units in Central America and in the Pacific during World War II.

"He is more than a friend," Eddy would write to his son, also a Marine officer, in the last months of World War II. "We entered the Corps together, had adjacent bunks at Quantico in 1917, and used to sit out under the stars and tackle theology (he is Roman Catholic) until taps. He is equally competent with hard liquor."

In his "Fitness Report" for this Quantico period, Eddy upgraded his skill level in Arabic to 3.8; on the question of which type of duty he would prefer, this time he listed only one: "Line Officer Infantry."

There is no way to know the reason for that change. Eddy was a prolific writer of letters throughout his life, but his papers contain virtually nothing from these first months in the Marine Corps. Even today young officers in training in the Corps have little time for introspective correspondence. In fact, Eddy's papers are skimpier with information about his World War I experience than about almost any other period of his adult life. But the files do contain a telegram he sent on October 4 to Mary Garvin back in Wooster: "Sail for france Monday leave quantico Sunday come on first train tonight to washington borrow money for ticket come at once with suitcase wait for me at union station washington will meet you there if you dont find me inquire for telegram at station wire reply here at once tomorrow the only day we can have together bill."

She did as he asked, and they were married the following day. For the rest of his life, his devotion to Mary was a constant theme. In public he was not a demonstrative man, but his private letters to her are rich in expressions of love and admiration.

On October 17, he sailed from Philadelphia aboard the USS *DeKalb*. Destination: France, epicenter of the war. Assignment: Headquarters Company of the newly formed 6th Marine Regiment, as intelligence officer. The 6th Marines were one of two regiments in the 4th Brigade, which in turn was a component of a combined Marine-Army contingent that formed the 2nd Division of the American Expeditionary Force, under the overall command of General John J. Pershing. The 2nd Division consisted of two regiments of army infantry and the Marines of the 4th Brigade—which itself consisted of the 5th and 6th Regiments and the 6th Machine Gun Battalion. Marine historians say this unusual combined force was created over the objections of Pershing, who was opposed to the deployment of Marines to the European battlefront.

"It was no great secret," George B. Clark wrote in *Devil Dogs: Fighting Marines of World War I*, "that Pershing was not in favor of

accepting any Marines in France and only took what he couldn't
refuse because of the political and interservice machinations" of
Major General George Barnett, commandant of the Marine Corps,
who was determined that the Corps would take part in the conflict.
Barnett, a career Marine who had served in China, the Philippines
and Cuba, became commandant of the corps in February 1914
and held that post throughout the war. Just from the stern-visaged
photos on his family's web site it is easy to understand that he
was not going to allow his Marine Corps to be excluded from the
action in France.

None of that Washington intrigue mattered much to Eddy
and the other young Marines who throughout that fall and winter
gathered and trained in France in preparation for the combat to
come. (Not until February 1918 would the entire 6th Regiment be
in place.) Green troops as they were, they were busy learning the
arts of war; even their experienced noncommissioned officers
had never faced mustard gas, which the Germans were firing in
artillery shells. As the regiment's units arrived, "Intensive training for trench warfare commenced at once," according to "A Brief
History of the Sixth Regiment," a document preserved among
Eddy's papers. (This is an anonymous typescript, but appears to
have been written by Eddy—a draft of part of it in his handwriting
is in the same file.)

> This training was very severe, due both to the strenuous
> schedule and the winter season which set in about this time.
> However grueling as it seemed then, it so hardened the men that
> they were able to bear up under the strain of continuous fighting
> which later became their lot. The schedule included hikes, close
> order drill, extended order, bayonet fighting, games, practice
> in both rifle and hand grenade throwing, rifle range practice,
> storming trench systems, taking strong points, defense against
> gas attacks and all modes of signalling then in use. Up to that
> time the uniform had been campaign hats, but now came the
> equipment that men at the front were never without: helmets
> and gas masks. The men were required to become proficient in
> doing everything both with and without gas masks.

The Marines' skill at accurate long-range rifle fire would come as a shock to the Germans a few months later.

Once assembled, the American forces were not thrown immediately into combat. The battlefield was largely static in the late winter of 1917. Millions had died over the previous three and a half years, to no conclusive effect. Victories in famous battles for one side or the other—Tannenberg, Gallipoli, Caporetto—changed the balance a bit here and there, at a soul-deadening cost in casualties, but no definitive outcome was in sight. At this point in the conflict the greatest danger for most troops came from disease, not enemy fire.

The French, battered by three years of trench warfare on their own territory, were impatient at the pace of the American buildup—they wanted the Americans to reinforce them in the trenches. The Americans under Pershing wanted to maintain independence of command, and Pershing saw no value in throwing American troops into the same inconclusive trench warfare that had inflicted so many casualties on the French and British. Thus by the time Eddy arrived in France, the American units were in a combat zone but not much in combat.

Nearly a century later, it often seems difficult to make sense out of the Great War, a conflict that involved Serbia, Romania, Belgium, Bulgaria, and several countries in Africa and the Middle East as well as the great powers; historians still argue about what caused the war and why the opposing sides lined up as they did. From the Arab perspective, it is useful to think of it as it was described by the historian Charles Issawi: the first great spasm of "the European Civil War of 1914-45," which "by fatally weakening European imperialism and stimulating Asian and African nationalism, allowed the [Middle East] region to regain both political and economic independence." That is, Muslim Arabs could think of the wars that wracked Europe more or less continuously from 1914 through 1945, including the Spanish Civil War, as one long fratricidal conflict among colonialists; the Arabs were largely indifferent to the outcome, but hoped to take advantage of it to gain independence.

And indeed those three decades of war in Europe did put an end to the era of European colonialism in the Arab world, but a new outside power appeared in place of the Europeans. By the end of World War II, the exhaustion and devastation of Europe after 31 years of nearly continuous bloodshed and turmoil would open a door for the United States—undamaged, robust, economically vigorous—to enter a part of the world where formerly there had been little opportunity.

THE GERMAN SPRING OFFENSIVE, 1918

By the time American troops arrived in France, the nature of combat was changing as motorized vehicles replaced the horse, the field telephone supplanted the courier, and submarines, tanks and airplanes were brought into service, but it was a political upheaval, not action on the ground, that shattered the stalemate. After the triumph of the Bolshevik revolution in the fall of 1917, Russia sought an armistice with Germany and withdrew from the war, freeing dozens of German divisions for redeployment to the western front. The following spring, beginning on March 21, 1918, the Germans unleashed five offensives along the lines from Ypres in northern Belgium to Rheims in France in a final all-out bid for victory.

The first, known as "Michael," achieved an advance of almost forty miles, a huge gain by the standards of this dug-in war, but then stalled. Then the German High Command ordered the attacks code-named Georgette, in Flanders, aimed at rolling the British forces there back to the English channel. This time the greatest gain was twelve miles. (Perhaps the most significant outcome of Georgette was the death of Manfred von Richtofen, the German flying ace known as the Red Baron.) The Germans were squandering their best troops without achieving a breakthrough. Then came the third offensive, known as Blucher-York, in the Marne Valley of France.

Among Eddy's papers is a small battered French datebook with a few handwritten notes from his service in France. On February 27, 1918, the feast of Saint Catherine, he wrote in pencil: "When spring comes 'round again, on some scarred slope of battered hill, I have a rendezvous with death." It was a rendezvous he came close to keeping several times that spring and summer. The 4th Brigade was about to get its first taste of combat.

The Marines were deployed across a large swath of territory southeast of Verdun, where the French introduced them to the reality of life in the trenches and then pulled back. According to *A Brief History of the 6th Marines* by Lieutenant General William K. Jones, "they learned quickly the grim realities of trench warfare—cooties, rats, 'wire parties,' raids, and poison gas. . . . They also learned the difficulties of relieving troops in front-line positions, how to coordinate the fire of their weapons with supporting artillery fire, and how best to deal with German raiding parties." Pershing wanted action, not static trench duty, but he was not the supreme allied commander and did not have complete freedom to control the AEF's deployment.

In his notebook, the young Lieutenant Eddy jotted notes on the men under his command: "3d battalion intelligence personnel, Sgt. Beckwith . . . in charge, Sgt. Barrett. . . . sniper." He listed the corporals and privates—Truitt, Dail, Kelly, Dunkelberger, Elliott, Deibel—and jotted down this observation. "3 scouts short. Scouts organized into 3 working groups. Have 8 expert riflemen with telescopic sights. Observers all experienced. Ready to go into line with present organization. Have 2 slightly wounded corporals about to return."

As an intelligence outfit, these men were responsible for keeping track of German troop movements and redeployments, assessing enemy combat strength, determining whether troops coming into view were friendly or hostile, and interrogating prisoners (a task facilitated by Eddy's knowledge of German). During much of April and May these tasks were relatively easy, despite frequent German ground probes and regular artillery barrages, because the front was static. Then all hell broke loose.

Frustrated by the failures of "Michael" and "Georgette," the Germans on May 27 suddenly began a massive attack against the Allied lines in the valley of the Marne, aiming to take Paris and deliver a fatal blow to the exhausted French. For the first time since the early months of the war in 1914, it seemed possible that Paris would fall. In the account of the renowned British historian

B. H. Liddell Hart, "at 1 A.M. on May 27th, 1918, a terrific storm of fire burst on the Franco-British front between Reims and north of Soissons, along the famous Chemin-des-Dames; at 4:30 A.M. an overwhelming torrent of Germans swept over the front trenches; by midday it was pouring over the many unblown bridges of the Aisne, and by May 30th it had reached the Marne—site and symbol of the great ebb of 1914. After nearly four years a menace deemed forever past had returned to a point that endowed it with demoralizing symbolism."

The historian John Keegan described the onslaught this way:

> For this third offensive the largest concentration of artillery yet assembled was brought to the front, 6,000 guns supplied from an ammuntion stock of two million shells. All were fired off in a little over four hours on the morning of 27 May, against sixteen Allied divisions; three were British, exhausted in the battles of March and April, and brought down to the Chemin des Dames to rest. Immediately after the bombardment ceased, fifteen divisions of the German Sixth Army, with twenty-five more following, crossed a succession of water lines to reach the summit of the ridge, roll over it, and continue down to the reverse slope to the level ground beyond. The plan required them to halt, when open country was reached, as a preliminary to renewing the attack in the north, but the opportunity created was too attractive to relinquish. [General Erich] Ludendorff [the German commander] decided to exploit the gains of the first two days and during the next five days pressed his division forward as far as Soissoins and Château-Thierry, until his outposts stood only fifty-six miles from Paris.

THE HOUR OF CRISIS

The French lines gave way. Château-Thierry fell. Now was the hour of crisis; the Americans were called upon to reinforce the French and turn back the German advance. The French retained overall command, but their military leaders were in a state of confusion bordering on panic and issued irrelevant and contradictory orders. The French were in retreat; all the Marines' training and instinct was to go forward. The Americans insisted on taking the field as self-contained units rather than as reinforcements for French battalions and regiments that were beyond saving. This set up the first great test of America's military performance in the war. It would be severe and lethal, and the outcome was in doubt for weeks.

The entire dynamic of the battlefront changed because suddenly everyone was on the move. For more than three years on the western front, everyone had pretty much known where everyone else was, and changes in position were measured in yards, not miles. Now, as the historical typescript in Eddy's papers noted, "there was considerable confusion of orders, many of them verbal, as to what French units were to be relieved. The result of this was that gaps in the line developed constantly. It was only by the almost superhuman efforts of intelligence officers and regimental and battalion commanders that liaison was maintained. The war of position had suddenly become a thing of the past. The war of movement, similar in some respects to the tropic fighting with which old Marine officers and men were familiar, had developed."

Before the Americans could confront the Germans north and west of Château-Thierry, they had to get there, redeploying on the run from their positions northwest of Paris. Eddy's notebook entry for June 2 gives an idea of what was involved. "Motorcycles go by rail. Infantry by bus at 5 A.M. . . . responsibility for embussing and entraining with unit commanders. HQ closes at departure of last train . . . only personal equipment on buses . . . no officers will proceed independently . . . arrive at entraining point 3 hours ahead . . . no animals will be shipped with harness on . . . water carts to be filled. Canteens filled: 8 hour trip, no chance to get water on the way."

This redeployment was greatly complicated by the fact that the roads, such as they were, were jammed with people going the opposite way: local citizens shepherding their children and their animals and clutching their belongings, and demoralized French troops driven back from their positions. This was the famous march toward the inferno during which a French colonel advised the Marines to turn back, only to be told by Captain Lloyd W. Williams of the 5th Marines, "Retreat? Hell! We just got here." (Other accounts have attributed the remark to other officers.)

Despite the obstacles, the Americans moved so quickly that they outran their field kitchens. Many of the American troops were hungry for days and even weeks after the redeployment. They foraged on local farms, and from French troops they scrounged tins of dark, unidentifiable meat imported from Madagascar. They called it "monkey meat."

Today the landscape of France's Marne Valley, from Meaux to Château-Thierry, could define the word "bucolic." It is idyllic terrain, a tranquil panorama of gentle hills, peaceful farms, tiny villages and the occasional small forest. It looks as if nothing bad could happen there. Yet it is dotted with military monuments and cemeteries and the occasional ruined tower or chimney that stand as silent witnesses to the horrors of June 1914. The Marines and the 2nd Divison would hold, the German drive toward Paris would be turned back and the prospect of a final German victory would be eliminated, but at a very high price in casualties. The reputation of the Marine Corps as America's most formidable fighting force would be forged in those few weeks, but many thousands would not survive to receive acclaim. By the time the war ended five months later, the 4th Brigade, with a total of 258 officers and 8,211 enlisted men, would suffer about 12,000 killed and wounded, more men than made up its original roster.

BELLEAU WOOD

The Germans had their own problems. By June 1 their advance units were 39 miles from Paris. They had reached the Marne, captured Soissons and surrounded Rheims. But their troops were exhausted, they had outrun their supply lines and they too struggled with congestion on the roads and disruption of the railways. Moreover, they were unaware that the Americans had at last entered the conflict in force, and they could not understand where the fresh Allied troops were coming from. They also could not comprehend the long-distance accuracy of the Marines' rifle fire: they thought their opponents were firing prematurely out of nervousness or inexperience, and were surprised when they began taking casualties at 800 yards.

"Our fire was too accurate and too heavy for them," one American participant wrote. "It was terrible in its effectiveness. They fell by the scores, there among the poppies and the wheat. Then they broke and ran for cover."

Unable to advance further, the Germans dug in across a small forest known as the Bois de Belleau, or Belleau Wood, an overgrown former hunting preserve of less than three square miles, just north of the Metz-Paris highway, between the villages of Bouresches and Lucy-le-Bocage.

As American reinforcements stabilized the lines, the French regrouped and ordered a counterattack. The Marines drew the assignment of taking Belleau Wood. The French told the Marines that the wood was only lightly occupied and American commanders above the brigade level apparently had no idea that it was held by heavily armed Germans in machine-gun nests. These machine

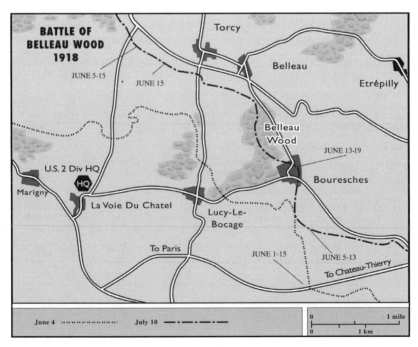

Battle of Belleau Wood from contact on June 4th to closure on the 10th of July.

gunners had clear lines of fire against troops moving toward the wood across the wheat fields that surrounded it.

The engagements of the last week of May and the month of June were recounted in dry but clear language in a narrative prepared not long after the war by a Marine Corps major, Edwin N. McClellan. These excerpts tell the story without embellishment:

> The Second Division, then in reserve northwest of Paris and preparing to relieve the First Division, was hastily diverted to the vicinity of Meaux on May 31, and early on the morning of June 1, was deployed across the Chateau-Thierry Paris road near Montreuil-aux-Lions in a gap in the French line, where it stopped the German advance on Paris. . . .
>
> The fighting of the Second Division in the Chateau-Thierry sector was divided into two parts, one a magnificently stubborn defensive lasting a week and the other a vicious offensive. The defensive fighting of the Second Division between May 31 and June 5, 1918, was part of the major operation called by the Americans the Aisne Defensive . . .
>
> On June 6, 1918, the Second Division snatched the initiative from the Germans and started an offensive on its front which did not end until July 1, 1918. The Marine Brigade captured Hill 142 and Bouresches on June 6, 1918, and in the words of Gen. Pershing, "sturdily held its ground against the enemy's best guard divisions," and completely cleared Bois de Belleau of the enemy on June 26, 1918, a major of Marines sending in his famous message: "Woods now U.S. Marine Corps' entirely."
>
> The American commander-in-chief in his first report calls this fighting "the battle of Belleau Wood" and states, "our men proved their superiority, and gained a strong tactical position with far greater loss to the enemy than to ourselves." In his final report he states: "The enemy having been halted, the Second Division commenced a series of vigorous attacks on June 4, which resulted in the capture of Belleau Woods after very severe fighting. The village of Bouresches was taken soon after and on July 1 Vaux was captured. In these operations the Second Division met with most desperate resistance by Germany's best troops."

During these 31 days of constant fighting . . . the Second
Division suffered 1,811 battle deaths (of which approximately
1,062 were Marines) and suffered additional casualties amount-
ing to 7,252 (of which approximately 3,615 were Marines). It was
that fighting and those 9,063 casualties that first made the name
Chateau-Thierry famous.

That dispassionate after-action account tells what happened in
the large view of commanders: the Marines stopped the Germans
before they could move much beyond Château-Thierry, then went
on the offensive and drove them back from their positions in Belleau Wood. The enlisted men who were doing the actual fighting
had the opposite perspective: at any given time they were able to
discern little of the big strategic picture, but faced constant confusion, fear, gas attacks, food shortages, crippling casualties and mis-
calculations by their senior officers. Lines of communication were
severed, field telephones failed, couriers were intercepted, orders
were delivered long after it was possible to carry them out, maps
were inaccurate, units lost track of each other and Germans were
everywhere, but no one knew exactly where, or in what strength.
For an intelligence officer such as Eddy, whose job was to compile
and distribute accurate information, usually while under fire, this
assignment could hardly have been more challenging, as evidenced
by one Marine's letter quoted by Gary Mead in *The Doughboys*.

"The second night we were here the Germans attacked us. It is
almost impossible to describe what we went thru," this young Marine
wrote. "The Germans came down the hill firing everything at us,
machine guns, rifles and hand grenades. We opened up immediately
with our rifles and threw hand grenades as if they had been baseballs.
We could not see them, but we knew that they were only a few yards
away and that they were set upon taking our trench. They would hold
up for a few minutes and start all over again. But we never let up with
our fire for a minute; kept throwing hand grenades. This lasted all
night, and they finally decided that there was too many of us for them
so they fell back to their old positions." That was the environment in
which Bill Eddy was running around trying to make sense of what was
happening and communicate his findings to headquarters.

If the Americans began the Belleau Wood campaign unaware that the Germans were taking strong positions there, it was not Eddy's fault. As the opposing lines stabilized on the night of June 4, Eddy and two enlisted men set out on a reconnaissance patrol. Dodging artillery shells that burst around them, they took cover in an uncut field of clover next to a gravel road, where they could hear German being spoken and the sound of tools digging trenches and machine gun nests. They set up an observation post in an unprotected tree, amidst shellfire that at times was so close and heavy they had to climb down and seek shelter. Some of the shells contained poison gas, which hung in the air. When they finally made it back to American lines, they reported the heavy enemy presence in Belleau Wood and on the road to the village of Torcy, just to the northwest.

For this daring escapade, Eddy received the Navy Cross and the Army Distinguished Service Cross, as well as a Silver Star, his first of two. The citations said his foray "transmitted information to higher authorities that resulted in heavy punishment to the enemy between June 6th and 16th. This [observation] post located between two batteries was not only in the line of heavy artillery fire, but had to be abandoned at times when the target of more direct fire. The abandonment was only temporary and throughout the operations he proved to be the medium of most accurate observation, although absolutely without cover from deadly fire. Lieutenant Eddy also performed conspicuous service in personally delivering and securing from points in the front lines vital information both to the lines and to our artillery. His conduct was distinguished to a [great] degree by unerring judgment, immediate action and a remarkable sangfroid."

As often happens in the confusion of combat, however, Eddy's heroism did not produce the desired results, because his information apparently did not register with the officers at the top of the chain of command, who persisted in believing that Belleau Wood was free of Germans. This error would have woeful consequences as the Marines tried to take control of the wood.

"As far as we can determine," George B. Clark wrote in *Devil Dogs*, Eddy's patrol "was the only attempt, during the first week, at reconnoitering the ground over which the brigade would fight, and it wasn't much . . . The only record of a reconnaissance was that performed by 2nd Lt. William A. Eddy. The disaster that would come on the morrow was directly caused by failure to reconnoiter the ground to be taken." According to Clark, Brigadier General James G. Harbord, the Army cavalry officer who—in a peculiar quirk of military organization—commanded the 4th Marine Brigade, "would be quoted later as saying something like 'I thought the French had done all of that.' If that was a resonably correct quotation, brigade head-quarters didn't know what was before them and consequently the regiments didn't know either. Worse, no one took it upon himself to do anything about it."

The question of what the Marines knew and when they knew it remains controversial, and military historians still argue about it. The commanding officer of the 6th Marines, Colonel Albertus W. Catlin, contributed to this argument when he later said that American commanders knew in advance that Belleau Wood was heavily defended. "We now stood facing the dark, sullen mystery of Belleau Wood," he wrote after the war. "That the wood was strongly held, we knew . . . that something was going on with those threatening woods we knew, for our intelligence men were not idle. Every day my regimental intelligence officer [i.e. Eddy] rendered a report of the enemy's movements to the divisional intel-ligence department and also to me, and I reported in turn to brigade headquarters." This is difficult to reconcile with Harbord's statements and with the assessments of Clark and other historians.

What is undisputed is that after the Marines blunted the German advance, Allied commanders decided to counterattack. At 2:05 P.M. on June 6, Harbord ordered the 4th Brigade to "take the Bois de Belleau" and to enter the village of Bouresches, take the railroad station, and "drive the Germans back from their positions along the line Bouresches-Torcy-Montecourt."

The attack on Belleau Wood began at 5 P.M. with the Marines advancing across 400 to 600 yards of open fields into the teeth of German machine gun fire and artillery bombardment. At 8:45 P.M. Major Berton W. Sibley sent this message to headquarters: "Unable to advance infantry further because of strong machine gun positions and enemy fire. Have given orders to hold present position at far end of woods. Losses already heavy. Await instructions." It was nearly 10 P.M. when Harbord responded: "Make no further attempt to advance tonight." By that time, the 4th Brigade had suffered more casualties— killed, wounded or missing in action—than the cumulative total of all casualties suffered by the Marine Corps since its founding 142 years earlier. The losses were 31 officers and 1,056 enlisted men.

A GERMAN OFFICER'S PERSPECTIVE

In a fascinating study published a decade after the war, a German officer, Lietenant Colonel Ernest Otto, attributed this disaster to the plan of attack devised by the French General Jean Degoutte:

"According to the German conception of the conduct of battle on June 6, the two fresh [American] divisions in full force, after a brief artillery preparation and gassing of the enemy artillery, should have rushed simultaneously in thick lines of skirmishers along the entire front. However, General Degoutte, commander of the French 21st Army Corps, to which the American 2nd Division was attached, had a different idea. He had the attack made in echelon, developing gradually from the left to the right in assigned periods of time, so that the different regiments followed one another into battle like the ribs of an opening fan. The right wing of the 4th Infantry Brigade did not advance until evening. This ingenious method of attack, well suited in view of possible flanking movements, had the great disadvantage of enabling the Germans to concentrate their artillery fire every time exactly on the attacking troops. If the Americans, notwithstanding their extraordinary bravery, did not meet with greater material success on June 6, the fault lies mainly in this arrangement of the French corps commander."

In his history of the war, writer Byron Farwell says that Degoutte was "the least popular of French generals in the eyes of Americans, who always found him too ready to expend American blood," but in this case General Harbord defended him. Harbord, who sent the Marines to be cut down by those German artillery barrages, wrote in a footnote to the English-language edition of Otto's paper, "I am obliged to acquit General Degoutte of any responsibility as to the tactical methods employed on that date . . . With the information we had that the woods were unoccupied by the Germans, we gave it no artillery preparation, thinking thereby to take it by surprise or find it unoccupied. Occupied as it was by machine gun nests well placed, the tactical formation of the time, which was to advance in successive waves as we had been taught, did entail considerable losses."

That was an understatement. As Otto observed, it had been a contest of "unexampled obstinacy. The American battalions set about their mission [of taking Bouresches and Belleau Wood] unconditionally resolved to the last man to do so, cost what it might. But the German battalions defended this, their main defense line, with equal determination. After bitter fighting the Americans finally had to give up the struggle, but with the village of Bouresches in their possession." He said the "heroic spirit" of the Marines was visible next morning when a single German company, the 4th of the 398th Regiment, found 100 American bodies in front of its positions. So intensely had the Germans fired, Otto wrote, that they ran out of ammunition.

THE ADVANCE ACROSS THE WHEAT FIELDS

Words can never fully convey the terror and confusion of combat, but a personal account of the Belleau Wood campaign by a participant, Captain John A. West of the 6th Regiment, gives a sense of what the Marines were up against. Here he is describing the advance across the wheat fields that lay between the Marines and the wood:

> Here we would lie in a shallow fox hole day and night. At intervals the German artillery would drop shells into us. At night, firing was more intense and more terrifying—big shells that came screaming down with a sound like whistling through the teeth, followed by a terrific bang and fire, then blackness and cries for first aid . . . More shells cracking down on us—they could not miss.

Cries of "first aid," "stretcher bearer," pitiful pleading cries, cursing, positive demands, 'Christ, Christ, Oh God.' Wounded men pleaded with me to kill them to put them out of their misery . . . Coming up in a black night we had been shelled heavily. Before we hit the woods gas shells had been exploded on us. We put on gas masks. Then one could see nothing. Men held to the shoulder of the man ahead or onto his rifle, a long line of men in single file. Men were hit, breaking that line, those in the rear hurrying blindly to catch up. The head of the column, not knowing what was happening in the rear, went too fast, men stumbled, fell, groping around in the darkness . . . When we hit the woods it was far worse. Here the way was continually obstructed by trees that had been knocked across it. It was impossible to keep a line with gas masks on. Off came the masks, gas or no gas . . . When we reached the far end of the woods, only half the company was there.

West added the observation that "In trenches you knew your objective, knew where machine gun fire came from. Here you knew nothing. It was a game of hide and seek.

This deadly engagement went on, with varying degrees of intensity, for three weeks, as the Marines forged through the German fire into the wood, where combat was often face-to-face and fought with bayonets. Eddy and other intelligence officers faced a daily challenge of determing where the Germans were and in what strength, and in getting that information back to commanders through the hail of artillery and machine gun fire. Given the primitive state of communications technology in those days, the transmission of information often required the bearers to run through the shells and bullets to deliver it in person.

On June 10, in anticipation of a major new thrust by the Marines the next day, Eddy tried to find out exactly where the German machine gun emplacements were. Accompanied by Sergeant. Gerald Thomas, he set out on another high-risk patrol.

Eddy "asked me to lead him to these machine gun nests," Thomas later told Robert Asprey. "I hadn't seen one up to this time, but [knew] about where they were located. We worked forward slowly through the dense wood. Finally we got to a place where I told Eddy I thought we'd gone far enough. He said, 'All right, you keep watch while I climb this tree and take a look.' He no more gotten up there when he turned loose and came down with a thump. 'My God,' he whispered, 'I was looking at a German machine gun nest right down there in front of us.' We got out of there fast. They evidently didn't see us—anyway they didn't open fire."

The American thrust of June 11 achieved better results than that of the 6th. In this encounter, which according to Otto was "fought with utmost bravery, both sides suffered great losses. The general confusion among [the German] defenders was increased by German-speaking Americans who in the thick woods called out 'Wo ist das Regiment 40?' and the like . . . Those who did not fall in battle were taken prisoner."

In that engagement the Americans gained control of the southeastern corner of Belleau, again with heavy casualties. Their attack began at 4:45 A.M. and lasted less than an hour. According to Asprey, "At 5:20 A.M. [Lieutenant Colonel Harry] Lee's intelligence officer [i.e. Eddy] notified Harbord: 'Action in woods deemed finished. Our barrage on woods is continuing. Guns are firing on enemy's batteries and towns. Only a few short bursts of machine gun fire noted during advance.'"

As similar reports filtered in over the next few hours Harbord came to believe the operation had succeeded, but his information was incomplete. The Marines had succeeded in taking only the southeastern portion of the wood, and the Americans had no clear idea of what still lay ahead to the north. There the German line remained unbroken.

By this time the Marines had been in combat without interruption for two weeks. The men were exhausted, food and water were scarce, clothing and bodies were filthy, there was no shelter from the rain, and all the time they faced explosive fire and poison gas from German artillery bombardment; and still the end was not near. On June 13 the Germans counterattacked, then dug in again. Not until June 26 would Harbord report to Division Headquarters, "Belleau Woods now U.S. Marine Corps' entirely." Colonel Otto attributed the outcome to "the death-defying boldness of the Americans, their impetuous onslaughts, and their tenacious endurance."

A few days later, General Degoutte, in tribute to the Marines' valor, issued an order renaming Belleau Wood as the "Bois de la Brigade de la Marine," and by 1923 there was a permanent American-owned memorial at the site. In dedication ceremonies for that memorial, General Harbord said emotionally that, "There were no better troops than our Marines in any army, and it is fitting that for this Memorial to American arms there should be chosen this battlefield, where they fought with such desperate valor, to redeem which so many of them gave their lives." Even today the thick forest beyond the memorial looks forbidding and impenetrable.

Taking Belleau Wood cost the Marine Corps 1,062 deaths—almost half the total of 2,455 Marines killed in the entire war—and another 3,615 wounded, some of them more than once. In the month of combat during which it halted the German offensive and retook Château-Thierry and its surroundings, the 2nd Division as a whole, including the Army regiments, reported a total of 1,811 battle deaths and 7,252 wounded.

Among the wounded was Bill Eddy. On June 25, the day before Belleau Wood was finally taken, fragments from an artillery round penetrated his boot and broke three toes on his right foot. He was hospitalized and did not return to active duty for a month. Upon his return, he drew a new assignment. As of August 1, he became aide-de-camp to Brigadier General Wendell C. Neville, newly appointed commander of the 4th Marine Brigade. (General Lejeune had taken that post in late July, but after only four days he was promoted to major general and assigned to command the entire 2nd Division, succeeding Harbord. Thus the command anomaly was reversed: instead of Harbord, an army officer, commanding Marines in a combined unit, Lejeune, a Marine officer, was commanding army troops. Lejeune and Neville both would later become commandants of the Marine Corps.) In addition to his duties as aide to Neville, Eddy was assigned as an intelligence officer of the 4th Brigade.

Exhausted and bloodied, the 4th Brigade stood down briefly after the Belleau Wood campaign. The war, now entering its final few months, had turned around as the desperate defenders of early June became the attackers. The threat to Paris had been negated. The British lines in the north had held. Unable to turn the reinforcements from the Russian front into a decisive break-through, the Germans had fired their last, best shot at victory, but they were not yet in retreat. Many weeks of horrifying combat lay ahead for the Americans, at places with hallowed names—Soissons, St. Mihiel, and Mont Blanc ridge.

The Germans still had one last bold offensive in them, and it came on July 15, along a front north of Château-Thierry and the Marne, around the town of Soissons. The U.S. 2nd Division, which had enjoyed a leisurely Bastille Day holiday away from the front lines, was suddenly rushed back into action. This was another nightmarish redeployment, by forced march, at night, under pouring rain and German artillery fire. Yet once in place, the Americans and French rolled back the Germans much more easily than they had at Belleau Wood. It took only two days.

"It was a glorious victory," General Jones wrote in his history. "Rather than the preliminary bombardment, massed American and French artillery, firing by the map, laid down a rolling barrage, and the picked American and French divisions charged. The attack inmediately broke through the most sensitive portion of the German line to the heights south of Soissons. The enemy infantry lines were overrun, as was his artillery. His communications were interrupted. The end result was a general, although stubborn, German withdrawal from the Marne in order to prevent disaster."

Eddy, recuperating from his wound, was spared participation in the Soissons battle. When he returned to active duty a week later, the Americans were preparing to move eastward, toward Germany. The end of the war was now in sight. None of the major combatant countries had surrendered, but in this war the definition of victory for the Allies was prevention of victory by Germany and Austria. That was soon to be accomplished. The entry of the Americans—fresh, courageous, disciplined troops, unscarred by the stalemate of trench warfare—decisively altered the balance of forces, outweighing Russia's withdrawal from the war.

ST. MIHIEL

The Marine brigade and the entire 2nd Division stood down from the front lines during August to rest, resupply and refill their depleted ranks. The wounded who had recovered enough to fight again returned from field hospitals. The 6th Regiment bivouacked near the city of Nancy, and some men were given liberty there. Then in September came the order to move eastward and confront the Germans again, this time at the St. Mihiel salient.

The town of St. Mihiel marked the westernmost point of an arrowhead-shaped bulge in the lines between the Moselle and Meuse rivers, southeast of Verdun, that the Germans had occupied since the early months of the war, defying several French attempts to eliminate it. It gave the Germans a bridgehead on the west side of the Meuse, and it interdicted the rail lines from Paris and Verdun to Nancy. "It was so apparent on maps," George B. Clark wrote in *Devil Dogs*, "that General Pershing saw it as a potential raison d'être, or objective for the fledgling American army, almost immediately upon arrival in France." This battle the Americans would fight on their own, not as auxiliaries to the French.

Pershing and his staff recognized that the British and French were fully occupied elsewhere along the long north-south front, and that St. Mihiel was an important target because, as Liddell Hart wrote in his history, "a thrust there needed to penetrate only a short distance before it would imperil the stability of the whole German position in France."

Among the officers Pershing assigned to plan an assault on the salient was George C. Marshall, a graduate of Viginia Military Institute who was then an unknown young Army captain. This was the same George Marshall who later became one of the country's most renowned military leaders and, after World War II, Secretary of Defense and Secretary of State, as well as winner of the Nobel Peace Prize for his sponsorship of the Marshall Plan to rebuild Europe. At the State Department, one of Marshall's senior counselors in the postwar beaureucratic battles over the organization of America's diplomatic and intelligence services would be the department's chief intelligence official, Bill Eddy.

For this campaign in France the 2nd Division was attached to the newly formed I Corps of the A.E.F. "On September 10th the regiment marched to Manonville, where regimental Headquarters was established and troops bivouacked in the woods in that vicinity," according to Eddy's anonymous typescript history. "Here on September 11th all battalion officers and company commanders received tank instructions. Emphasis was laid on maintaining liaison between tanks and infantry," an assignment in which no one had any experience because the tank was a new weapon. "It was clearly indicated that this was to be one of the great offensives of the war. Troops were massed in every woods. The amount of heavy artillery, especially long-range guns mounted on railway trucks and well camouflaged, exceed that of any former offensive. On September 11th a number of replacements were received, bringing the regiment approximately to full compliment."

On that same day, Colonel Lee issued this order: "Tomorrow, September 12th, is 'D' day. 'H' hour is 5:00 A.M. The artillery preparation will start at 1:00 A.M. and continue for four hours. During the bombardment, it is absolutely necessary that all men be kept under cover in designated positions."

This was one of those relatively rare occasions in combat when the battle proceeded as planned. The artillery opened fire at 1 A.M., and kept it up for the prescribed four hours. During that time the troops huddled in trenches and foxholes under heavy rain near the village of Limey. At 5 A.M. they began their advance and found that the artillery had done its work well.

Advance reports of German strength in the salient "were not exaggerated," according to Eddy's anonymous typescript. "Only the terrific four-hour preparation of the morning of September 12th made the first stages of the operation possible without serious opposition." German positions were well fortified, but proof of the artillery's effectiveness in knocking them out could be seen in "the havoc brought upon them. The enemy had been driven into dugouts and trenches by the bombardment, and those who did not retreat as the barrage advanced were taken prisoner." The 6th Regiment quickly seized the village of Thiaucourt, five miles inside the German lines at the start of the assault, and set up field headquarters there. It had been in German hands since September 1914.

According to Liddell Hart, the Germans anticipated the American attack and sought to limit its effect by withdrawing during the night of September 11-12, which "has led to a satirical description of St. Mihiel as 'the sector where the Americans relieved the Germans.'" Nevertheless, what mattered was the outcome. The Americans drove the Germans back toward their final line of defense in France, and captured 15,000 prisoners and 443 artillery pieces, in five days, with relatively light losses of their own—for the 4th Brigade, 132 dead and some 600 wounded.

On September 16, the last day of the assault on St. Mihiel, Eddy wrote from "Somewhere in France" to "My precious darling Mary." This letter is one of the few extant accounts by Eddy himself of what he had been going through.

"I hope that before many months have past [sic], I will be heading my letters 'somewhere in Germany,'" he wrote. "Anyway we just got back today from our part in the American offensive, in which we removed the Saint Mihiel pocket. It is the first time I have had a chance to write to my dear little wife in 10 days . . . This was the first big fight since I was made the general's A.D.C. [aide-de-camp.] Hence I was in an entirely new situation. Instead of conducting reconnaissance patrols and observation of enemy activity I was at Brigade Hqts. keeping the operations maps of the general up to date and collecting all information that was available. Except when the Germans shelled our hqts., I felt quite out of the war. As you know the drive was a complete success. We advanced 11 miles and our division alone took 300 prisoners and 50 officers. It was pathetic to see the joy of the French civilians who had been living with the Germans on their hands since 1914. We ourselves captured Remenauville, Thiaucourt, Rembercourt and Saulny. I was in Thiaucourt 2½ days. I went ahead of the brigade and got there as our Marines were still clearing out groups of Germans from dugouts, cellars and behind walls."

Evidently there was more to his work than that terse narrative would indicate. Shortly after hostilities ceased, Neville wrote to General Lejeune to recommend Eddy for a Distinguished Service Medal, saying that "his energy, accuracy and faithful devotion to duty relieved the Brigade commander and the Adjutant from all worry as to details regarding proper functioning of the Intelligence personnel." And later, in a separate letter of commendation, he wrote that Eddy "served with me in Marbache sector and afterwards in the battle of St. Mihiel. During that battle he worked ceaselessly night and day, with no regard for himself, was particularly successful, and rendered important services in gathering and systematizing valuable information from the enemy. Captain Eddy was also cited in Second Division Orders as follows: 'An officer of exceptional ability. He was brigade Intelligence Officer from August 9th until evacuated on September 24th for pneumonia contracted during the performance of his duties in the operation of St. Mihiel, with no regard for himself, he worked ceaselessly night and day."

As that citation indicates, Eddy was felled right after St. Mihiel not by enemy shellfire but by illness, described in military records as pneumonia but probably the Spanish flu, which swept the world in 1918 in a pandemic that killed more people than the war itself. Troops in the field—exhausted, irregularly fed, unwashed, living in constant close contact, with improvised sanitation—were particularly vulnerable. The 2nd Division and the Allies faced two more months of combat as they forged eastward toward the German border, but Bill Eddy's war was over. He was again in mortal danger, this time from the virus that was causing global havoc.

By October 3, he was too ill to write to Mary himself—he had to dictate. From Base Hospital 45 he sent this note: "My dearest Mary, Have not been able to write to you for some time because I have been in a hospital. Do not worry it is only pneumonia not a wound, though it is not a bit comfortable at that. Isn't the war news great. Everybody is very good to me here at the hospital. Today I got roses by my bed. Miss Meyer, who is writing this letter for me, has been as nice as she could be." At the bottom of the page was a note from Stella Meyer, a Red Cross nurse: "I am sure you will be glad to know that your husband is indeed improving daily and we trust will soon be quite well." She was wrong; his condition deteriorated rapidly. Fluid filled his lungs, and he developed an abscess in his groin and an infection in a hip joint.

He sent Mary a brief note on October 26: "It has been disappointing after four weeks in hosp. to have the doctors find that it was necessary to operate on me. My left chest began to fill up and they had to cut my back open and put in a drain. It only means the time lost, for I'm in the best of care." The good news was that he had been promoted, so her family allowance would increase to $100 a month from $75.

His condition worsened. His military medical records say he developed "empyema," which is an accumulation of pus in the chest cavity, and "ankylosis," or fusion of the hip joint where doctors had made an incision in his groin area to lance the abscess. "X-ray shows an abscess extending from the inner surface of the ilium, downward across the neck of the femur to a pocket of about 3" long in the adductor muscles," the doctors found.

On January 14, 1919, two months after the armistice, he wrote a despairing letter to Mary, this time from Base Hospital 71: "Dearest precious Mary, I am suffering tonight but I am not thinking of that. My heart is aching for you, or at least for a word of love from your hand." He asked for reassurance that she would stay with him even if he was an invalid and they lived in poverty. "I force myself to eat when I detest it," he wrote, "that I may keep myself strong. I move as much as I can in bed at great pain when it would be much easier to lie still, that I may not become mere skin and bones. I have fought away the grave time and time again—all that I may see you again. I have been this way 4 months less 3 days today, without seeing anyone who cares, or hearing a loving voice. It is what I need more than medicine. My great solace was your letters and now they have been astray for a month."

The uncharacteristically self-pitying tone of this and similar letters alarmed Mary and other family members back home. Something had to be done, but what? Bill Eddy was too sick to stay where he was and too sick to move. And now that the war was over, he was just one of tens of thousands of Americans who needed to be brought home from Europe; people in official channels were too busy to worry about one solitary Marine.

Chapter 2

NEW YORK

"*I* wonder if you ever heard the story about how President Woodrow Wilson saved Dad's life in World War I. It's a great story," Mary Eddy Furman said. Her father would have died in the military hospital in France, she said, because he was too ill to be moved, only his connections to Princeton got him out of there.

Wilson, a graduate of Princeton, became president of the university in 1902. "When he went to the White House," Mary Furman said, "he took several Princetonians along with him as aides. And one of them was a Close."

This was Gilbert Close, class of 1903, Wilson's personal secretary. The Closes, like the Eddys, were longtime mainstays of the American Protestant community in Lebanon, and of Princeton. Gilbert's brother, Harold Close, class of 1910, was a prominent professor and dean at the missionary-founded American University of

Beirut. Harold's wife, Dora Eddy Close, was Bill Eddy's sister. Harold and Dora's son Ray (Princeton '51) spent a distinguished professional career as a CIA agent in the Arab world, where his work and that of his uncle Bill would overlap in later years.

In Mary Furman's recounting of the story, "One day Gilbert said, 'Mr. President, my sister-in-law is getting very worried because her brother is in a hospital in France and the family is getting incoherent letters from him, saying why aren't you coming to visit me?' So President Wilson took a sheet of paper and addressed it to the War Department: 'Find Captain William A. Eddy, United States Marines, and have him sent home immediately.' I love that nineteenth century way of doing business.

"Eventually when the truck arrived at the hospital where dad was in France, the doctor refused to let him get in that truck because he wouldn't live to make it to the boat. And they said, 'We have this letter from the President of the United States and we're going to take him.' So they took him to Paris, and when he arrived at the ship that was going to bring him to the States, they went through the same routine. The ship's doctor didn't want to take him because he wouldn't make it across the ocean, and they said, 'We've got this letter from the president, you've got to take him. When dad arrived at the Brooklyn Navy Yard, he weighed 99 pounds."

As dicey as his evacuation was, it was no guarantee of recovery because medical services back home had been severely overtaxed by the combination of war casualties and Spanish flu victims. Many who survived the flu did so because they were lucky, not because medical practitioners were able to cure them.

By the time Eddy sailed into New York harbor aboard the SS *Matsonia*, it was March 24, 1919, more than four months after the armistice. He was ill and emaciated, but for him the crisis had passed—he was out of danger. Now in tedious months of slow recuperation at a military hospital in Brooklyn, he fretted over what would become of him once he was able to return to civilian life. There was no question of making the Marine Corps a career, even though superior officers recommended him for a permanent commission.

Endorsing that recommendation, Lieutenant Colonel Earl H. Ellis, a comrade in arms from what he called "the American offensive against the Bosche in the St. Mihiel salient," wrote on Feb. 12 that "Lieutenant Eddy came to the Brigade Staff with an excellent record with troops. His record as a staff officer was equally good. He showed intelligent energy, judgement and knowledge far beyond that warranted by his age and length of service. After an excellent opportunity to judge, the undersigned considers Lieutenant Eddy one of the best young officers that he has ever known and peculiarly fitted for service as an officer of the U.S. Marine Corps." But the Corps did not really need Eddy— reserve officers were being discharged in droves—and his injury and illness had left him with a disfigured leg and a severe limp that would have disqualified him for anything other than office duty.

On June 10, Eddy wrote to Mary's mother about his concerns, not only for himself but for his wife. "We are all glad that I am back in the States and improving gradually and can be put into a wheel chair for a while each day," he said. "I hate to think of Mary staying in the hot city all summer. She does mind the heat so much. But it seems nothing on earth could persuade her to go off on a vacation and leave me." Mary Eddy's inability to tolerate prolonged hot weather would later have a direct impact on her husband's career in the Middle East.

In that letter Eddy noted that he was still being paid by the Marine Corps, but was worried about what would happen when that income ceased. "It is a real question what we will do after I leave the hospital (probably next fall) as you know I will be a cripple all my life. There will be something I can do, I know," he wrote. In fact, Eddy's correspondence files show that he haggled with the Navy Department for years afterward about the extent of his disability and the amount of retirement pay due to him.

On July 28, a Marine Retiring Board convened at the Brooklyn Navy Yard to review Eddy's case. Asked by the board if he wished to be retired, Eddy said yes. "I have had Ankylosis of the joint, the right hip, since October 1918," he said. "The ankylosis in the joint in the right hip necessitates the use of crutches to get along." A medical officer testified that this disability was permanent and listed his condition as "unfit for service."

Three weeks later the acting secretary of the Navy, Frankin D. Roosevelt, accepted the board's finding that Eddy was "incapacitated for active service by reason of septic infections of the right hip joint, following pneumonia and abscess, which resulted in complete loss of motion in the joint, and that his incapcity is the result of an incident of the service." Eddy was "retired from active service" at his current rank, captain. He was a civilian again, but he had no job.

From his letters it is clear that Eddy had always expected to pursue a career in the church, like his father and grandfather, or in the academic world, or some combination of the two. His entry in the 1917 Princeton yearbook said that "Eddy expects to enter the ministry." Indeed, he had little preparation for any other line of work. He was not attracted to industry, finance or science. His military service had instilled in him a love of the Marine Corps and an appetite for action, but in the shrinking armed services of the post-World War I years there was no room for a demobilized reserve officer with a permanent disability.

His solution was to accept an offer from Charles Robinson to teach German at the Peekskill Military Academy in New York to earn a bit of cash so he could go back to Princeton to pursue the advanced degrees he would need to find a position on the tenure track at a college or university.

He received his doctorate from Princeton in 1922. His Ph.D. thesis was titled "A Critical Study of the Literal Relations of Gulliver's Travels with Special Reference to *Lilliput* and *Brobdingnag*."

The subject was *Gulliver's Travels* as an example of what Eddy called "the philosophic type of Imaginary Voyage literature," which he described as "a didactic treatise in which the author's criticism of society is set forth in the parable form of an imaginary voyage made by one or more Europeans to a non-existent or little-known country, including an account of the traveller's journey and adventures, together with a description of the imaginary society visited." Like most doctoral theses, this one was destined to be archived and forgotten, but for Eddy it was more than an academic exercise; the topic reflected his lifelong interest in the fantastic, the humorous, the satirical and the magical. The serious scholar was also a wit—he performed sleight of hand tricks for children, compiled the tales of a mythical Arab wiseguy into a book, and peppered his correspondence with sardonic commentary on people and events.

By the time he received his doctorate, Bill Eddy was a very well educated young man, erudite and multi-lingual, steeped in the classics and in history. Yet in later years, when he was in government service and when he was a business consultant trying to influence government decision-making, it would become unhappily apparent that all the environments in which he had come to maturity—the missionary community, Wooster, Princeton, and the Marine Corps—had left an important gap in his understanding of American life and politics: these environments were largely devoid of Jews. In that era Princeton and other elite colleges maintained quotas to limit the number of Jews who could attend, and Jews were scarce at the eating clubs. There was a sizeable Jewish community in Sidon, but nothing in his correspondence indicates that Eddy ever had much contact with those Jews. This lacuna left Eddy—and many of the men from similar backgrounds who would later be his diplomatic colleagues—with a peculiar lack of sensitivity to the concerns and interests of Jewish Americans and an inability to comprehend their political influence. He was by no means alone in this fallibility, but he was particularly affected by it because of the positions he would hold in later life. The views he would espouse, especially during his period of U.S. government service, might have been different if he had some input from Jewish friends and neighbors. The same was true of many members of the State Department cadre known collectively as the Arabists.

DESTINATION CAIRO

Eddy's completion of his studies and his search for an academic position coincided happily with the creation of a new institution that appealed to him on several grounds—the American University in Cairo, a private institution with instruction in

English. It was modeled on the American University in Beirut, which Eddy's missionary ancestors and their colleagues had been instrumental in founding during the previous century. (His grandfather, William W. Eddy, was a member of the original board of managers of Syrian Protestant College, which later became AUB, and delivered the invocation at AUB's first prayer service in 1866.) AUC was and remains a less ambitious and less renowned institution than the Beirut school, but at the time it offered Eddy an opportunity to get in on the ground floor of an institution that would give him college-level teaching experience and a chance to return to the Arab world.

His application for a position at AUC received a rousing endorsement from his former Marine Corps commander, General Neville. In November 1921, while Eddy was working on his dissertation, Neville wrote to Dr. Charles A. Watson, AUC's founding president: "I know of no man whose personal qualifications so appeal to me as did those of Captain Eddy in the short time we were together. Captain Eddy's personal character is all that could be desired. His capacity for leadership, his influence upon others, and his ability for efficient administration are beyond praise. To me he showed intelligence, energy, judgment, and knowledge far beyond that warranted by his age and length of service." The young scholar was hired and the Eddys decamped to Egypt with their first child, Bill Jr., who was born in 1921.

Details of the Eddys' life in Cairo are sketchy and the paper trail is thin, but there is no doubt that those were productive years for him, and that he met people and learned things that would be useful throughout his life. Appointed chairman of the English department in 1923, he "performed pioneer work in education and developed a progressive program of teaching English to Egyptians who were preparing for civil service and the professions," according to an American University document. He drafted bilingual textbooks. He also studied classical Arabic, to supplement the Lebanese street Arabic he had spoken as a boy in Sidon. Two decades later, when he returned to Cairo as a military intelligence agent just before World War II, his former students from the university were among the first people he sought out.

Even in those early years at AUC, he exhibited the mischievous sense of humor and flair for ironic discourse that would characterize his writings and his conversation throughout his life. One day he teased the venerable shaikh who was tutoring him in Koranic Arabic. "What would you Muslims do," Eddy inquired, "if you lived up inside the Arctic circle and it was six months before the sun set? What would you do in Ramadan?" (Ramadan is the holy month in which Muslims are required to refrain from food and drink from sunrise to sunset.) After a moment's reflection, the aged scholar asked, "Have you ever actually seen that yourself?" When Eddy confessed he had not, the man instructed him, "Do not believe it." It was just the sort of tale Eddy loved to tell over bourbon and pipe tobacco after dinner, his nephew Ray Close recalled many years later. "From the time he was a child until the day he died, he was a teaser and a joker," Close said.

Eddy had retained his love of basketball, which he had played in those early years of jump balls and two-handed set shots, although because of his severe limp he could no longer be competitive. He and his American colleagues on the AUC faculty introduced the game to Egypt, encouraging Egyptians to play and teaching them the rules. He coached an AUC team that won the championship of a private-school league in 1925. A copy of an Arabic-language rule book printed during those years is among Eddy's papers at Princeton. Friends and colleagues would later credit Eddy with writing that rule book—as did his obituary in the New York Times—but he described himself as "only one of several who cooperated in promoting the sport in its early days in Egypt."

In addition to teaching, Eddy pursued mastery of classical Arabic, the language of the Koran, almost a different language from the dialect spoken on the streets of Cairo.

"Dad knew huge sections of the Koran by heart," his daughter Mary recalled. "In Egypt he used to stand on the street corners with holy men and they'd chant forever. People would gather around and listen and say, 'Here's this American who knows the Koran.' And see, his accent was good. He knew the dialects. He knew pages and pages of the Koran by heart."

His instructor tried to convert him to Islam. Many years later, Eddy recalled their conversation. "'Why don't you become a Muslim?'" the scholar asked. "'You were born amongst us, live with us by preference, speak our language and like our customs. Why not come all the way?' I replied that I was satisfied with my own religion. But, said he, yours is only a Western, materialistic religion. Our Prophet was the greatest and the last of all the prophets, of whom Jesus is one. Islam is the only religion valid all over the world." Here Eddy tried again with his mischievous query about how Muslims could fast all day in the months-long sunlight of the Arctic summer.

"The teacher looked at me severely and said quietly, 'Have you been in the Arctic Zone?' No, I admitted. 'Nonsense,' he said, 'don't believe such nonsense; everyone knows that night and day follow each other every twenty-four hours. Go home and get some sleep; you must not believe old wives' tales.'" One reason Eddy was so esteemed by the Arabs throughout his life was that he never argued with such people, and he never laughed at them or belittled them in their presence or in the presence of other Arabs. On the contrary, he admired their faith and the steadfastness of their beliefs.

As gratifying as they were for Eddy professionally, these were difficult years for the young family. They soon had two more children: Mary Garvin, born in 1922, and John Condit, born in 1925. A fourth, Carmen Frances, would arrive in 1933, after their return to the United States. (Having been briefly a member of the AUC faculty half a century later, when my wife and I had two small girls, I can attest that Cairo is not an easy place to raise American children and keep them healthy, even with the university's support.) In the 1920s, there were few Americans in Egypt other than the handful at the university, and the Eddys found the British, who controlled the country, to be chilly and standoffish. In addition, as they had discovered during Eddy's recuperation in Brooklyn, Mary Eddy did not do well in the heat. Cairo is comfortably cool in the winter, but from April through October the temperatures are searing.

"She really hated being in Cairo," their daughter, Mary Eddy Furman, recalled decades later. "It couldn't have been worse for an American woman—no air conditioning, we had to wear veils over our heads, and the British were terribly snobbish."

Overwhelmed, Mary Eddy eventually fell ill, to the point where she was unable to care for the children or maintain the family life in

Cairo. The two younger children, Mary and Jack, were dispatched to the care of relatives in Lebanon; Mary Eddy and the oldest boy, Bill Jr., retired to a Garvin family farm in Illinois where she could regroup. It was time for Bill Eddy to seek a job in an environment his wife would find more congenial, which he did in 1928 when he accepted a position on the faculty of Dartmouth College in Hanover, New Hampshire.

"She loved living in New Hampshire," Mary Furman said of her mother. "She thought Princeton was flat and boring, but as soon as she got to Hanover, she thought she'd died and gone to heaven in this beautiful college town. "With the marvelous skiing and the winter sports, she didn't mind the cold a bit. She wore the first pair of women's ski pants ever seen in Hanover."

CAMPUS LIFE

Bill Eddy was now in a position that would be the envy of any young scholar with academic ambitions. Armed with his degrees from Princeton and fluent in three languages besides English, he was on the tenured staff of a renowned institution of higher learning, popular with students and well regarded by colleagues, in a community where his family thrived. After a decade of difficult environments on the battlefield, in the hospital and in Cairo, Eddy was able to focus his erudition on his students and on the subjects that engaged him intellectually—literary criticism and satire as social commentary.

His class notes show detailed, painstaking preparation and a difficult syllabus. He set and insisted upon high standards, and believed in requiring the students to write, write and write some more, even if they were engineering majors. He followed his own dictates, turning out essays for scholarly magazines and church-centered reviews, mostly on academic subjects but also on religious and moral themes. He edited and wrote introductions to new editions of Swift's works and Samuel Butler's *Erewhon*. These are of little interest today except to specialists, but at the time they enhanced his reputation as a scholar and thinker.

One of his Dartmouth courses was "Principles of Literary Criticism," in which he and the students addressed such questions as, "How does Byron's concept of liberty differ from Shelley's?" and "To which emotion do Pope, Goldsmith, Shelley and Poe appeal primarily? Which is most fertile soil for literature?"

He also taught "Satire in the Drama," in which the lecture topics and assigned readings reflected his love of satirists and of satire as an art form: Swift, Juvenal, Twain, Cervantes, Chaucer. "Satire on parlour hypocrisies long ago taught us to see more beauty in the hands of a washerwoman than in the manicured hands of a courtesan," he observed. "My thesis is that Satire as an art, as a habit of mind, is neither destructive nor inhuman, that it will enrich the experience of the scholar and the skilled workman, the poet and the plumber, the banker and the bell-boy."

As well situated as the Eddys were, he was restless as he approached his fortieth birthday. He wanted to leave a mark on education that went beyond the classroom. In 1936 he became the fifteenth president of Hobart College, a well-respected if not first-tier school for men in Geneva, New York. Simultaneously, he was installed as the fourth president of Hobart's sister institution for women, William Smith College.

This might have seemed an excellent position for Eddy: scholarly environment, pleasant community on Seneca Lake in New York's Finger Lakes region, weather that was congenial to Mary, a good place for children to grow up. "We loved the house," his daughter Mary recalled. "It was wonderful—eight bathrooms, and a whole back section for the butler and the maid."

It was a good life, at least on the surface, a life of security and comfort. The United States was still mired in the misery of the Great Depression, but the Eddys were comfortably insulated from it—so much so that family correspondence from those years contains little mention of the nation's grim condition. Yet the appearances turned out to be deceiving; the presidency of Hobart, or of any college, was a job Bill Eddy should never have taken, because he was a man of action. Though trained at the highest levels of scholarship, he was not temperamentally suited to the management of an institution where tenured professors resisted direction and pursued their own agendas. It would not be long before he found himself trapped and thrashing about on the tarpaper of academic politics.

SEMPER FI AT HOBART

One of Eddy's first official acts upon taking up the Hobart post was to write to General John H. Russell, commandant of the Marine Corps, who had sent a note of congratulations upon his appointment, to seek some connection between the Corps and Hobart; he said the school had fine young men who would profit from Marine training and "bring credit to the Corps." Thus in 1937 Hobart was added to the schools providing candidates for the Platoon Leaders Class, Marine Corps Reserve. As always, Eddy valued his Marine connections, and he encouraged promising students to enter the Corps. With the rise of Nazi Germany, the threat of a new war loomed in Europe, and Eddy could see it coming. Most of his time, though, was occupied by more mundane concerns.

Like any college president, Eddy was expected to assume a certain number of social and community obligations, and to promote the college in speaking engagements. He undertook these dutifully, but it is easy to see why—after the breath-catching fear and exhilaration of the battlefield and the exotic life of Cairo—he found them boring, especially in the hinterlands of upstate New York.

His schedule of speaking appearances for February 1937, for example, is filled with such entries as: Feb. 2, annual dinner meeting, Church Club of NY, New York; 15, Geneva Women's Club; 19, Monroe County Teachers Association, Rochester; 24, Ladies Night, Geneva Rotary Club; 25, Banquet, American Legion Post 396, Geneva. An entire folder of his papers deals with his efforts on behalf of the Western New York Apple Blossom Festival of 1939, which was held at Hobart. Nobody at these events spoke Arabic or shared Eddy's sense of romance and commitment about the Middle East. Quickly, he grew restless.

Although Eddy and his family were not directly affected by the economic disaster of the Depression, he developed an acute sense of its demoralizing effect on the population. It was partly because of this that he sowed the seeds of trouble for himself and the college in his inaugural address to students and faculty on October 2, 1936. As a citizen, a patriot, and a moral man who believed in the ethical values instilled in him by his parents, he was distressed to see young people of privilege in comfortable academic enclaves studying their classics and their sciences as if all were well in the world outside the campus. He envisioned Hobart as his laboratory for doing something about this complacency.

"Our remarkable victories in technology are contemporary with our humiliating defeats in mental hygiene and political economy, as we see our hospitals overcrowded with nervous wrecks, and our government paralyzed by the collapse of diplomacy and credit," he stated according to a text published later by School and Society magazine. "Throughout the country, educators are coming to agree that progressive education must be characterized by (1) personal guidance and (2) integration of the curriculum to bring ordered minds to bear upon the chaos and bewilderment of modern life."

He proclaimed, "Every student who lives among us unmoved, who graduates without becoming profoundly disturbed by the predicament of modern society, will mark one complete failure for Hobart."

Then, to the apparent surprise and distress of a faculty that he believed had already consented to the course he was about to set, he made a dramatic announcement: beginning immediately, every Hobart student would be required to take "a continuous, four-year course in responsible citizenship," which would become a cornerstone of the undergraduate experience.

He described a citizenship curriculum in which studies in economics, history, political science and social psychology would be "organized to constitute an ordered and progressive preparation for civic responsibility. Our chief business will continue to be the arts and sciences. But experience has proved that the average college graduate does not lead in civic affairs in his locality. The bosses in our wards and precincts are seldom educated men . . . aloof, fastidious scholars will not turn into alumni impassioned for social justice"—the kind of alumni he wanted.

Since it was October, the new first-year students were already on campus and in class. A philosophical revision of their curriculum on short notice represented a difficult proposition for the faculty; and resistance soon developed, but Eddy forged ahead.

The curriculum developed over the next two years began the first semester of freshman year with "Responsible Citizenship, an introduction to the traditions of American economic and political life," and progressed through "Government in a Democracy," "Contemporary Economic Problems" and "American Government" to senior seminars on some "enterprise of the community, social, cultural, political, economic or philanthropic," to give each student "practical experience in the technique of leadership."

This innovative program brought Eddy a certain amount of acclaim beyond the Hobart campus. He was invited to publish his ideas in several respected journals, and in 1940 the New York State Board of Regents appointed him "State Counselor on Civic Education and National Defense for Out of School Youth." He took a three-month leave from Hobart to devise a program in response to this mandate. Aimed at motivating dropouts and other perceived slackers to take productive places in their communities, it would "raise and attempt to answer the following questions: What must we Americans defend? Why? Against what? With what?" This program would mobilize "community resources" to produce young people who would be better educated, more physically fit and more socially responsible. It was to be community based, rather than statewide, and tailored to attract the interest of young people with such suggested topics as "Am I equipped to be an intelligent voter and tax-payer?" and "What will happen after the war?"

These aspirations were lofty, as were Eddy's goals for his students at Hobart and William Smith. The problem he faced as college administrator was that the new curriculum was by its nature interdisciplinary: it required members of the faculty to devise and teach courses that were outside their academic specialties, incorporating material they might not know much about or be interested in. These courses were often unrelated to the specialized knowledge that was the basis of their tenure—and thus of their career aspirations. Everyone knew what should be taught in chemistry or French class; it was not clear what should be taught, or by whom, in these citizenship classes. The course Eddy had set for the college, rather than inspiring teachers and students to broaden their horizons and serve the country, trapped him in a maze of academic politics and faculty intrigue, which erupted into public view on February 25, 1941.

"Three Members of Hobart College Faculty Resign," said the big headline in that day's *Geneva Daily Times*. "Differences over Policy Cause Withdrawal of Citizenship Teachers. President Eddy also Hints at Possible Resignation."

In lengthy articles, the paper ventilated the entire conflict within the faculty and administration. "Unwillingness of a majority of the Hobart faculty to continue support of the present four-year citizenship requirements unless the general faculty has a choice in shaping the program and a share in the selection of the future teaching staff was said to be behind the resignations of the head of the Citizenship training course and two of his assistants," the lead article said. "Coincident with the announcement of the resignations came word of the appointment of a special committee to make recommendations on the future of the Citizenship program."

In other words, everything Eddy had tried to accomplish was in jeopardy because the faculty did not buy into it. "It was explained today," the *Geneva Times* article said, "that the Citizenship training program is not a department but inter-departmentalized and this crossing of lines into the three regular departments of humanities, sciences and social sciences is believed to be the main source of this controversy."

The newspaper printed an exchange of correspondence between Eddy and Dr. J. Raymond Walsh, a professor of economics who had been one of Eddy's faculty allies as director of the citizenship program and was one of the three who resigned. In his letter of resignation to Eddy, Walsh said he was leaving because "there is little chance of our efforts becoming effective in the years ahead, and this for one reason: The faculty will not allow it. They seem not to be possessed of an adequate reservoir of personal goodwill, professional loyalty, and educational responsibility to sustain such a program." In a bitter response, Eddy said he fully understood why Walsh was bailing out, agreed with his analysis of the faculty's attitude, and made clear his feelings about this turn of events.

"My disappointment is very keen indeed. I should have been quite willing to continue as a leader of the faculty in spite of all these differences if there had been a will on both sides to respect and trust each other," Eddy wrote. "This will is lacking and you have concluded rightly that any temporary evasion of the issue in terms of the faculty vote of personal confidence in me would be futile as well as undemocratic. I am therefore tired of the role of arbiter of the purposes of others and shall exercise my prerogative as a citizen of carrying out some of my own purposes in life, since I am neither successful nor happy in the job of trying to help others carry out their purposes."

As for what would happen next, Eddy told Walsh, "I shall welcome active service with the Marines if that comes next summer, and, if not, I shall ask for it a year later if the world emergency continues to be acute." If the war already under way in Europe should end and the growing clamor for the United States to get involved recede, Eddy said, he would be willing to return to teaching but not to the presidency of Hobart or any other college, "a profession with which I am definitely out of love."

Three months later, Eddy sent a letter to family members and friends with the news that he would indeed leave Hobart to return to military service: "Under the date of May 14th, I have just received instructions to report for active duty as soon as the college year is over. I have applied for a leave of absence from Hobart College for the duration of the emergency." He would never return to academic life.

The United States was not yet at war; the U.S. military had no great need for Eddy's services, especially because his severe limp limited the duties he could undertake. If family were his first consideration, he would have stayed at Hobart, perhaps giving up his administrative duties to return to teaching, so that he could be with his children as they grew up. But he never made career decisions based on what was best for the children, and only once, some years in the future, would he do so for Mary.

———◆❖◆———

Chapter 3

CAIRO

*N*ow that Bill Eddy was back in his beloved Marine Corps uniform, where would he serve? The United States was not officially at war and was not engaged in combat. Even if it had been, Eddy's World War I injuries would have ruled out a battlefield assignment. His knowledge of Arabic, German and French and his intelligence background made him better suited for another role. It was the State Department, as much as the Navy Department, that developed a grand design to make use of Eddy's talents. Despite his years in small-town academia, he was known to interesting and powerful government men and to a network of well-placed Princetonians because of his gregarious nature and his involvement in public causes, and senior people in Washington had plans for him. On June 23, 1941, Eddy was formally designated Naval Attaché and Naval Attaché for Air in Cairo.

At U.S. diplomatic missions around the world, military officers are regularly assigned as "attachés." Their duties include reporting on the military planning and armed forces deployment of the host country, monitoring weapons acquisitions and training programs, and evaluating defense planning and security issues. In major posts such as Cairo, there is likely to be more than one such officer, each from a different branch of the military, each reporting to a higher-ranking officer who holds the title "Defense Attaché," who in turn reports to a civilian diplomat, namely the ambassador or chief of mission. These attachés are members of the armed forces, not of the Foreign Service, but as members of the embassy staff, they are protected by diplomatic immunity—if caught breaking local law or offending local authorities, they can be deported but they cannot be arrested or interrogated.

On July 1, the State Department's Wallace Murray wrote to Alexander Kirk, the chief of mission in Cairo, to tell him about his new staff member. "Major Eddy, you will find, is more than a Naval Attaché," he said. "The Navy Department envisages using Major Eddy not only in Egypt but in nearby Arabic speaking countries such as Saudi Arabia, Palestine, Syria and Iraq. From our own point of view we not only see no objection to such an arrangement, but heartily approve of it. Major Eddy has many close friends among high-placed Arab officials and Arab families throughout these territories, and I believe he he can make contacts with these groups that would be impossible for almost any other American. We should like to have him have as much opportunity as possible to travel around freely, make contacts and observations and submit reports."

These Arab countries were not combatants, but by this time official Washington was waking up to the strategic importance of a region to which it had paid scant attention in the past. It was crucial to the Allied war effort to keep the Suez Canal and the Arabian oil fields out of Axis hands. It is to the credit of the War and State Departments, normally turf-protective organizations reluctant to share assets, that they were sufficiently flexible to sign off on Bill Eddy's unusual arrangement because they needed the information they believed he could deliver.

Once Eddy was on the ground in Egypt, however, Murray's grand vision of his role went largely unfulfilled because of the day-to-day demands of his official job as Naval Attaché. Not until well after the war would Eddy take on such a wide-ranging mission in the Arab world, and by then he was working for a very different employer.

Egypt had nominally been independent since 1922, but in 1941 the most important power in the country was still the British Army, which by treaty had the right to keep troops in Egypt to protect the Suez Canal. Because of Egypt's long Mediterranean coastline and the canal, the country was an obvious strategic prize, and by the time of Eddy's arrival in Cairo the war had come: British forces were struggling to halt the eastward march out of Libya of General Erwin Rommel's redoubtable Afrika Korps. Rommel would drive to within 60 miles of Cairo before being stopped at El Alamein the following summer.

Eddy set out for Cairo on July 15, 1941. This was not a routine trip, because by that time much of the world was at war. The Battle of Britain had saved England from invasion by Germany, but most of Europe was under Nazi domination, and Hitler was marshaling his forces to invade the Soviet Union. Japan, Germany's Axis partner, occupied Korea, Thailand, and much of China, was taking full control of French Indochina and was preparing to march on Singapore and Indonesia. Civilian ships were torpedo targets, airplane seats were scarce, fuel was in short supply, ports and airfields that were secure one day were under enemy attack the next. It seemed as if the entire world outside of Latin America was caught in the vast cataclysm.

Because the United States was not yet in the war, Americans could still travel to areas under Axis control. To reach Cairo, Eddy went by way of the Pacific, through Singapore and then Bangkok. By that time both cities were under Japanese occupation, but Eddy's skimpy correspondence about his voyage is oddly devoid of commentary on what must have been a peculiar experience. From Bangkok he made his way to Egypt via Rangoon, Calcutta, Karachi, and Basra in Iraq, finally arriving in Egypt on July 30. Cairo was not a combat zone, but the war was everywhere around it as the British struggled to hold off Rommel and secure the Suez Canal.

Eddy immediately found himself at home in a city he knew well. "I find unused Arabic vocabulary comes back fast as I hear it constantly," he wrote in a journal shortly after arriving. "Many of my favorite students [from the American University] are around whom I shall see as time permits."

He was still nominally president of Hobart, but the Cairo posting thrust him into the action he craved when he escaped the confining life of the campus. "I see nothing temporary about my job," he wrote to Mary in August, "and it was agreed with the trustees that unless I could return by next summer, they would select and appoint a successor."

His career as an academic was behind him, but not his affection for the students. Not long after arriving in Egypt, he sent a letter to "all my undergraduate friends" at Hobart and William Smith to tell them about his new life. It exudes the exhilaration he found in his work and his surroundings, so different from the cloistered life of academia, and his delight at being part of a team that was working to a common great purpose instead of quarreling over campus politics.

"I wish I could tell you what it means to be a member of a team that is pulling together as a team for the greatest cause in history," he wrote. "And what a team. Britons, South Africans, Greeks, Free French, Poles, Anzacs, Sikhs from India, Canadians, Serbs, American volunteers, men from all corners of the earth, uniforms of every pattern, all working in closed ranks for our common freedom. No personal considerations are allowed to impede the common enterprise, which is simply this: that the lovers of freedom, who have been bred to domestic pursuits of peace, must now match and throw back the Nazi machine of war which is the most efficient and ruthless engine of destruction man has ever seen. The issue is still in doubt, but I have been moved to tears by the inspiring sight of these comrades in goodwill, who have gathered themselves for the fight."

He urged the students not to be persuaded by Americans who wanted to stay out of the war. "Do not believe the defeatists or the isolationists," he wrote. "The fight will go on as long as there is one square foot of ground, or one man of courage alive. When I see these exiles of fifteen conquered countries who have lost all, not quitting but enlisting in the shock troops of freedom, I am ashamed of the caution and compromise and fear for security which control so many of our fellow countrymen."

To Eddy, the issues in the war were unequivocal: the Allies were good, the Axis was evil, and it was the duty of right-thinking people—including the people of the United States, who had not yet been attacked—to ensure that good prevailed. In one letter home, pondering the fact that Germans who were otherwise normal people were carrying out atrocities in Greece, he said, "This illustrates the utter inhumanity of the Nazi system and shows what it does to its followers, something much worse than what it does to its enemies. It kills the body of the enemy but it kills the soul of the Nazi."

THE ATTACHÉ'S DUTIES

In letters to Mary, Eddy reported details of his new assignment and described his life in Egypt.

"I wear khaki uniform, long pants and shirt, but only put on the blouse and Sam Browne belt if I have to report to very high officials like the Minister of Defense etc. Even for my two daily conferences at HQ Royal Navy Middle East, I wear only the shirt . . . I do not wear shorts (which four out of five do) for the good reason that the distribution of my anatomy leaves much to be desired," he told her. For social events in the evenings he wore civilian clothes except at "official legation dinners, at least once a week, where I wear white uniform."

Most of his letters from this Cairo period concern family matters—his love for Mary, the children, chitchat about his living arrangements, news of friends. But Mary wanted to know what he actually did all day. Without going into operational details, about which he was always discreet, he gave her this account:

I rise at seven daily, reach the ofice between 8:30 and 9, study radio press summaries and transcription from the Arab press, communiqués and GHQ Bulletins for an hour or so. At ten daily the legation secretaries, the Military and the Naval attachés meet in the Minster's [Kirk's] study for daily conference, to exchange information and to receive instructions on any special jobs he wishes done. Either late in the morning or in the evening I visit the royal Navy hq, RAF hq, and about every other day the Royal Marines and the Egyptian Ministry of Defense. At these offices there are intelligence or operations officers designated for me to visit, to secure information on events. Sometimes, when transcribing notes for a full report to the US Navy on some completed operation, I am given a desk there temporarily and work for the major portion of a day or more on papers that cannot be removed. For example, I prepared thus a detailed study of the part played by the Royal Navy in the spring campaign, bombardment of the coast, landing parties, etc. . . . I am now completing a statement of the effective strength and disposition of all units of the Italian fleet that survive, and of the French fleet. The nature of the information on naval matters which I seek (and sometimes find) concerns the enemy more than the allies and covers: naval operations, trade, merchant marine, suspects and agents, technical devices and inventions (interesting developments recently in the mining of the Canal), bases, mine fields, mutinies or disaffection among personnel or in ports, contraband being shipped to enemy by or thru neutrals, arrivals and departures of all vessels, volume of supply going to for example Dardanelles or North Africa, sailing routes. I suspend all routine investigations of course for emergency work such as attacks on US shipping where immediate and full identification of the attackers, their tactics, ammunition, etc., are urgently requested . . . strength of harbor and canal defenses, naval supply facilities, storage, fuel sources, camouflage etc. . . . I have listed naval items, but as you know I am charged with political errands too, counter-espionage, study of Axis propaganda, personnel, organization, sabotage, blacklists . . . I have developed sources of information in several cities. Nothing on this sheet should ever appear in print unless you are in a hurry to become a widow. Entirely apart from these duties above I have sole responsibility for coding and decoding all Navy cables.

Despite his cautionary note to Mary about the need to keep all this information confidential, there was nothing secret about the nature of his duties. The Naval Attaché of any other country, asked to guess Eddy's job description, would have given a reasonably accurate list of his duties; what he was doing was what Naval Attachés do in wartime. Less obvious was his role as intelligence agent outside his military duties. Egypt at the time was full of officers and politicians who sympathized with Germany in the war, not because they viewed Hitler favorably but because they thought a German victory would put an end to British dominion over Egypt and other Arab countries. (Among these German sympathizers was a young army officer named Anwar Sadat.) Eddy apparently failed to discern this sentiment in the army, reporting unequivocally to Washington that "the officers are pro-British," but he was aware of pro-German sentiment within Egypt's small political and business elite and he wanted to infiltrate this community.

"One of my most interesting duties," he wrote to Mary, "was membership in the Royal Egyptian Club, which I got into through knowing Arabic and some native officials who belong. It is a hotbed of pro-German propaganda, with nightly dinners and meetings of fifth columnists. My official position excluded me from the inner councils of the conspirators but I did enough 'agreeing' and 'cursing the British and the Jews' to get quite a bit of information." His boss, Chief of Mission Alexander Kirk, "disapproved of counter-espionage by any of us, saying it would end diplomatic immunity, but I had other instructions from my primary boss, the director of Naval Intelligence, and I went my own way."

That "primary boss" was Admiral Alan G. Kirk, a career officer and a committed internationalist who had been Naval Attaché in London. When the United States entered the war, Kirk gave up his desk job in Washington to participate in combat operations in the Mediterranean and commanded U.S. naval forces in the invasion of Normandy. After the war he served as U.S. ambassador to Belgium and the Soviet Union.

Eddy's reports were often detailed to the point of tediousness, and it is questionable whether all of them were valuable to the Allied war effort. One confidential memo, for example, reported that "Convoy WSIX, consisting of seven supply ships and the auxiliary BRECONSHIRE arrived in Malta from westerward Sept. 28 A.M. The eighth ship IMPERIAL STAR (White Star line) was torpedoed from the air the evening of Sept. 27 at 37⁰ 31' N; 10⁰ 46' and was taken in tow." Interesting information, perhaps, but this was an Allied convoy, and it can be assumed that London and Washington already knew that the *Imperial Star* had been torpedoed.

At other times, however, he contributed information that any military planner or commander would want to have. In one detailed report to the director of Naval Intelligence, for example, he reviewed the state of mine-laying in the Gulf of Suez by the Germans, noted that Egyptian troops had been deployed to unload cargoes in the port of Ismailia because air raids had frightened off the civilian workers, and described the defense network of the Suez Canal. There he found that two of every three antiaircraft guns visible from the air were fake, "the distribution, however, being changed frequently so that raiders cannot be sure which guns are dummies."

Eddy was not a combat officer, but neither did he hide behind his desk. The war and its dangers were all around him, and he regarded it as part of his duties to see it up close.

In September, he investigated an attack by German bombers on a Panamanian-flag freighter, the *Honduras*, which was carrying a load of coal up the gulf of Suez. Once aboard, Eddy realized that three bombs had failed to explode and were embedded somewhere in the cargo, primed to detonate. The coal had to be offloaded carefully before the bombs could be recovered.

In his report about the *Honduras* incident to the director of Naval Intelligence, Eddy took the risk of going well beyond his writ to express views about a subject that mattered a great deal to him and would eventually become the arena of his most enduring accomplishments: Saudi Arabia.

At the time, President Roosevelt and his advisers were beginning to recognize the future importance of Saudi Arabia, which was neutral in the war. The State Department's interest was clear from Wallace Murray's memo about Eddy's original assignment, but in most of official Washington, the Kingdom was still virtually invisible—so much so that the U.S. government had recently turned down a request from King Abdul Aziz ibn Saud for a $10 million loan to tide him over during the very severe economic stress that the war was inflicting on his country. Exports of the oil discovered in the 1930s by Standard Oil of California had begun only in 1939, and they were cut off after six months by the outbreak of the war. The loss of this revenue, coupled with a sharp decrease in the number of taxable pilgrims to Mecca, also because of the war, left the Kingdom virtually destitute, but the Roosevelt administration took the position that it was more properly up to Britain to provide financial aid.

Eddy was more prescient, and even at this point in his life, before he ever went to Saudi Arabia, he was a voluble advocate for its king and his kingdom. He volunteered the opinion that "cordial relations and our favorable position have been damaged seriously by ths blunt refusal [of economic assistance] which was accompanied by implications suggesting that Ibn Saud and his country are not of great interest to the United States. I consider, on the contrary, this territory to be very strategic to the Allied cause in the Arab world, and I am presuming therefore to offer the following considerations for the information of the Office of Naval Intelligence which may be disposed to assert an influence to change the foreign policy of our government regarding Saudi Arabia.

"(a) Surrounded by countries torn with dissension, he [the king] has kept his country at peace at home and with others, and he has kept it free from Axis control.

"(b) With his prestige among his co-religionists and fellow Arabs he is a constant restraint on extremists on his borders . . . As he goes, so will go the Arab countries and Islam.

"(c) The development of the resources of his country, begun so largely by Americans, lies ahead in the future. The only question is who will furnish him with the technical and financial assistance. We have there, at present, an unparelleled opportunity, America's one priority in the Arab world . . .

"I find no reassurance, but only cause for alarm, in the suggestion that a division of spheres of influence has taken place under which the U.S. resigns to Britain all initiative in Saudi Arabia. It is not impossible that the war may be followed by a general emancipation of Near and Middle Eastern countries from the Franco-British system of colonies, mandates and protectorates . . . In such a day, through Ibn Saud we might exert great influence. Not, however, if he has been told long since that he and his country don't really matter to the United States."

This appears to have been the first time any employee of the U.S. government with any policy input expressed such a vision of an alliance with Saudi Arabia. Toward the end of the war, Eddy would have the opportunity to put these views into practice, and he would play an important part in the process of prying Saudi Arabia out of Britain's sphere of influence and into the American camp.

Eddy had no way of knowing in 1941 that Roosevelt was already coming to agree with him on this subject. The president was actually quite intrigued by the prospect of forging some sort of long-term relationship with Saudi Arabia and by the possibility that Saudi Arabian oil might be useful to the Navy. Behind the scenes in Washington, the president had privately asked the State and War Departments for ideas about how a partnership might be developed to benefit both countries. Not being privy to those early discussions, Eddy assumed that the denial of immediate financial assistance represented the end of the story, not a beginning, so he fired off his brilliantly accurate but unsolicited and premature bit of policy advice to his superiors.

Then he returned to his job. He went to sea for a couple of weeks of observation with the Royal Navy, an especially dangerous environment because German U-boats were everywhere in the waters around Egypt. He was first aboard the destroyer *Jackal*, for "a run to Tobruk to take in troops and supplies." (The *Jackal* was later sunk by the Germans.) Then he sailed aboard the RMS *Jupiter* for "two night bombardments of the Libya coast; a successful submarine hunt; and a rescue of crew from a bombed and sinking British mine-layer, the *Latona*." The *Latona*, an Abdiel-class mine-layer commissioned only six months earlier, was carrying reinforcements and ammunition to the besieged British garrison at Tobruk, in Libya, when she was attacked by Axis aircraft on October 25. The cargo of ammunition exploded, followed by the ordnance in her own magazine, and she sank in two hours. Recounting this time at sea to his children, Eddy wrote that "the Tobruk run was thrilling, the bombardments fun, the sub hunt very gratifying, but the rescue horrible, with 84 dead, and 150 terribly burned, of whom 18 died on the way back to Alexandria."

Thus Eddy, who in upstate New York had been out of place as a convivial pipe-smoking academic and raconteur, went back to war and was in his element. As he would write to his son Bill, a young Marine officer, later in the war, "Nothing can equal the thrill of leading men in combat." He was not leading men in combat, but he was living on the edge of it for a cause to which he was committed, and doing it in the Arab world, where he felt at home.

But now, after he had been in Egypt only a few months, he was suddenly redeployed. Busy as he was, and however useful his reports may have been to Washington, a greater need for his talents was developing a thousand miles to the West. The United States had still not entered the war, but General William Donovan, who was building the American intelligence and espionage organization that would be known as the Office of Strategic Services, or OSS, could already see that however events unfolded, the United States would be engaged strategically in North Africa. He wanted an operative in place in that region who could prepare the groundwork for military action in which the United States would participate, if it came to that, or for espionage to subvert the Germans if they got there first. French North Africa was politically and ethnically complicated and dangerous. Donovan needed an agent who spoke the languages, understood military thinking, and could be counted on to be discreet. On the basis of Eddy's work in Cairo, Donovan concluded that he would be the right man. "By an appeal to [Navy] Secretary Knox," an official OSS history recorded, "Donovan secured Eddy's appointment as Naval Attaché in Tangier in December 1941 (a post which had not heretofore existed)."

This new assignment, which carried with it a promotion to lieutenant colonel, seems to have come as a surprise. On November 1, Eddy wrote to Mary, "I returned from my two weeks observation cruise with the Navy to find a bombshell in the form of telegraphic orders awaiting me: 'Immediate return Washington for instructions regarding other foreign duty.' I have no idea what the orders mean, whether I am later to return to Cairo or to some other duty in the Near East."

He was gone from Cairo in less than a week, even before his new appointment was official, and before the Japanese attack on Pearl Harbor propelled the United States into the war. On November 4, Alexander Kirk wrote him a "Dear Eddy" letter to say, "I wish to tell you again how deeply I personally deplore your transfer and what a loss to this Mission the termination of your service here constitutes . . . I feel that in your departure the prestige of American representation in Egypt is reduced and that my own task is made harder." That was not Eddy's problem; he was replaceable in Cairo. He was about to take on an assignment of far greater scope and complexity, in which the danger would come not from German submarines but from human treachery.

———◆◆✖◆◆———

NORTH AFRICA

*T*he Hollywood moviemakers who depicted the exotic environment of Morocco in the early 1940s in the classic film *Casablanca* were not making it up. North Africa in early 1942 was a conspiratorial hothouse of spies, double-agents, desperate refugees, Spanish fascists, Nazi provocateurs, Vichy French officers, anti-Vichy French officers, British and American agents of influence, and assorted military attachés, arms merchants, and opportunists, male and female, of every origin—Arab, Berber, French, German, Spanish, Portuguese, African and even a few Japanese. Dozens of indigenous tribes and clans pursued their own rivalries. No one told the truth about anything. Some of the intriguers were skillful, some were buffoons. Some were principled, many were unscrupulous. The characters played in the movie by Paul Henreid, Ingrid Bergman, Claude Rains, Sydney Greenstreet and Peter Lorre would have fit right in.

In the words of Robert D. Murphy, the North African political representative of General Dwight D. Eisenhower, supreme Allied commander in Europe, "It was estimated that at least two hundred thousand Europeans had come to French North Africa since the outbreak of war, some of them very rich, many very poor. Bankers and businessmen were clandestinely transferring their money and investments to Africa to avoid inflation or confiscation; paupers found shelter in rude, makeshift camps. Scattered among these fugitives were hundreds, perhaps thousands, of restless and even dangerous men and women, most of them anti-Nazi, but also anti many other things." It was still the same old story, a fight for love and glory.

Into this garden of evil in January 1942 walked William Alfred Eddy, posted to Tangier, an outpost of Spanish rule on the Atlantic coast of Morocco, just west of the Strait of Gibraltar. In his Marine Corps uniform, now a lieutenant colonel, he was ostensibly the Naval Attaché at the U.S. consulate. In reality he was a combination spy, saboteur, political agent and military planner. He knew as well as anyone how high were the stakes: for individuals, life and death, freedom and oppression; for the countries and organizations that sent them there or chased them there, control of North Africa and the Suez Canal, and the future of France and its colonial empire. Tension was high and a misstep could be fatal, not only to Eddy but to others, including the Allied troops who would stage an amphibious landing later that year, but as usual Eddy's sense of humor served him well. He described wartime Tangier as "a cute, compact musical comedy set peopled by as strange a crowd as ever gathered on an opera stage."

The city's 100,000 inhabitants, whom Eddy referred to as "Tangerines," included about 80,000 indigenous Arabs and Berbers, or "Moors," as he called them. He estimated that there were 10,000 Spaniards, 5,000 French citizens and about 2,000 Britons.

The American presence in Tangier is as old as the republic, perhaps the only place in the Arabic-speaking world of which that could be said. Morocco was the first country to extend recognition to the rebel nation in the New World, in 1777, and American ships put in frequently at its port.

From the roof of the U.S. legation building in the old walled medina, which is now a museum, the Rock of Gibraltar is visible on clear days across the narrow strait. As would be expected from such a critical position on the global maritime map, the U.S. Marines have a long history there, beginning with the struggle against the Barbary pirates.

According to the museum's web site, "Early in the Civil War, Confederate ships called at Tangier. After the Union government called this indiscretion to the attention of the Moroccan authorities, life at the Legation was occasionally disturbed by hostile crowds protesting the U.S. Navy's interference with Moroccan trade. On several occasions it became necessary for U.S. Marines to come ashore to move prisoners which had been taken from Confederate ships, through town to U.S. warships."

By the time of World War II, Eddy wrote, Tangier "was full of persons who had been, or ought to be, in jail. As Lisbon was for Europe, so Tangier was for Africa—the escape hatch from prison, banking laws, justice, persecution, morality (there was no neighborhood without sin fit to cast the first stone)."

Eddy arrived in Tangier on January 26, 1942, only seven weeks after Pearl Harbor, at a time of policy chaos in Washington and London. Axis forces were on the march in Europe and Asia; Britain and the Allies were reeling. No one knew where Hitler would strike next, and there was no coherent Allied war plan. The State Department and the War Department often had conflicting priorities, and neither had much esteem for Bill Donovan's fledgling intelligence operation, which itself played by no rules; when diplomats and generals referred to Donovan by the sobriquet "Wild Bill," it was not necessarily a compliment.

It was possible that the Germans, already in Libya, would take over French North Africa as well. It was also possible, but by no means decided, that the Allies would invade to prevent the Germans from moving. And it was possible that ostensibly neutral Spain, which controlled its own small slice of Moroccan territory, would enter the war on the side of the Axis, a development the Allies wished to prevent. What, then, was Eddy's assignment?

In a memo to Roosevelt on December 22, 1941, just two weeks after the U.S. declared war, Donovan said he had given Eddy these instructions: "That the aid of native chiefs be obtained, the loyalty of the inhabitants be cultivated; fifth columnists organized and placed, demolition materials cached; and guerrilla bands of bold and daring men organized and installed." He told the president that Eddy had been instructed "to maintain a line of demarcation, in so far as practicable, between operations and intelligence."

Eddy wrote that he was "sent out with a double-barreled directive: Prepare a network of agents and seven clandestine radio stations (a) to leave behind in case the Axis occupies North Africa (b) to prepare intelligence and sabotage in case the Allies should land an expeditionary force. I tried in vain to read between the lines of type, and the lines of Wild Bill's careworn brow, which eventuality was the more likely. I assumed that for security reasons I was not being told." From what he heard in Washington and upon arrival in Tangier, he believed an Allied evacuation, which would leave Morocco and Algeria in Axis hands, was more likely. Eddy said Donovan instructed him to take orders only from himself and Murphy, the senior U.S. civilian representative in Algiers.

Murphy, a fluent speaker of French, was already an experienced diplomat but still in the early years of a remarkable career in which he became a sort of Zelig of American diplomacy. He had already served in Germany, Switzerland and France; ahead were assignments in Belgium and Japan and at the United Nations, as a senior official in the State Department, and as a foreign policy troubleshooter for Presidents Eisenhower, Johnson, Kennedy, and Nixon. He and Eddy, partners in North Africa, would work together again in the Lebanese political crisis of 1958.

Before Eisenhower sent him to North Africa, Murphy had been the American envoy to the Vichy government in France. That government, established after the Germans took Paris, represented one of the greatest uncertainties facing Murphy. Eddy, and other Allied planners.

The provincial town of Vichy was the capital of the defeated and emasculated France that remained, under the terms of the armistice imposed by Hitler, nominally independent and neutral in the war. In reality, French military and civilian officials in North Africa, whatever their personal sentiments, had little choice but to implement whatever instructions came from Berlin and Rome. A "German Armistice Commission" in Morocco, an "Italian Armistice Commission" in Tunisia and a combined commission in Algeria were in place to remind the French that they had been routed by the Germans on the battlefield and to ensure that the Axis-friendly terms of the German-imposed armistice were carried out. The police officer portrayed by Claude Rains in *Casablanca* personified the ambiguities and divided loyalties among the so-called "Free French"—were they to follow orders of the only French government they had, namely the collaborationists in Vichy, or resist and go over to the Allies, in effect turning against a beloved but defeated France that had cut the best deal it could to survive?

In these treacherous political waters, Eddy had tactical decision-making power, but strategic questions were to be resolved at a higher level. "I was to do what Murphy, the policy man, ordered or approved, and nothing else," Eddy said.

In Washington and London, where military strategists often disagreed about how best to deploy their forces, it seemed clear that one side or the other would soon send troops to occupy Morocco and Algeria—either the Germans, to seize full control of the Mediterranean and reinforce their designs on the Suez Canal, or the allies, to prevent the Germans from doing so. If the former, Eddy's task was to create a network of saboteurs, spies and clandestine operatives who would make the German occupation difficult and tie down as many German units as possible; if the latter, Eddy's mission was to create a similar network of friendly or at least acquiescent agents and groups who would facilitate an Allied landing.

"Eddy's work thus included the establishment of a network to collect intelligence from various agencies and technical means of funneling it to Tangier for transmission to Washington," according to a narrative in the OSS archives. "It also included equipping the resistance groups of North Africa with arms. This was done through the diplomatic pouch, with [OSS agents] bringing the arms over from Gibraltar or obtaining them locally, and a number of individuals carrying them to their destinations. It also included the transmission of printed propaganda material aimed at the French. Furthermore he selected individuals to guide in the fleets" in the event of an Allied landing, and smuggled these maritime pilots out of Morocco to join up with Allied navies.

According to Tom Braden and Stewart Alsop, OSS agents who later gained prominence as journalists in Washington, Eddy "was to set up intelligence posts in the principal cities. He was to establish a chain of communications between them, and with America. He was to prepare the beachheads and landing fields, and he was to try to nullify French opposition or, if possible, win French support. In the meantime Eddy was to encourage the French to resist the Germans in the event that Hitler beat the Allies to the draw by invading North Africa himself."

"Our purpose in organizing subversive groups in Spanish Morocco," according to a fascinating narrative by Eddy's sidekick in these operations, the anthropologist Carleton Coon, "was to prevent the Germans from taking this country in event that they (a) moved west from Tripoli or (b) moved south through Spain. Later on we added to this the purpose of facilitating the success of American and British arms in case the United Nations should make a landing in international or Spanish territory, or both, or in case the Spaniards should try to close the Straits of Gibraltar. The British SOE had much the same idea, but early in the game we agreed on a division of labor whereby the British should handle the Christians in Tangier and Spaniards in Morocco, and we, Moslems."

The uncertainty of the moment was reflected in a letter Eddy wrote to Murphy on March 1, 1942, in which he used analogies from the global trading marketplace to throw a thin cover of code over what he was talking about. He said it appeared from a telegram he had received that the proposed invasion, which he called "the big contract," had been postponed.

"Our speculators had decided to invest their money on it when I left home and told me so, but it may be that their reserve funds have been depleted by the commercial losses in the Middle East and in the sugar plantations in the Philippines," he wrote, in transparent references to Axis advances in Libya and Japanese gains in the Pacific. "I take the telegram to state quite clearly that we cannot count entirely upon the big contract but must be prepared for any other eventuality by establishing chain stores of groceries," Eddy wrote. Distributing supplies—that is, weapons—through such medium-size groups of operatives was preferable to the "five-and-ten-cent roadside hot dog stand" scale of operations they had discussed previously.

Eddy was only stating the obvious when he wrote to Donovan on March 18 that "my own thinking would be a great deal clearer if I knew whether or not large scale operations in North Africa are being contemplated for this spring."

There was a high potential for disagreement in a team that paired strong-willed men with a high opinion of their own abilities such as Murphy and Eddy, reporting through different chains of command; Ray Close, Eddy's nephew and a longtime CIA agent, told me that Murphy was Eddy's "nemesis" in the North Africa assignment. But there are few hints in their correspondence of the tensions that must have arisen.

At one point Eddy expressed dismay over the "strong undercurrent of impatience and irritation" he perceived in a letter from Murphy, and in March 1942, Eddy surprised Murphy by reporting that he mistrusted and would no longer work with a French agent code-named "Augie," to which Murphy replied brusquely, "Our people have used Augie for years. I see no reason for discontinuing that practice." When Eddy learned that food was running out for the civilian population on Malta, he agreed to a proposal by the British to divert to the island a French cargo vessel carrying food from Algeria to the French mainland. Murphy objected that such an action could ignite naval warfare between the French and British because the Vichy French, while nominally neutral, could not simply give the British a free hand to oppose the Axis.

Other than these scattered episodes, Eddy and Murphy appear to have been on the same page, sharing their frustrations as well as their successes. Murphy's papers contain letters to various other agents giving them specific instructions to keep Eddy informed. "He is entitled to know everything we are doing," one of these letters said.

Eddy, in a retrospective narrative he wrote some years later titled "Spies and Lies in Tangier," called Murphy "a truly legendary hero of the war." Murphy, in his memoir *Diplomat Among Warriors*, wrote that Eddy "was invaluable throughout the various stages of the African operation. Eddy was always meticulous in coordinating his activities with mine, and no American knew more about Arabs or about power politics in [North] Africa. He was one of a kind, unique; we could have used a hundred like him."

WHO'S IN CHARGE HERE?

Despite the comic opera overtones of the Tangier environment— clumsy car chases, sleeping powders in cocktails, sexual liaisons in diplomatic villas—Eddy and his agents were engaged in serious and sometimes deadly business. Smuggled weapons blew up. People disappeared. At one point Eddy began to carry a pistol and took shooting lessons to guard against the possibility of an attack on the street. Newly arrived Americans who knew nothing about the Muslim holy month of Ramadan were thrown into panic when Spanish batteries fired to signal the evening start of the Iftar sundown meal and local citizens ran through the streets.

The political geography of Tangier and Morocco by itself created a murky, ambiguous environment, in which it was never entirely clear who was in charge. Everyone had divided loyalties and multiple agendas, and no one could be trusted. German agents and Axis sympathizers were everywhere. Even the British could be troublesome as they competed with the Americans for power and influence within the alliance. In May Eddy complained bitterly to Murphy that British Intelligence had told Washington that the French officers he was negotiating with about arms supplies "are not to be trusted." He characterized this as "a stab in the back, a resentment that we should be dealing with French groups at all, rather than thru [sic] the British." Eddy threatened to play a "trump card" with the British, which was that the Americans controlled the distribution of British diplomatic correspondence in the region because they had maintained diplomatic relations with Vichy while the British had not.

Tangier was nominally a neutral international zone and as such had the only cable and mail service in North Africa not subject to

Axis censorship. Spanish troops dispatched by the Falangist government of Generalissimo Francisco Franco—the victor in Spain's civil war a few years earlier—had occupied Tangier in 1941, but as Eddy noted in a letter to his son Jack, "the USA has not recognized the occupation, making our relations with the Spanish rather strained." Among the Spanish residents of Tangier was a colony of sullen losers from the Republican side of the Spanish war, many of them communists. This was a group that Eddy would recruit to his advantage.

Beyond Tangier lay the protectorate of Spanish Morocco. Franco's Spain was ostensibly neutral in the war, although its sympathies clearly lay with the Axis, and Eddy's work was complicated by Washington's desire not to anger Franco and bring him into the conflict on the side of Germany and Italy. Franco was the only ruler with the power to close the Strait of Gibraltar to Allied shipping, which would cut Britain off from the Suez Canal. Moreover, if Spain entered the war or collaborated openly with the Germans, it was possible that German control of North Africa could create a southern route to an invasion of the United States by way of the Canary Islands.

Complicating Eddy's calculations was the fact that he and his nominal boss, Consul General J. Rives Childs (later his successor as ambassador to Saudi Arabia), liked and respected the governor general of Spanish Morocco, General Luis Orgaz. They concluded that Orgaz was first and foremost a Spanish patriot who did not share Franco's sympathies for the Axis. Orgaz believed that the Allies would win the war, and therefore he labored to maintain Spain's distance from Hitler, despite the policy in Madrid.

"It is by no means improbable," Childs cabled to Washington on September 1, "that General Orgaz might, under favorable circumstances, be induced to decline to agree to the use by the Axis of Spanish Morocco as a base of operations even if permission therefor might be granted by the Madrid government under pressure" from Berlin. Eddy wanted to encourage Orgaz in this attitude without being so obvious about it that it would cost the Spaniard his job.

The rest of Morocco and all of Algeria and Tunisia, as well as French military units operating there, were still under the control of France—which meant not Paris, then occupied by the Germans, but Vichy.

A year earlier Roosevelt had dispatched Murphy on a reconnaissance tour of French-controlled Africa, a vast swath of the
continent's northern and western regions. Defeat and capitulation
in Europe had left all these colonial outposts in an anomalous
position, still loyal to France but divided about whether to support
the Vichy collaborators or to embrace the fledgling resistance. On
this tour, Murphy wrote in his memoirs, "I was delighted to meet
Frenchmen who were strongly anti-Nazi, who were much more
pro-British than I had anticipated [despite a clumsy, doomed Brit-
ish-sponsored effort to capture Dakar, in Senegal] and who acted
as if they really would fight for their independence in their African empire. It seemed to me that the least we Americans could do
was to give these Frenchmen the modest economic support they
required. If the United States later entered the war, the French
military establishment in Africa and the area's strategic importance could be of immense value." This became, in effect, the policy Murphy and Eddy were assigned to implement as the United
States prepared to go to war.

The armed forces of France had been defeated quickly in
Europe, but under the peculiar terms of capitulation Germany did
not dismantle the military units in France's overseas territories
and did not dismiss the officer corps. As a result the French units
in North Africa were in place and intact, but with divided loyalties. Eddy and Murphy aspired to turn them decisively against
Vichy and win them over to the Allied side; at the very least Eddy
was to ensure that they would not resist an Allied landing even if
they did not support it.

Then there were the native populations of these zones, Arabs
and ethnic Berbers from the southern mountains. Mostly indifferent to the conflict between European powers, which these
Muslims viewed as a civil war among Christians, the Arabs and
Berbers wanted an end to colonial rule and were willing to aid
whichever force held out the greatest prospect of delivering that
outcome. This was the same phenomenon Eddy had observed in
Cairo among Egyptians who favored Germany not because they
approved of Hitler but because they saw a German victory as a possible way to end British military control over their own country.

Carleton Coon, who had done field work in the rebellious Rif region of the Atlas Mountains and been kidnapped by Riffians, described the attitudes of the local people with mixed sympathy and contempt.

"They realize that they cannot get the French out," Coon wrote. "Like almost all North Africans, they despise the French for taking away their lands and privileges and treating them as inferiors. Yet they know that the French are firmly entrenched and that they cannot live without them. So what they want is political equality, relief from economic exploitation and above all the opportunity for education. They want to become modern people, like the Turks and Iranians and other Moslems who realize that the Moslem Middle Ages are over, and they know that the key to this change is education. The French (and I have heard many of them say this) think that Moroccans are not sufficiently 'evolved' for education or modern life." No wonder the local Muslims supported neither the Axis nor the allies but instead sold their services to the highest bidder of the day. Eddy himself did not view the Arabs of North Africa with the same respect he would later accord to the Arabs of the Arabian peninsula, whose ethical code was largely uncorrupted by colonial occupation.

Eddy and Coon hoped to foment an uprising among this discontented native population, much as T.E. Lawrence had done in Arabia in the first war. They talked of organizing tens of thousands of men under the leadership of a Rif chieftain known as Abd-el-Krim, a troublemaking Berber leader of opposition to colonial rule, whom they aspired to bring back from exile on France's Reunion Island. But these plans came to nothing, for several reasons. The State Department opposed any such endeavor because it would amount to undermining a government with which the United States maintained correct relations—that is, Vichy France. The War Department, in an oddly prophetic assessment that might have envisioned the world of 2007, feared that it could lead to a civilizational conflict between Muslims and Christians. And the local leaders weren't having it anyway; much as they loathed the French, they were reluctant to commit their own credibility and positions of leadership to a different group of Western Christians.

As for Abd-el-Krim, who had been in exile since his rebels were defeated by a combined French-Spanish force in 1926, he never returned to Morocco before his death in 1963.

This was a cutthroat environment in which the mutual hostility of the participants was masked by a veneer of protocol and diplomatic courtesy. In one letter to Jack, Eddy described a diplomatic reception in which the nominally neutral Spanish hosts moved back and forth across the salon, chatting alternately with the Americans on one side, the Germans and the Italians on the other. Eddy took the opportunity to strike up a friendship with Hassan Muhammed, the Khalif, or native chief, of Tetouan, the town that served as the administrative capital of Spanish Morocco. As Eddy spoke to him in Arabic, the hosts were upset, Eddy observed, because "they do not like to see us friendly with the Moorish leaders." The Khalif, he said, "has the Moors solidly behind him and would probably hold the balance of power if there were ever any European strife in the Spanish Moroccan zone."

Thus was formed another link in the chain of alliances and connections that Eddy forged in Tangier. This was a pattern Eddy would follow throughout his later career in the Arabian peninsula, Lebanon and Syria: treat the Arabs as human beings worthy of respect, identify those of political or cultural importance, and cultivate their friendship by conversing with them in their own language.

Donovan had chosen well. The assignment in North Africa called on all of Eddy's knowledge and skill: his knowledge of Arabic, German and French, and his familiarity with Islam; his Marine Corps and military intelligence training and experience; the ego-management tactics learned from academic politics; his impenetrable discretion; his ability to inspire loyalty in subordinates; his sense of humor; and his ability to follow orders while improvising on tactics.

"Now I was to begin an association with a person whom I consider one of the greatest men I have ever met," Carleton Coon would write of his work with Eddy, "one of the happiest associations of my life."

In Tangier, Eddy lived in the Minzah Hotel, the city's best. It was intrigue central, the Rick's Cafe of Tangier. He also maintained a villa outside of town where conspirators could rendezvous unobserved.

"We are followed everywhere we go," Eddy wrote to Jack in February 1942, "so we have to be very careful about meeting our confidential agents. I know the men who follow me because I have photographs of the 55 Axis agents in Tangier and Spanish Morocco. It is lots of fun to turn on them and stare them in the face. They dare no overt action because the Germans are most unpopular here. The people of Tangier want only to be left alone, they do not want anybody bringing violence to the town. Our telephones are all tapped. We never say anything confidential over the phone so it is lots of fun to say, 'I'll meet you for lunch at the Minzah Hotel but we will not invite the damned German who is listening to this conversation.'"

On one occasion, Eddy wrote to his wife, he heard a noise in the room next to his at the hotel, obtained a key from a house-keeper, and walked in to find a German agent "pretending that he was making repairs in the closet."

In fact, Eddy wrote to his daughter Carmen on March 27, "We have quite a time with counterespionage. The head telephone operator in the Minzah Hotel (a very well educated man on our side who prepared for months to disguise himself as a mere tele-phone operator) has just been offered 5,000 francs a month by the Germans to report to them all telephone conversations at the Minzah between British or American residents. He promptly told us. We are taking the francs and composing fake conversations for him to report to them, conversations which should give the Ger-mans plenty of phony information." At the office, he added, they would deliberately leave the safe open "by mistake" and permit the theft of phony documents by "one of the native messengers" who had been recruited by the other side.

In a letter to Jack ten days later, Eddy recounted with char-acteristic humor the tale of one of the "Heinie agents" he had encountered. She was "a super Mata Hari," he wrote, "one of Hit-ler's confidential blondes who goes around spying on other agents. She cut a swathe here for a few days riding around in a deluxe lim-ousine and throwing her weight around. But she recently went home with a black eye, which will cramp her siren style for a while. It seems she was in a night club, where in a loud voice she made some insulting remarks about the British, at which point one of the Gibraltar boys got up from his table, went over to where she was sitting with two Germans, bowed politely, and then calmly pasted her one in the snoot. There was a dead silence, then the Heinies looked around and decided to do nothing, and they left with their damaged queen. She left town the next day." Think of Victor Laszlo, the Paul Henreid character in *Casablanca,* silencing the German singers in Rick's Café by instructing the musicians to "Play the Marseillaise!"

These anecdotes are about as close as Eddy came to revealing any operational details of his work. For security reasons, he was not allowed to keep a journal. The discretion that made him suitable for the job constrained him from writing to Mary and the children about what he actually did all day; that information must be reconstructed mostly from the writings of his colleagues and others, whose once-secret files are now in the National Archives of the United States. Even with that material it is sometimes difficult to figure out exactly what Eddy and his team were up to because they used code names for everyone—"Robinson Crusoe," "Kingpin," "Tweedledum," "Fifty Cents."

"Col. Eddy told no one anything he did not need to know," Carleton Coon wrote in his own colorful narrative.

For Eddy, the Tangier assignment carried danger but also excitement, challenge and the camaraderie of combat. He was unhappy only in the absence of Mary, who had remained in Hanover. Just as Eddy was arriving in Tangier, Donovan wrote to Mary with bad news about this separation: "I very much regret that we were not able to have you join him in North Africa. I have taken up the mattter with the highest authorities in the Navy and have been advised that because of the unsettled conditions there the Navy could not make any exception to their rule of not permtting members of officers' families to join them on foreign stations . . . I do not know when Colonel Eddy may return, but doubt that it will be soon," Donovan cautioned her.

OPERATION TORCH

In the policymaking and organizational disarray that broke out in Washington after Pearl Harbor—the State Department pulling one way, the War Department another, and Donovan's newly established OSS making up its own rules of the game as circumstances and opportunities dictated—one critical decision by Roosevelt and his advisers made possible the work of Eddy and his agents and the ultimate success of Operation TORCH, the Allied landings of 1942. This was the decision to maintain diplomatic relations with the government of Vichy France.

Roosevelt was strongly criticized at home for recognizing a government that was essentially a puppet of Nazi Germany, especially because Britain took the opposite position. On July 3, 1940, British warships shelled the French fleet at Mers el Kebir, Algeria, killing nearly 1,300 French sailors, and Vichy's president, Marshal Philippe Pétain (who had led the force that defeated Abd-el-Krim in 1926),

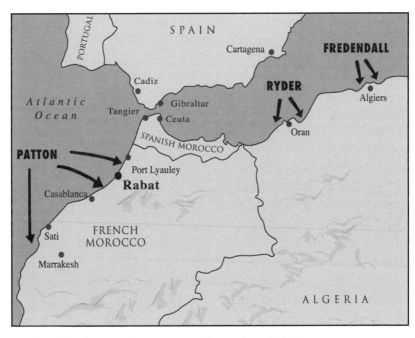

The deployment of Operation TORCH,
the Allied invasion of Vichy North Africa—November 8th, 1942.

responded by severing relations. Britain thus took the position that Vichy was a tool of the Axis and should be regarded as an enemy; as a result, all British diplomats and agents were expelled from French North Africa. The United States, which at the time still had correct relations with Japan and Germany, did not follow the British lead.

Within the Roosevelt administration, the links to Vichy were opposed by dissidents who favored the French resistance leader Charles de Gaulle, who from his exile in London was presenting himself as the legitimate leader of France. Embracing de Gaulle was politically appealing, but from an operational perspective would be useless because de Gaulle had little if any support among the French officers in North Africa.

The contest between de Gaulle and Vichy divided even Eddy's operatives in the field. "Of the new arrivals who joined Eddy's staff during the spring, some 'were convinced that de Gaulle, whether we liked it or not, had popular support in France and was the man we would have to reckon with in postwar France. Others were smart enough to follow the White House-imposed official line regardless of its merit or consequences,'" one participant in these events told R. Harris Smith, a historian of the OSS. Eddy himself "fell in with the official line [of maintaining ties to Vichy], no matter what his personal conviction may have been." That was because Eddy could easily see that Vichy officers could help him and the allies, whereas de Gaulle had nothing material to offer.

Because the United States maintained diplomatic relations with Vichy France, Eddy had a ready-made network of agents in place when he arrived in Tangier.

While Bob Murphy was still the senior U.S. diplomat in Vichy, he had negotiated an agreement with Maxime Weygand, a French patriot who was Pétain's chief of North African affairs. The United States would provide raw materials and commodities to assist the people of North Africa. American officials would be permitted to take up station at key cities in French North Africa to monitor the delivery and distribution of these commodities to ensure that they were not diverted to military use or to the benefit of Axis forces.

According to Murphy, "the essence of the Murphy-Weygand Accord was that French officials should be permitted to use French funds, then frozen in banks in the United States, to buy a limited amount of non-strategic American goods acutely needed in French North Africa; and be permitted to ship such cargo through the British naval blockade which was enforced after the rupture of Anglo-French diplomatic relations in July 1940. The Weygand group beseeched me to try to obtain supplies immediately because they believed the Germans were planning to occupy French North Africa early in the summer of 1941, and consumer goods were urgently required as an incentive to Arab cooperation in defense of this area." (It is not clear why the Germans permitted this arrangement to continue even after Hitler forced Pétain to get rid of Weygand in November 1941.)

The American officials dispatched under the Murphy-Weygand agreement were ostensibly consular officers assigned to U.S. diplomatic missions in the region, at Algiers, Oran, Casablanca, and Tunis. There were twelve of these agents, who inevitably were dubbed the "Twelve Apostles." They came from diverse backgrounds, but all were fluent in French. The Germans of course knew that monitoring cargoes was not a full-time assignment and had their suspicions about what the Apostles were up to, but because the United States maintained diplomatic relations with Vichy, the twelve had diplomatic immunity and could not be arrested by the Vichy French police. Their diplomatic status also allowed them to send and receive sealed pouches that were not subject to customs inspection—a ready-made conduit for weapons, ammunition and radio parts.

While war planners in London and Washington argued over how to stem the Axis advances and where to counterattack before the end of 1942, Eddy and Murphy became convinced that Germany was preparing to move on French North Africa. In April, Pétain was replaced by the pro-German Pierre Laval, who they believed would acquiesce in the German maneuver. If that happened, they believed that all French military assets in North Africa would fall under German control. Therefore they sought to encourage a resistance movement among anti-German French officers, and begged Donovan and the War Department to support it. This was one point at which Eddy's commitment outran his judgment, because it was by no means certain that there was in fact any viable resistance movement among the French officers in North Africa, and de Gaulle—who at least had credibility with the British—was hundreds of miles away.

Weygand might have organized French Army officers in North Africa to join the Allies in resisting a German invasion, but his recall to mainland France in the fall of 1941 took him out of the picture, as the Germans intended. Murphy and Eddy, more convinced than ever that a German invasion was likely, still believed "that if the French were armed, they would resist it. Thus they believed that by arming the French, the United States might save North Africa for the Allies," Braden and Alsop recounted. "It was this conclusion, and its logical consequences, which led to Murphy's castigation in the United States press as a dealer with fascists, and even as a fascist. It was this conclusion which led to Eddy's fruitless arguments with Donovan, as he begged for supplies for the French."

"We will not find such leaders elsewhere," Eddy pleaded with Donovan, "and we dare not lose them now . . . They are taking all the risk; they will receive, distribute, and use the supplies, every step being taken with the threat of execution as traitors if they are uncovered. The least we can do is help supply them on their own terms, which are generous and gallant."

In April 1942—that is, before he and Murphy knew that there would in fact be an Allied invasion—Eddy sent to Washington a request for a half million dollars and a substantial shipment of arms, including motorcycles, planes and howitzers, for this supposed gallant resistance. "If Murphy and I cannot be trusted with a few million francs in an emergency then I should be called back and someone who can be trusted sent," Eddy told Donovan with uncharacteristic petulance that reflected the tensions of the moment. "We have days before us, not weeks" before the anticipated German move on Morocco and Algeria.

Military planners in Washington were unimpressed. They decided not to furnish arms to the French, and urged instead that limited funds be used to build up a guerrilla resistance group among the local population—a proposal that other departments in Washington did not encourage. That same month Laval replaced Pétain as Vichy prime minister, but even then Washington did not break relations, and therefore the State Department continued to oppose any direct assistance to anti-Vichy French conspirators, however much Eddy and Murphy might promote them.

This was a revealing episode. Eddy, a field operative with a necessarily narrow focus, failed to understand that decision makers in Washington had many more issues to deal with, in a much more complicated political environment, than he could possibly grasp from his vantage point.

Murphy, with years of diplomatic experience in the field, understood what was happening: the policy vacillation "at the whim of every pencil-pusher in Washington" created something of a siege mentality in the field. "As sometimes happens in the Foreign Service," he wrote, "these experiences produced in our little group in French Africa an acute case of 'localitis,' meaning that the local situation seemed to us the most important in the world, and we could not understand why so many outsiders failed to recognize its earth-shaking importance."

The reality was that Eddy's equipment requests were unreasonable, given the limited U.S production capacity at this early stage of the war and the more pressing demands on other fronts. The British, America's most important allies, favored de Gaulle, and therefore wanted any Allied military support to go to him, not to shadowy officers of dubious allegiance in North Africa. After Hitler's Germany attacked the Soviet Union, Allied commanders were under pressure from Stalin to counterattack somewhere—anywhere—before the end of 1942, but as of April no decision had been reached as to where. Rejection of Eddy's requests for money and arms did not necessarily represent rejection of him, his team, or his assessment of the situation in North Africa; it represented the best judgment at that moment of men charged with waging an enormous global war and deploying their limited resources to greatest effect, and was not necessarily final.

As Murphy noted, it is not uncommon for military officers or diplomatic representatives in distant outposts to fail to understand the political environment at home or the importance of domestic opinion among the elected representatives of the people, including the president, in weighing their options. Career foreign service officers especially tend to be dismissive of public opinion as uninformed, and resentful when it outweighs their views. Eddy and his colleagues in the State Department would experience this phenomenon on a much larger scale later in the decade, when the issue was not whether to supply some weapons to a resistance group but whether to partition Palestine and create a Jewish state.

Washington's rejection of the plan to arm the French resistance in North Africa was thus a political setback for Donovan and the OSS, but the always ebullient Donovan chose not to be discouraged, and he urged Eddy to carry on as well. "If we are right," he wired, "it will work out right."

The difficulty of Eddy's mission was compounded not only by the ambiguity of objective but also by inter-service and inter-agency rivalry and mistrust of a sort that he had not encountered in the first war, when he was a junior officer with limited command responsibility in a Marine unit that functioned more or less effectively under the command of an Army general. The Tangier assignment was oddly more similar to what he had faced at Hobart than it was to his first wartime experience.

In simplest terms, the War Department did not trust the OSS, an untested organization hastily thrown together by Donovan without military input. The OSS was rich in talent, even genius, but most of its agents and operatives, however accomplished, were amateurs; and some were, to put it politely, eccentric. The military historian Edward Hymoff wrote that the agency was "staffed by geniuses, screwballs, misfits and just plain people" who were resented by the military professionals because their OSS jobs carried military commissions that the brass did not think they had earned. And some of Roosevelt's closest advisers were wary of Donovan, who was a Republican and a wealthy Wall Street lawyer. Donovan was a supporter of New York's Republican governor, Thomas E. Dewey, who would challenge Roosevelt for the presidency in 1944.

The prominent people Donovan recruited from academia, the literary world, business, journalism and the law constituted a virtual Hall of Fame of American distinction in the mid-twentieth century. In addition to Braden, Alsop and Coon, the roster included Allen Dulles, Paul Mellon, Arthur Goldberg, Charles Kindelberger, Herbert Marcuse, David Bruce, both sons of J.P. Morgan, and such

"When we reached the far end of the woods, only half the company was there."
— CAPTAIN JOHN A. WEST USMC OF THE 6TH REGIMENT

TOP LEFT: *The U.S. Army fighting with Renault FT-17 tanks—1918.*
BOTTOM: *German prisoners march past Allied wounded—1918.*

TOP RIGHT: *American machine gun nest in the French woods—1918.*

Bill and Mary in Jeddah, Saudi Arabia—1945.

As Naval Attaché—photo taken in Tangier, 1942.

TOP: *The landing of Operation TORCH—November 8th 1942.*
BOTTOM: *Algiers liberated from the Vichy.*

Eddy (right) with US Army officer (center) and a Free French officer (left) in Algiers.

future stars of the intelligence firmament as Richard Helms, Frank Wisner and Ray Cline. But the military professionals were not much interested in flashes of brilliance from the world of ideas, which in Donovan's unorganized, make-it-up-as-you-go OSS alternated with harebrained schemes. The generals and admirals had landings to organize, equipment to move, troops to deploy, weapons to develop, and they were more comfortable with the career intelligence analysts who worked within the military chain of command.

On the other hand, Eddy had military intelligence experience and he had assets on the ground in North Africa, which the War Department did not, and the generals planning the landing to be known as Operation TORCH would need all the reliable information they could get about what the troops would face when they hit the beaches. The key to meshing the military planners and the intelligence agents for a successful invasion was a meeting in London in late July of 1942 at which Eddy won the confidence of senior military strategists.

Eddy went to London for the nominal purpose of seeking support for his hoped-for pro-Allied uprising among the French and the Muslim natives of North Africa, but the outcome was quite different. Colonel Edward Buxton, assistant director of the OSS, arranged a dinner party at which Eddy was introduced to Generals James H. Doolittle, George S. Patton Jr., and George Strong. Strong, who had recently been appointed director of military intelligence, was a rival of Donovan's and dubious about the competence of the OSS agents and the reliability of their information.

Eddy, in his Marine Corps uniform with the rows of medals and ribbons he had won in the first war, cut a dashing figure as he limped into the room. "Do you know Bill Eddy?" Buxton asked as he introduced him to Patton, the swashbuckling commander with the cavalry boots, twin pistols and volcanic temperament who would command U.S. troops in North Africa. "Never saw him before in my life," said Patton, with his flair for colorful language, as he eyed Eddy's medals, "but the son of a bitch's been shot at enough, hasn't he?"

According to Braden and Alsop, who provided the most extensive narrative of this encounter, "They took chairs in the room, and Eddy began to talk about Africa. Before he could get fairly under way, Strong interrupted him.

"'Now wait a minute, Eddy,' Strong said, 'I'm G-2 [intelligence chief] of this army and I'm going to tell you something. If you're going to tell us what you think instead of what you know, you might find yourself contributing to the murder of thousands of your own countrymen. Now for God's sake, tell us the facts.'"

Eddy, who by this time had been in Tangier six months and had developed an extensive network of contacts, knew what he was talking about, and proceeded calmly to lay out the situation for his rapt audience. He described the political sentiments among the French military and the possibility that French units would acquiesce in an Allied landing even if they did not openly support it. In the Braden-Alsop account of this conversation (about which Eddy's own papers are predictably silent), "He named the groups he had trained outside the Army, and his plans for them. He told of his own organization and of the intelligence on ship movements and defenses which his group had already assembled." This information was detailed and specific; Eddy's agents had even measured the height of the surf along the Moroccan and Algerian coastlines. He described to Doolittle the airfields of the region, and the possibility that they could be delivered intact to an Allied landing force.

As Harris Smith, a historian of the OSS, put it, even the skeptical Strong was impressed by "Eddy's seemingly factual, detailed account of the French underground—its strength, organization, leadership, and potential. All three [generals] took particular note of Eddy's conclusion: 'If we sent an expeditionary force to North Africa there would be only token resistance.'" Less than a month later, Eddy and Murphy were informed of the decision by American and British planners to invade North Africa, under Eisenhower's command, before the end of the year. Thus, at this critical juncture of the war, Eddy—who had never won Washington's assent to the Lawrence-of-Arabia-style native uprising envisioned by the OSS and had never persuaded Donovan or other senior Roosevelt administration officials to arm sympathizers in the French military for a rebellion against Vichy—nevertheless established sufficient credibility with the generals to persuade them that an invasion was feasible and that he and his OSS teams could create the conditions for its success. Doing that became his full-time mission; the days of uncertainty were over. It was now a time of clarity.

THE SECRET RADIOS

With the U.S. entry into the war the previous winter and the centralization of intelligence work under Donovan's control, the Twelve Apostles—nominally State Department personnel—had been placed under Eddy's command. With the aid of a Navy radio expert named Joe Raichle, they installed clandestine shortwave radios, each with a distinctive code name, such as "Yankee" at Algiers and "Pilgrim" at Tunis. Through this network they transmitted whatever they learned about French military activities, political sentiment among the European and local populations, airfields and aircraft, coastal gun emplacements and possible landing points for Allied troops, tides and surf, the availability and reliability of guides and marine pilots, and the crucial question of what the French officer corps would do when the Allies landed: support, resist, or stay neutral.

The existence of these radios, Carleton Coon recounted, was a secret even from most of the regular State Department diplomats assigned to these outposts. In Tangier, the operator, known by code name Stork, worked at night on the roof of the legation, which was also the residence of J. Rives Childs and his wife. She heard the sound but was unaware of its origin. "Mrs. Childs complained that the tapping of the key at night disturbed her sleep," Coon wrote, "so Mr. Childs ordered the set removed from the legation. It is idle to point out that the success of the invasion was more important than Mrs. Childs' sleep." The transmitter was moved to a small villa outside of town that Eddy rented from a retired British diplomat.

Eddy and his OSS team monitored cargo shipments by land and sea, mapped roads, and smuggled out by sea agents who had been blown or local contacts who had come under suspicion. One of these was the chief maritime pilot of Port Lyautey, who several months later would guide Allied landing vessels to safe harbor.

"Remember how, to get them out," Eddy recalled after the war, "we would enlist the cooperation of Tangier prostitutes who, for a consideration, would earlier stroll around and take the Spanish sentry off into the woods for half an hour to (1) the saving of Allied lives and (2) the delight of the Spanish soldier and (3) double pay if not the delight of the prostitute. Well, she worked anyway, and why not in the woods as well as in the sheets?"

Eddy and Coon cultivated a key contact known by the code name Tassels, described by Coon as "a general in Abd el Krim's army and . . . one of the most influential leaders, under cover, in the Rif." Their meetings were clandestine, and Tassels wore a disguise, sometimes as a woman. According to Coon's droll account—which features a tale of his lying in the bushes outside a house where these meetings took place, waiting for Tassels while a Spanish couple copulated energetically on the other side of a reed fence—Tassels was a one-man lode of valuable information. "During these meetings we made our plans for the revolt of the Riffians if needed, and plotted the landing troops, the dropping of parachutists, the delivery of guns, the cutting off of roads and garrisons, etc.," Coon wrote in his secret narrative. They also enlisted the support of an indigenous sheikh code-named Strings, the leader of a fundamentalist Muslim group. This band of local consipirators was "to do for the western Spanish zone what Tassels and his gang were going to do for the Rif."

Eddy, on his own and without informing anyone on his team or in Washington, also built up a clandestine network among Spanish malcontents from the losing side in the Spanish Civil War. Nothing was known publicly about this group at the time—even Coon was kept in the dark—and Eddy described it only after the war in a secret memo intended only for the OSS files. This memo of September 1946, later declassified by the National Archives, provides a good example of how he analyzed people and how he operated:

> Very soon after my arrival at Tangier in January 1942, the American Chargé d'Affaires, Mr. J. Rives Childs, told me that his chauffeur, a Russian Communist, was in touch with a group

which he believed could render secret service to the Allies. Mr. Childs offered to turn over this contact of his chauffeur to me and I accepted.

To make a long story short, the contact was with a very closely knit and well-organized network of Spanish Communists, mostly embittered veterans of the defeated Spanish Repubican Army, who had escaped to Spanish Morocco and were engaged in planning their revenge. The network for communication purposes consisted of over 200 human post offices which relayed messages from Tangier to Marrakesh repeatedly in less than 15 hours and from Tangier to Melilla in 8 or 9 hours. So far as I know, no message ever went astray or was intercepted during the months when we were in touch with this network. These post offices were in all the principal Spanish Army units, civil and military headquarters in Spanish Morocco, and curiously enough in the Spanish Catholic churches, not of course as priests but as lay employees and even as theological students. The result was we were furnished with a remarkably accurate and fairly complete steady stream of intelligence regarding the activities of the Falange Party, military movements, and official Spanish Government propaganda. This same chain of agents gladly undertook special commissions for us, such as reporting on coastal defenses of the Straits in areas barred to all civilians. Although we used them to deliver confidential messages to French Morocco, we requested from them only intelligence on Spanish affairs, the only field in which they were thoroughly reliable from our point of view. They did not like the French and they distrusted the British, who they considered had betrayed them during the Civil War, but they hated above all Franco and all of his government, and we could therefore count on them never to color their reports in favor of Franco, who was the only person capable of closing the Straits to the Allies.

According to Eddy's memo, these operatives also engaged in acts of sabotage against Spanish installations, but the OSS did not participate in or support those "in view of the very strict orders that there should be no overt acts in Spanish Morocco to attract

Axis attention or create Axis alarm and reinforcements . . . The only direct use we made of the Spanish Communists apart from intelligence was on three or four occasions to hide individuals whom we were smuggling through Spanish Morocco. The Spanish Communists kept and cared for them and delivered them at the appointed beaches or frontier rendezvous without mishap."

These Spaniards never asked for money, nor did Eddy give them any. "It was a movement dominated by fanaticism, ideology, or patriotism, however the indivdual wishes to regard it, but they did not work for money," he wrote, "We did occasionally secure for them items of equipment of which they were in need for their intelligence work, items which they did not dare to secure locally where the supplies could be traced." The equipment included a typewriter and a Ditto machine for their underground newspaper.

These Spaniards, Eddy added, "had no connection whatsoever with our clandestine radio establishments throughout North Africa."

EXPLODING TURDS

As the stories of the Tangier prostitutes and the Spanish dissidents illustrate, Eddy and his colleagues used people for their own purposes, with little consideration for the interests of these individuals or the dangers they might face. That was to be expected in the atmosphere of the time, in which there was little room for scruples or ethical considerations. If people could be persuaded to be helpful, by argument, bribery or coercion, well and good. And if they got in the way, they were to be neutralized or removed, by violence if necessary.

The historian Harris Smith described General Donovan as an incorrigible improviser who would try anything, disdained organizational detail and valued only success—that is, the antithesis of the military, which operated by the book. "Standard operating procedures were almost taboo in OSS," Smith wrote. "Effective action was the sole objective." In keeping with that spirit, Eddy, even while wearing his military uniform, gave his operatives wide latitude to do whatever was necessary to carry out their assignments; improvisation and freelancing were encouraged. War was serious business and the spying game was dangerous, but the unstructured nature of the operation—and the exotic setting— lent themselves to escapades of high humor as well.

Eddy assigned a team headed by Coon to reconnoiter a highway across French Morocco that would be used, the OSS hoped, by advancing Allied forces or retreating German units. The OSS operatives were to note every building along the route and mark every bridge and culvert that could be blown up or booby trapped by the Germans.

They were also to collect samples of rocks found along the route, so a laboratory in London could make plaster-of-Paris copies that could be packed with explosives to be detonated by German trucks passing over them.

"On this trip, which was difficult to arrange at a time when gasoline was scarce, we discovered that there are very few stones along the roads," Coon wrote in a droll after-action report, "but that mule turds can be found in great abundance." Thus the meager rock collection was supplemented with a package of mule droppings, which could be copied to the same purpose.

"We took care to explain that the full, rich horse dung of the British countryside would not do in Morocco; it was the more watery, smaller-bunned mule type that would pass there without suspicion," Coon explained in unnecessary detail. "Also, it was important to have a deep sepia color, sometimes with greenish shades, the produce of straw and grass, not of oats and hay. In due course of time the British London office made up explosive turds from these samples, and we used them to good effect later in Tunisia."

The mule turds caper was characteristic of Coon, who—unlike Eddy—was flamboyant to the point of danger. He was an adventure-loving, pistol-packing professor of anthropology at Harvard who spoke French and Arabic—as well as several other languages— and the author of several serious and well-respected books about human society and social development. He lived among the tribes and people he wrote about, occasionally ran guns to local groups, and developed a firm confidence in his ability to understand people of different backgrounds and skin color. He came under suspicion when a pistol that had belonged to him turned out to be the murder weapon in the assassination by one of his pupils of Admiral Jean Louis Darlan, a reviled figure as Vichy commander in chief in North Africa, but he convinced authorities that the gun had been stolen from him and that he was out of town at the time.

In the general atmosphere of danger and treachery, exploits such as the construction of exploding mule droppings endangered no one, at least until the bombs detonated under German trucks, and provided fodder for amusing recollections that are still cherished by surviving OSS veterans. Other episodes were less benign, as Eddy noted in a letter to Mary in May 1942.

"Our seven secret transmitters, short wave, which we have scattered about N. Africa, are doing good work. We signal to Gib[raltar] and Malta the departure of cargoes for Libya, for the information of Allied subs and planes. The other day I got particular satisfaction in a very rapid transmittal of information about the departure for Berlin of a plane carrying nine German officers. The plane did not reach its destination." At every opportunity, OSS agents put sugar into the fuel tanks of German planes, and celebrated when these planes went down into the Mediterranean.

In the spring and early summer months before the Allies committed themselves to Operation TORCH, Eddy and his agents busied themselves with tasks that would suit either of the two eventualities they faced: expedite an Allied landing, or stymie a march westward across Tunisia by Axis troops coming out of Libya.

They organized clandestine groups of railroad workers "with the purpose," as David King, one of the Apostles, wrote, "of putting the railroads out of action temporarily should they be used to bring up troops to resist us. At the same time these men were to protect such railroad bottlenecks as tunnels, bridges and switching yards" for possible later use by the Allies.

In French Morocco, King recounted, "it was arranged that the radio station transmitters could be cut off from the studios and connected with a secret radio, so that if the chiefs of 'Radio

Maroc,' who were hostile to us, began to broadcast, they would speak into a dead microphone and our men could issue proclamations from the secret studio."

The OSS team enlisted the chief technician of the Moroccan telephone company, who knew the locations of all the wires between command posts and firing batteries, to cut them. Technicians in electric power plants were similarly recruited, so that electric trains, radios and search lights would be shut off.

"Over and above these groups," King wrote, "local strong-arm squads were organized; for instance, in Casablanca we had a group of twelve men, all of whom had bicycles. Each of these men commanded a group of ten, for whom we smuggled in arms, hand grenades and explosives. Their object was to seize or eliminate the German Armistice Commission after having created the necessary commotion by the use of explosives. Not one of these men had served less than three years in a German concentration camp."

AMPHIBIOUS LANDING

On June 11, Eddy informed one of the Apostles that the decision to invade North Africa had been made and that "time of attack is 0400 hrs GMT Nov. 8th." That message was probably premature, because the United States and Britain were still arguing over which theater of operations would be the scene of their first counterattack against the Axis. Roosevelt and Churchill had agreed to strike against Germany first, rather than Japan, but where? Roosevelt wanted to invade directly across the English Channel; Churchill felt that German forces were too heavily dug in on the French side. He argued that an invasion of North Africa would bottle up Rommel and, if successful, provide a strong base for Allied strikes into southern Europe. Churchill prevailed, and in July Roosevelt gave his formal assent to the North African operation. Eddy's June 11 message turned out to be correct, down to the hour.

Now invasion planning began in earnest. TORCH would deploy more than 80,000 American and 10,000 British troops, in addition to a naval force of three battleships, twelve cruisers, nine aircraft carriers, and sixty-four destroyers, plus minesweepers and support vessels—a total of more than 107,000 men, 400 warships and 1,000 planes. President Roosevelt and his advisers insisted that the invading force consist mainly of American troops, and that the visibility of British participation be minimized, because they feared that the hostility of Vichy officers to Britain would encourage resistance. Churchill accepted their argument.

The invasion force was divided into a Western Task Force, commanded by Patton, that would aim for Casablanca; a Central Task Force, under Major General Lloyd R. Fredenhall, aimed at Oran, on the Algerian coast; and an Eastern Task Force, commanded by Lieutenant General K.A.N. Anderson, which would strike at Algiers, then attack German forces in Tunisia. All American aircraft were under the command of General Doolittle, who would later gain fame for his daring air raids over Tokyo. Eddy successfully opposed a proposal to include Free French forces commanded by de Gaulle in the invasion force, fearing it would incite resistance among Vichy officers. It was still uncertain—and it would remain uncertain right up to the day of the landing—how the French military forces would respond. Would they resist, cooperate, or sit it out?

It would be up to Eddy and his agents on the ground to secure fuel supplies, arrange to seize airfields, neutralize potential opposition, provide navigational data and ensure reliability of communications across a vast strip of North Africa, from Casablanca to Algiers—all the while maintaining secrecy, because the Allies wished to maintain the advantage of surprise. Eisenhower's pre-landing orders to Eddy and to his senior OSS operatives in Casablanca, Oran, Algiers and Tunisia stressed the importance of this: "You will appreciate that it is vital to the success of the whole operation that there should be no leakage as regards the nature and date of the operation. . . . The actual date on which each agent is instructed in his duties should be postponed as long as possible and will be dependent on the individual's reliability and the time he will require to prepare for his assignment."

"In those days before the landings," Eddy wrote some years later, "it was imperative that one neither cancel nor increase normal engagements of any kind lest he give the alert. One must plan to go to the tailor as usual to be measured for a suit, or to a barber for a haircut, or to invite Spanish friends in for a cocktail party which will never come off, just as though nothing were to happen."

Eisenhower instructed Eddy to transfer his operational head-quarters from Tangier to Gibraltar three days before the landing date, so that the work could be coordinated with that of the military commanders. The general left it to Murphy to continue negotiating with the Vichy French military in an effort to minimize their potential resistance. "The success of these negotiations," Eisenhower wrote in his orders to Eddy, "may greatly reduce, or even make unnecessary, the tasks given you in these instructions," such as blowing up rail lines and bridges if large-scale armed conflict developed.

Coon was already in Gibraltar, decoding and distributing incoming messages and encoding and sending out originating messages—the volume of which rose sharply as D-Day neared, to the point where the communications network was breaking down.

Coon was under orders not to share the codes with the British, and therefore had to do all the work himself. "The messages were coming in 24 hours a day and I was getting but one and two hour snatches of sleep," he recalled. "Col. Eddy's arrival was a great relief. . . . When Col. Eddy arrived I was able to put my files in order; I had been working at such a tempo that I had simply thrown the messages in the box; now under Eddy's direction it was possible to bring some order into this tangle. Also, he was there to make the decisions." Coon noted that Eddy's departure from Tangier "required considerable planning not to give the show away. He kept his rooms in thc Minzah, and left most of his clothing there; he told them that he would be gone a few days."

On the night of November 7, Eddy, Coon and all their agents at the radio stations were waiting for a message to be broadcast on the French language program of the BBC. It came at half past midnight: *Ecoute, Yankee, Robert arrive, Robert arrive.* Listen, Yankee (or Franklin, Lincoln or Pilgrim for other radios), Robert is arriving. The flotilla is on its way. Every half hour thereafter the BBC broadcast a message from Roosevelt, secretly recorded at the White House, urging the French not to resist. "We come among you solely to destroy your enemies and not to harm you," the president said. "Do not obstruct, I beg of you, this great purpose."

As they waited in Gibraltar, Coon recalled, "We ate ham sandwiches and drank beer, and soon came this historic broadcast in several languages—I remember most clearly the German, *Achtung, Achtung*—and then, Franklin Roosevelt in his Grotonian French, making his announcement [of the news] to the French people. Then the Marseillaise and the Star Spangled Banner. Eddy and I, groggy with excitement and lack of sleep, went back to the office and made out a message to General Donovan. And then we slept."

Eisenhower's orders to the OSS team came in three versions: actions to be taken if the French forces supported or at least acquiesced in the landings; actions to be taken if the French resisted; and "Action required in the event of German counter-invasion into Tunisia." For each there was a list of military equipment that would be provided when the operation was set to go: hand grenades, Sten guns and ammunition, anti-tank mines, rifles and even parachutes.

What if the French resisted? "You should bear in mind," the orders said, "that it is possible that diplomatic relations between the United States and France may be broken off, and you should, therefore, ensure that the necessary machinery exists for carrying out your plans even were the United States consulate closed." In the event of a German thrust, the OSS teams were to "immobilize the harbors of Bizerta, Tunis, Sfax and Gabes by wrecking the power stations and burning fuel dumps," destroy the telephone exchanges, and blow up bridges and tunnels on roads and rail lines. How simple it sounded. In the end, these actions turned out not to be necessary because the Germans, caught by surprise, made no counter moves; they did not even deploy their U-boat fleet to attack the Allied convoy carrying the invasion force.

As for the French, they briefly put up fierce resistance in Algiers, where shore batteries crippled an American destroyer that later sank, and at Port Lyautey, sixty miles northeast of Casablanca, where a premature demand for capitulation alerted the French, who were waiting in machine gun nests on the beach, but Allied air power soon put down these French efforts. Elsewhere there was much confusion and sporadic resistance, but also some helpful

French cooperation. The entire operation lasted only three days, and of the 107,000 soldiers, sailors and airmen who participated in the operation, 82,600 of them U.S. Army personnel, the Allies took only 1,469 casualties, mostly in U.S. Army units: the Army lost 526 killed, 837 wounded and 41 missing. As always happens in large-scale military operations, the casualty figures include personnel killed by accidents and mistakes, such as the four soldiers who were electrocuted when a severed power line fell into a ditch where they had taken cover, rather than from actual engagement with the enemy.

THE EDDY TEAM'S ACHIEVEMENT

On the Moroccan and Algerian coasts the United States Army and Navy conducted operations for which their history offered no preparation: large-scale amphibious landings under hostile fire, even though that hostile fire was much less intense than it would have been if the French had committed themselves to resist the invasion. TORCH secured a North African base for future operations in southern Europe, and it enabled the Allies to bottle up Rommel and his fearsome Panzer divisions, now caught between the Allied forces in Morocco and Algeria and the British troops advancing westward from El Alamein in Egypt. Whatever threat the French military posed to the Allies was eliminated. As in 1918, the entry of the United States as a combatant had turned the tide of the war. Five months earlier the U.S. Navy had defeated a Japanese armada at the battle of Midway in the Pacific; TORCH now represented the first great Allied victory in the European or Mediterranean theaters. As a relatively easy triumph over a feeble and divided opponent, TORCH did little to prepare the American fighters for the epic battles against Germany and Japan that lay ahead, but it was a massive—and much-needed—political and psychological boost for the Allies.

What was the contribution of Eddy and his OSS team? Military historians have noted that the landings themselves, in which the Allies were inexperienced, exposed weaknesses in amphibious operations that a stronger French defense would have been able to exploit. Once ashore after the collapse of French resistance, however, the troops encountered a relatively benign environment in which neither the local Muslim people nor any other group caused trouble, and airfields, support bases and communications networks were largely intact and quickly secured. Spain remained neutral. For those outcomes, the OSS deserves much of the credit. Here is the OSS's self-assessment:

> At the eve of D-Day, therefore, we find 80,000 Moslems ready to throw off the Spanish yoke; an indeterminate number of Spanish Loyalists with the same end in view, and with things so arranged that the Moslems and Loyalists would not come into serious conflict. We find intelligence networks operating smoothly and completely in all strategically important parts of North Africa. We find a complete network of clandestine radio stations funnelling their information to Tangier, whence they received orders. We find resistance groups organized in all these places, ready to take over the government long enough to let the invaders in with a minimum of opposition. We find special agents drawn from these places on the high seas with the fleets, guiding them into their landing places, and advising the commanders on the geographical, military, and political situations in their destination. We find [the Apostle] Gordon Browne sitting out on the bleak plain between Tafaroui and Le Senia, ready to guide in the paratroop planes. We find men on the beaches with flares at all landing places. We find Eddy and Coon in Gibraltar, sending and receiving messages around the clock, Eddy consulting with General Eisenhower, who is lodged with the Governor of Gibraltar, while Coon keeps a Riffian costume hidden in his cubicle . . . in case the Spaniards resist and he has a chance to beach at Ajdir, where Tassels and his Riffians await him. [The agents] Holcomb, Hoskinson, and Williams sit in the Naval Attaché's office in Tangier, armed to the teeth, ready for all comers. Charlie MacIntosh's gang is ready to take out the battery at Algeciras. The preparation is complete, and the TORCH personnel is ready for any eventuality.

This is self-congratulatory, but not wrong for that reason. Professional historians such as Joseph E. Persico agree with it. As Persico wrote, "The OSS had played a respectable role in TORCH. Colonel Eddy's team had amassed an Everest of logistical data on tides, currents, depth of ports, location of bridges, tunnels and airfields, placement of coastal guns, the strength and deployment of French forces, and the most favorable landing sites. On certain beaches, OSS agents, waiting to greet the troops, handed them French military maps and guided them inland. The enemy was where these agents said it would be, armed as predicted, and in the numbers estimated."

Nor was the success of TORCH important in military terms alone. According to Kermit Roosevelt's official history of the OSS, it was decisive in the strategic infighting in Washington. The OSS operations in North Africa "were the main reason OSS survived," Roosevelt wrote. "Without this evidence to the Joint Chiefs of Staff of its value it would most likely have been dismembered" and the military would have taken full control of U.S. intelligence work for the duration of the war.

Eddy's accomplishments in his OSS assignment were manifest and brought him great acclaim. His citation for the Legion of Merit said that he "performed exceptionally meritorious service to the government from January 1942 to October 1943. . . . Apart from the activities of the invading forces themselves, much of the success of the landings may be attributed to the competence with which he discharged his vital duties."

As an ethical person, though, Eddy was sometimes uncomfortable with the methods employed to achieve those victories—the duplicity, the moral ambiguity, the treachery, the alliances with reprehensible people. Conventional war was one thing: Men in uniform killed other men in a different uniform. It was the opposite of ambiguous. The campaign waged by the OSS in North Africa was war of a different sort, a war in which the combatants probed for weaknesses not of armament or position but of character, and if the struggle claimed innocent victims, so be it.

"I regret that I cannot record any special moral superiority for the Allies in wartime Tangier," Eddy wrote in "Spies and Lies in Tangier."

Reflecting on the campaign some years afterward, Eddy recounted a disturbance in the streets, with gunfire and surging mobs, in the early autumn of 1942. It had apparently been incited by the Germans.

"Could we really complain if the Germans had bought the Moors first?" he asked. "Did we not all employ native informers and touts? The Moors, the depressed have-nots of Tangier, would sell anything to anybody. When you stepped out of the hotel any morning, a tout would whisper, 'You want nice girl, very cheap? I bring my sister.' While neither as Naval Attaché nor as chief [of] OSS would I rent his sister, I would, and too often did, rent his brother as an informer. The brother might be a wife-beater or an opium addict, it mattered not if he knew how to get around. It is permitted to walk with the devil until you have crossed the bridge. The OSS was in a death struggle with the Gestapo, and like Churchill, aligned itself with devils to survive. We deserve to go to hell when we die. We used Communists, telling them that we would help them overthrow Franco, which we did not do. We falsely promised Riff Moorish officers to work for the independence of Morocco from Spain. Civil life has some of this cynicism: one will patronize a skillful dentist, even though he is a 'queer,' but not a banker who is a known embezzler. The OSS had no conscience," he concluded. "It is still an open question whether an operator in OSS or in [the] CIA can ever again become a wholly honorable man."

He had no such ambivalent feelings, however, about the crucial decision of President Roosevelt and his advisers to maintain diplomatic relations with the collaborationist government of Vichy—a decision which he supported during the war and afterward—and to work with French officers of dubious allegiance. "The military advantage of collaboration with [the Vichy officers] Giraud and Darlan," he said in an address to the Naval War College in Newport, Rhode Island, in 1953, "was not that the landings were made with little bloodshed; they could have been made anyway at the cost of a few hundred more Gold Star Mothers. The advantage was that, on landing, U.S. troops could speed immediately to fight the Germans in Tunisia, without the need to occupy and police all of

Morocco and Algeria, which would have cost many months and the pinning down of several divisions." In this case, the end justified the means.

In the wake of TORCH, American troops were in combat in Muslim lands for the first time since Stephen Decatur and his warships broke the tribute demands of North Africa's pashas and the Barbary Pirates in 1815. The emergence of the United States as a strategic and economic power in the Arab world, commenced a decade earlier with the arrival of the first geologists from Standard Oil Company of California to look for oil in Saudi Arabia, was now fully under way.

With the success of TORCH, Eddy's work in North Africa was largely done. He stayed on in North Africa until October 1943, by which time the Allies had taken Tunis and Bizerte and put an end to the German threat to Egypt, but during those months, he was much in demand among senior officials in Washington because of his performance in Tangier. He wanted to stay in uniform. The OSS wanted to keep him, but the State Department had its own plans. In a bureaucratic three-cushion shot that reflected the esteem in which he was held, the Navy Department, OSS and State Department cut a deal by which he remained an active-duty Marine Corps officer on loan to the OSS, which in turn detailed him to the State Department. Now he was to enter upon the most challenging and rewarding assignment of his colorful career, and the one that would have the longest-lasting and farthest-reaching consequences. He was going to Saudi Arabia.

SAUDI ARABIA, PART ONE

*D*uring the grim years from 1942 to 1945, few countries would seem to have had less claim than Saudi Arabia to the attention of President Roosevelt. The president and his military and foreign policy advisers had many more urgent concerns. Europe, North Africa, the Soviet Union, most of Asia, Canada and Australia were locked in the epic combat of World War II. The countries of sub-Saharan Africa were also involved, as colonies of the combatant states. Even Latin America required vigilance as a traditional region of U.S. interest where enemy agents were active, and Brazil sent troops to fight in Europe. Why, then, would anyone in Washington be thinking about Saudi Arabia? It was an impoverished backwater, known to the rest of the world only for the annual Muslim pilgrimage to Mecca, never colonized and thus unaffiliated with any European nation, and neutral in the war.

The country was at the opposite pole of industrial development from the United States, without electricity, roads, schools or hospitals. It was true that Standard Oil Company of California, later known as Chevron, held a concession to explore for oil in Saudi Arabia and had begun producing for export in 1939, but those exports were quickly cut off by the outbreak of war, and Saudi Arabia's output was negligible in the world oil market. Fewer than 150 Americans lived there.

The United States had granted diplomatic recognition to the new Kingdom of Saudi Arabia soon after the creation of the unified country was proclaimed in 1932 by its founder, King Abdul Aziz ibn Saud, but there were no resident U.S. government officials; the senior American diplomat accredited to the Kingdom was based in Cairo and seldom went to Saudi Arabia. Nor did Saudi Arabia have an official representative in Washington. And yet Roosevelt was interested. He was curious about the country and about King Abdul Aziz, whom he had never met. Indeed, the Saudi King at the (approximate) age of 63 had never met the leader of any country except neighboring Kuwait, and had never traveled much beyond the Arabian peninsula. Nevertheless, this semi-literate, half-blind desert monarch was remarkably well informed about the issues of the world that mattered to him—he had court interpreters who translated radio broadcasts from New York, London, Rome, and Berlin—and he had a serene confidence about his accomplishments, his abilities and his position as ruler over the holiest places of Islam. He was not awed by the power of an American president or of any other man.

Roosevelt began thinking about the King as early as 1938, when Abdul Aziz first wrote to him to complain about perceived U.S. support for Zionist aspirations in Palestine. We want to be your friends, the letter said in effect, so don't give Palestine to the Jews—a blunt message that put on the table an issue that would entangle Roosevelt and his successor, Harry S. Truman, for the next decade. The president had responded noncommittally, but signed his letter "Your good friend, Franklin D. Roosevelt."

In January 1939, Roosevelt's interest was piqued by a letter about the King from a plumbing fixtures heir named Charles R. Crane. Crane, bored by sinks and bathtubs but fascinated by the

Middle East, had busied himself in the region's affairs since the presidency of Woodrow Wilson. He was one of the first Americans to visit King Abdul Aziz, and in 1931 he financed an expedition to Arabia to look for water and mineral resources led by an industrious engineer named Karl Twitchell. Twitchell's findings were instrumental in persuading the King to overcome his aversion to infidel foreigners and allow Chevron to come in to look for oil.

"The papers out here [in California] say you have had a communication from Ibn Saud,"[1] Crane wrote to Roosevelt. "I should like to tell you a few things about him that are not very well known, at least not in the western world. He is the most important man who has appeared in Arabia since the time of Mohammed, is severely orthodox, and manages his affairs, his life and his government as nearly as possible as Mohammed would have done." In establishing his dominion over the Arabian peninsula by conquering rival tribes, Crane said, Abdul Aziz was always "guided by the old desert doctrine of *hilm*, which Mohammed emphasized so much, of doing everything possible, in the most affectionate manner, to reconcile his enemies once he had conquered them."

According to Crane, Abdul Aziz's treatment of vanquished foes was the opposite of the vengeful spirit that had prevailed at the Versailles treaty conference after World War I, which rearranged the geography and power structure of the entire Middle East.

Crane was fully familiar with the work of that conference because President Wilson had appointed him, along with Oberlin College president Henry King, to advise him about the future status of Palestine. The Great War of 1914–1918 had ended centuries of Ottoman rule in Palestine, but the land's new status remained to be determined. Even then Zionist leaders were claiming Palestine as a future Jewish homeland, an objective King and Crane said in their prophetic 1919 report could be achieved only by force and only at the expense of Palestine's Arab population.

President Roosevelt was intrigued by Crane's portrayal of the King. "All I have heard of [Abdul Aziz] fully confirms your own impression

---

1. King Abdul Aziz ibn Saud, or son of Saud, was for many years referred to in the West as Ibn Saud. Now it is customary to refer to him by his given name, Abdul Aziz. The Arabs use the given name in reference to all princes of the House of Saud.

of his fine character and personality," he wrote in response, adding that he hoped an opportunity would arise to learn more.

Thus was planted a seed that would germinate throughout the war and culminate in a legendary meeting between the President and the King at which was forged the unique alliance between the United States and Saudi Arabia that still endures. History has generally depicted that meeting as an afterthought to the great-power summit conference at Yalta that preceded it, and has described the encounter of F.D.R. and Ibn Saud as if they were discovering each other for the first time. In fact, the meeting of the two leaders and the alliance they forged were years in preparation, and the two men knew quite a bit about each other before they met. Throughout the years 1941 to 1944, Roosevelt gradually became convinced that Abdul Aziz and his kingdom could be economically and strategically useful to the United States, as well as interesting, and that it was worth the effort to reach out to the King to align him with American interests. The person eventually designated by the president to carry out that policy was Bill Eddy.

In those years of global crisis, Roosevelt displayed a gift for looking beyond the urgent issue of the moment to think about the future. Before the United States entered the war, the president was thinking about how the United States could win it, because he saw U.S. involvement as inevitable. Once the United States did enter the conflict, Roosevelt began thinking about postwar strategies and alliances. He came to envision Saudi Arabia not as an irrelevant curiosity or perpetual backwater but as a country with possibilities, a country that could develop to meet the needs of its own people in a mutually beneficial partnership with the United States.

In April 1941, six months before Pearl Harbor, Roosevelt asked J.A. Moffett, a New York-based executive of Chevron's Saudi Arabian operation (known as the California Arabian Standard Oil Company, CASOC) and a prodigious campaign fundraiser for the president for "a memorandum covering the situation in Saudi Arabia and what the King might be able to do in furnishing finished petroleum products" to the U.S. Navy. Roosevelt had to ask CASOC for information because the oil company had people inside Saudi Arabia, while the U.S. government did not.

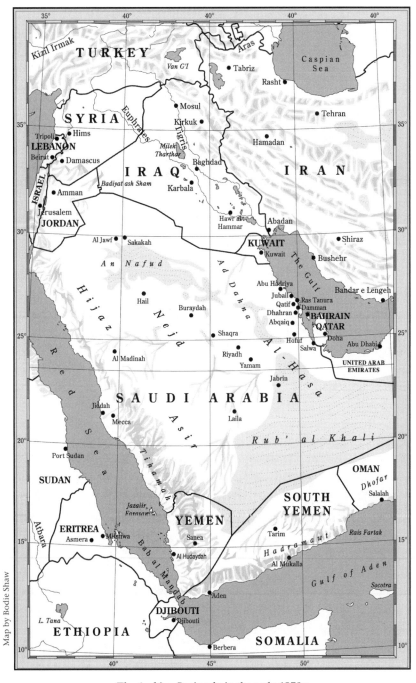

The Arabian Peninsula in the early 1970s.

Moffett replied on April 16. "Our representatives have had numerous conferences with the King," he wrote. "His financial situation is desperate." It may seem strange now to think of Saudi Arabia as destitute, but such was the case in the early 1940s. The huge country had few resources other than oil, and the outbreak of war had cut off revenue from that source just as it started to flow. The Kingdom's other principal source of income, a tax on pilgrims to Mecca, had also been reduced because the war limited travel. A drought was devastating the country's limited agriculture. The King, who was accustomed to handing out cash to maintain the loyalty of tribal leaders in the unruly land he had unified only a decade before, was indeed in dire fiscal straits. Moffett informed the president that Britain had given the King some money, but not nearly enough to meet his anticipated needs.

"If the United States government will advance to the King of Saudi Arabia $6,000,000 annually for the next five years, we feel confident that we can work out with the King an arrangement whereby he will deliver through us the following quantities of petroleum products, at the prices mentioned," Moffett proposed. He listed 1.8 million barrels of gasoline, 2.66 million barrels of diesel fuel, and 3.4 million barrels of heavy fuel oil, "totalling approximately $6,000,000 worth of petroleum products annually." It was urgent to accept this offer or find some other way to provide aid, Moffett said, because "unless this is done, and soon, this independent kingdom, and perhaps the entire Arab world, will be thrown into chaos."

What was really driving Moffett and his oil industry friends was the fear that Britain, which had supported Abdul Aziz and his desert warriors as they rode to conquest thirty years earlier, still harbored designs on Saudi Arabia and its oil. If the United States government failed to support the King in his hour of need, they feared that the British would entice Saudi Arabia into the sterling currency zone, the King would revoke the American oil concession and transfer it to the British, or both. This tension between American and British interests in the Kingdom was an underlying theme of all that would happen in U.S.-Saudi Arabian relations— and in Bill Eddy's work—for the next several years.

The issue as explained by Moffett raised the obvious question of why, if Saudi Arabia was so important, Standard Oil of California did not advance the money itself, to protect its investment. Moffett anticipated questions from the White House and Congress on this point, telling the president that the company had indeed already given the King advances against anticipated postwar royalties of $6.8 million through CASOC. "It has now come to a point where it is impossible for the company to continue the growing burden and responsibility of financing an independent country, particularly under present abnormal conditions. However, the King is desperate," he wrote.

The president asked the State Department for comment. In a political background memo, the department said it was aware in general terms of the King's fiscal difficulties but had no details because it had no representative in Saudi Arabia. "King Ibn Saud is unquestionably the outstanding figure in the Arab world today," this memo said. "All of our recent reports from our own officers and the British indicate the King favors the Allied cause"—aside from his objections to Britain's longstanding commitment to the creation of "a national home for the Jewish people" in Palestine.

In principle, the State Department said there was no objection to the arrangement proposed by Moffett. The alternative, it said, was to supply aid directly to Saudi Arabia under the Lend-Lease program. This program, created by Congress in March 1941, authorized the president to provide vast amounts of equipment and supplies to allies in the war against the Axis powers. Some $50 billion worth was distributed over the next four years, mostly to Britain and the Soviet Union. The problem with using Lend-Lease to assist Saudi Arabia was that Saudi Arabia was at best neutral in the war, not an ally. By some accounts, the King was actually pro-German, as were many Arabs who saw the prospect of a German victory as putting an end to British and French colonial rule. Abdul Aziz opened diplomatic relations with Hitler's government in 1939 and according to the British author Robert Lacey "sent a messenger to Berchtesgarten with a personal letter assuring Hitler 'that it is our foremost aim to see the friendly and intimate relations with the German reich developed to the utmost limits.'" It could be argued that the King said that sort of thing to any foreign leader who expressed a desire for friendship, but it was certainly a stretch in Washington to think of the King as some sort of principled beacon of liberty.

Roosevelt sent Moffett's memo and the State Department's comments to Secretary of the Navy Frank Knox, asking him to try to set up some arrangment along the lines proposed by Moffett. In May, Knox replied that it could not be done: "I have had an investigation made of the oil produced in Saudi Arabia and find that its quality is not suitable for Navy use" because of its high sulfur content.

A few weeks later, Roosevelt's adviser Harry L. Hopkins sent all this material to Jesse Jones, administrator of the Federal Loan Agency, with a note saying that "The president is anxious to find a way to do something about this matter." Perhaps food aid could be sent under Lend-Lease, Hopkins said, "although just how we would call that outfit a 'democracy' I don't know." Jones, who was not an admirer of the King and steadfastly rebuffed overtures on his behalf from Chevron, replied that "There appears to be no legal way we can help the King" and suggested that the British provide what the King needed. Roosevelt accepted the argument that the King, a desert autocrat who was sitting out the war, was not a candidate for U.S. government financial assistance. In a famous note he told Jones, "Jesse: Will you tell the British I hope they can take care of the King of Saudi Arabia. This is a little far afield for us."

But the president did not let the matter rest there, despite all the more urgent things on his mind. On February 13, 1942, he wrote to the King to inform him that he was sending, at U.S. government expense, Karl Twitchell and two experts in desert agriculture to examine prospects for increasing agricultural output in the Kingdom through irrigation. (This was the same Twitchell who had been dispatched to Arabia by Charles Crane a decade earlier. He was present on the shore when the first Chevron geologists arrived in the Kingdom by boat in 1933, and was later introduced to Roosevelt by Wild Bill Donovan.)

In his letter notifying the King that he was sending the agricultural team and that the U.S. government would pay for it, Roosevelt was elaborately flattering of Abdul Aziz and his people, to the point of finding in them a "love of liberty" not readily discernible to others. The president extended best wishes to "the Government and people of Saudi Arabia, who have a long and noble history, and whose love of liberty finds a particularly warm response in our hearts at this time. . . . As Your Majesty is doubtless aware, my countrymen, in association with the other peoples comprising the United Nations, have pledged their lives and their fortunes to the eradication of the evil forces of Germany, Italy, and Japan, which seek to destroy the world's liberties in accordance with an utterly selfish plan, pursued in a cruel and dishonorable manner. However bitter the struggle may be, the final outcome is not in doubt, and, in view of the bonds of civilization and the common aims which unite our Peoples, I am confident that Your Majesty will assist in the attainment of freedom, security and progress in such manner as your wisdom and judgment may determine." In a handwritten postcript to his official letter, the president said, "I have just seen some very interesting films of various places in your kingdom which have pleased me. I wish that I could visit your country."

In response, the King expressed his gratitude, and added: "Your excellency's expression of the fact that you would like, if you had the chance, to visit my country, which has been made nearer to other countries by the modern means of communications, has caused me great pleasure. I will look forward to the realization of this desire, which is also mine, with satisfaction, delight, and pleasure."

Among Roosevelt's papers is a memorandum from the State Department asking him to approve the Twitchell mission to court the King's favor because the Army Air Corps was considering "the desirability of requesting the permission of the Saudi Arabian government for the installation of airfields." This was raising the stakes in Saudi Arabia. The United States was by now engaged in war in Asia and Europe, and Saudi Arabia was between the two fronts; the War Department was looking for bases in the Persian Gulf region that would shorten the distance between the Mediterranean and South Asia, would be out of German reach, and would not be under British control. Roosevelt told Secretary of State Cordell Hull that it was time to open a permanent U.S. diplomatic mission in Jeddah to begin talking directly to the King and his advisers. On April 13, 1942, a career diplomat named James S. Moose Jr. arrived in Jeddah as chargé d'affaires of the first resident U.S. diplomatic legation in Saudi Arabia.

Moose was not part of the State Department's Ivy League elite—he grew up in a small town in Arkansas and attended Kentucky Military Institute—but as a young Foreign Service officer he studied Arabic and became a full member of the State Department group known collectively as "The Arabists." He had a long and successful career, capped by a term as ambassador to Syria, but unlike his colleagues became disillusioned with the Arabs and is probably best remembered for one quotation: "Arabic is a language that opens the door to an empty room."

From the day of Moose's arrival in Jeddah, the United States and Saudi Arabia moved steadily closer to each other—despite British delaying tactics—and closer to the point where their leaders would meet in the historic encounter that led to their permanent alliance. On February 18, 1943, just ten months after Moose took up his station, Roosevelt declared Saudi Arabia to be strategically vital to the defense of the United States and thus eligible for Lend-Lease assistance. The following month, Secretary of State Hull recommended that the position held by Moose in Saudi Arabia be elevated to "minister resident," raising the occupant's status with the King. Moose was promptly promoted. (Not until 1949 was the mission elevated to full embassy status.)

By June 1943, the war was raging almost around the world, from the plains of Russia to the Italian islands to the Aleutians off Alaska to the mountains of China. The Allies could sense that the tide had turned in their favor, but victory was not yet in sight. In the midst of this cataclysm, Roosevelt sent his personal foreign affairs adviser, Brigader General Patrick Hurley, to Saudi Arabia to talk to the King.

Hurley's specialty was China, not the Middle East, and he was a Republican—he had been secretary of war in the administration of President Herbert Hoover. But Roosevelt trusted his judgment, as he had that of another prominent Republican, Bill Donovan of the OSS. On June 9, Hurley sent the president a long report about his conversations with the King.

"Ibn Saud is the wisest and strongest of all the leaders I have met in the Arab states," Hurley wrote. "He is a man of vision and executive ability ready to lead his people in keeping pace with the progress of the world. He is, however, sensitive to the primitive outlook of his countrymen and their reluctance to accept foreign influence too readily. Ibn Saud acknowledges frankly that his country for its own safety and welfare needs the friendship and the assistance of a strong foreign power, but he distrusts and fears foreign imperialism. He is determined that his country will not become a ward or a mere instrument for profit of some foreign government. The King has, however, great faith and confidence in the United States. . . . He expressed complete confidence in your leadership and sincerely pleaded for your friendship."

Hurley said the King told him he wanted the oil resources of his country to be developed exclusively by American enterprises. "Saudi Arabia is potentially one of the greatest oil areas of the world. . . . The development of the situation in Saudi Arabia gives you, Mr. President, the possibility for a complete answer to the critics who tell us we are exhausting our oil resources at home without any hope of replacement. The development of the great oil resources of Saudi Arabia will give you a supply of this essential commodity in a strategic location," he added. The King, he said, was looking forward to postwar American assistance in irrigation, road construction, transportation, communications, education and public health. Hurley also observed that Saudi Arabia's economic distress was compounded by the fact that its silver riyal coin, the basic unit of currency, had silver content higher than its monetary value and therefore disappeared over the borders as soon as it circulated. He recommended that Saudi Arabia switch to paper money, which it resisted doing until Americans introduced the concept a decade later.

This remarkable document, from a mid-level envoy in the middle of a world war, conveys concisely many of the essential elements of the unique relationship between the United States and Saudi Arabia in the ensuing six decades: the Saudi preference for

American involvement over European because the United States was not a colonizer; the tension between Saudi Arabia's need for outside assistance to develop its resources and protect itself and the aversion of the Saudi people to infidels and outsiders (reflected most dramatically in popular resentment of the U.S. deployment for Operation Desert Storm in 1991); and the sensitivity of the proud desert Arabs about their material backwardness.

Separately, Roosevelt dispatched Lieutenant Colonel Harold B. Hoskins, an Arabic-speaking intelligence agent who was Bill Eddy's cousin and Princeton classmate, to sound out the King on the subject of Palestine; pressure was building, as the reality of the Nazi Holocaust was revealed, to permit thousands of traumatized Jewish refugees from Europe to migrate to the Holy Land. The Arabs uniformly opposed additional Jewish migration to Palestine, and the King rebuffed Roosevelt's overture, telling the president that it was a nice of him to send a "tactful representative" to talk about it but there was no give in the position he had already stated in two previous letters: Palestine is Arab land. In his report to Roosevelt, Hoskins concluded with this warning: "Not only you as president but the American people as a whole should realize that if the American government decided to support the establishment of a Jewish state in Palestine [as Zionists were demanding], they are committing the American people to the use of force in that area, since only by force can a Jewish state in Palestine be established or maintained." This echoed what the King-Crane Commission had told President Wilson, but somehow even this blunt assessment from a trusted analyst, and many similar memos Roosevelt was receiving from a strongly anti-Zionist State Department, left the president with the belief, or the hope, that he could charm the King into flexibility on this subject.

While he was in Saudi Arabia, Hoskins conveyed to the King an invitation to visit the United States or to send a member of his family if he could not come himself. In September 1943, two of Abdul Aziz's sons, princes Faisal and Khalid—both future kings— were invited to Washington and were well treated (although by some accounts they were upset when told that wartime restrictions made it necessary to deny their request to acquire 14 automobiles).

Vice President Henry A. Wallace attended a splashy dinner for them at the White House. They stayed at Blair House, the official government guest house, and were provided with a special train to carry them on a sightseeing trip to the West Coast. Upon their return home, they reported favorably to their father, and also informed him that they had been told President Roosevelt enjoyed collecting stamps, a personal detail that Hoskins had also told the King. These messages gave the King an opening to approach the president directly. He assembled a set of 160 current and old-time stamps from the Arabian Peninsula, then quite rare in the West, and sent them to the president as a gift.

During that same summer of 1943, on August 10, Roosevelt received a memo from Harold Ickes, the wartime oil administrator, alerting him to the urgency of securing new supplies of oil because the United States was already at peak production. Ickes was a flamboyant political brawler of progressive leanings who served Roosevelt throughout his presidency as secretary of the interior and, during the war, as a trusted counselor on all matters dealing with oil. He was renowned for blunt talk, and his memo to the president reflected it: "Despite everything," Ickes wrote, "our supplies are falling below demand. Therefore, it behooves us to find supplies of crude oil elsewhere. . . . We have assumed obligations in the world upon which we must make good. This means that we should have available oil in different parts of the world. I believe that the time to get going is now." The logical conclusion to be drawn from this was that Saudi Arabia would become increasingly important to U.S. strategic and economic interests; the oil reserves of the other countries around the Persian Gulf were under British control.

On February 10, 1944, Roosevelt sent the King a letter thanking him for the stamps. He expressed regret that he had been unable to meet the King during a recent trip to Cairo and Tehran—a trip on which he flew over part of Saudi Arabia and conceived the idea of bringing irrigation and agriculture to the region's vast deserts—and expressed the hope of meeting Abdul Aziz on some future journey. "There are many things I want to talk to you about," the president said.

The King took this as a commitment from the president to visit, and began asking Moose when he could expect Roosevelt's arrival. The president's forthcoming journey to Yalta, in the Soviet Crimea, for the crucial meeting at which he would discuss postwar arrangements with Churchill and Stalin, was to provide the opportunity for the president and the King, so different in background but in many ways kindred spirits, to come together at last.

ASSIGNMENT: ARABIA

At the end of 1943, his work in North Africa done, Bill Eddy was instructed to return to Washington for "temporary additional duty." This turned out to be an assignment from the Secretary of State to report to Saudi Arabia by February 15, 1944, "where you will be attached to the American Legation at Jidda in the capacity of Special Assistant to the American Minister resident," James Moose.

As for his duties, "It is desired that you visit other parts of Arabia, including Bahrein and Kuwait, also Iraq, Syria, Lebanon, Palestine, Transjordan, and Egypt. Your capacity in each of the countries above mentioned to which you will go will be that of Special Assistant to the Chief of Mission or to the principal consular officer . . . . Your duties are in general to establish contact with both official and nonofficial persons for the purpose of acquainting yourself with local personalities, problems, currents of thought, wants, needs, and aspirations, both political and nonpolitical, with particular reference to American interests, friendly and helpful relations between the United States and the local governments and peoples, and the attitude of their governments and their respective nationals regarding these matters. Your estimates, interpretations and proposals in these respects will be of especial value to the department." He was authorized to travel as much as he wished, by any means available. A copy of this order was sent to the U.S. diplomatic mission in each of the countries mentioned, to make sure that the personnel there understood the scope of Eddy's mandate and did not undermine him.

This was an amazingly broad writ for one individual; it was even broader than the mission that the State and Navy Departments had envisioned when Eddy was first sent to Cairo in 1941. As on that earlier occasion, however, Eddy was diverted away from this wide-ranging assignment because a more urgent task came up.

In April 1944, the State Department's Wallace Murray met with Hafiz Wahba, an Egyptian schoolteacher who was Saudi Arabia's ambassador to Britain. (The Saudis at the time lacked a diplomatic corps of their own and often used favored foreign-born Arabs in this role.) Murray said the U.S. government was "very anxious to have direct contact" with the King. Wahba replied that "We would certainly welcome that idea," but he told Murray there was an obstacle: James Moose was not showing sufficient enthusiasm. He said Moose had missed opportunities to work more closely with the Saudis and with the King himself, leaving the field of influence to the British.

Four months later, in August 1944, Moose was recalled. Who better to replace him than Bill Eddy, who was already in Saudi Arabia, spoke the language, knew the Arabs well and had demonstrated his interest with his memo about the *Honduras* attack four years earlier? With the upgraded title of Envoy Extraordinary and Minister Plenipotentiary, he became President Roosevelt's emissary to the King, with a salary of $10,000 per year. Roosevelt wrote to the King to tell him of Eddy's appointment: "He is well informed of the relative interests of the two countries and of the sincere desire of this government to cultivate to the fullest extent the friendship which has so long subsisted between them." The wily president was exaggerating for effect, to flatter the King. Far from being longtime friends, the United States and Saudi Arabia had no relationship whatsoever before 1932 and were only beginning to grope their way toward alliance.

Eddy's promotion effectively terminated his regional reporting assignment; he was now the president's full-time emissary to Saudi Arabia. Thus it fell to Eddy to carry out the unprecedented task of orchestrating the meeting of the president he served and the King to whose government he was accredited. Given that the two leaders were so far apart in background, education, language, religion, and knowledge of the world that they might have been from different planets, it was going to require all of Eddy's skill and experience to bring it off.

EARLY DAYS IN JEDDAH

Bill Eddy was still technically an officer in the Marine Corps during his first five months in Saudi Arabia, until his discharge from active duty upon his promotion to succeed Moose as head of the upgraded U.S. Legation. His duties were diplomatic and administrative in nature rather than military, but he frequently wore his Marine uniform, and the Marine Corps was very much on his mind for another reason: his eldest child, Bill Jr., was a Marine lieutenant fighting his way across the Pacific islands in the great campaign against the Japanese, and the Eddys went many weeks without knowing whether he was alive. The younger Bill Eddy saw combat on Iwo Jima, Saipan and Tinian, where his gallantry earned him the Navy Cross and a Bronze Star. In an eerie replay of his father's career, Bill Jr. was promoted to captain and selected as the aide de camp to his division commander, Major General Clifton B. Cates.

When Bill Eddy finally got word that his son was alive and out of danger, he wrote a letter of congratulations on this new assignment, a position he of course knew well, having held it himself in World War I. "A general wants the best officer available to be his aide," he wrote, "because he wants him to be an AIDE not a hazard. I am sure they picked the best man they could find, one whose combat record entitled him to a change of duty, and whose combat record would make him understand the real business of Headquarters. Apart from the honor to you, we are also happy about your new job because it will give you an entirely new and revealing experience in the war. . . . You will now have a different and more intellectual satisfaction in knowing the whys and wherefores of what is done. And in meeting the top men, you will meet some very fine men whose friendship you will prize all your life, just as they will be the better for knowing you."

With the anxiety about his son out of the way, Eddy was able to throw himself into the challenging assignment of nurturing the incipient relationship between the industrial superpower he represented and the impoverished but promising country to which he was posted. Eddy's papers and correspondence and the diplomatic record for this period describe a difficult, often bizarre but rewarding life of eye-opening experiences, frustrating communications, and accommodation to local customs and traditions.

Unlike a European nation or any outpost of European colonialism, Saudi Arabia was a country where the book on diplomatic protocol and embassy management was being written as the Eddys went along; many decisions were made through trial and error. On the Saudi side, only the King had true decision-making power, and cultivation of the ruler was essential to Eddy's mission.

In April 1944, a month after his arrival, Eddy traveled to Riyadh and met the King for the first time. Like all foreign visitors to the capital in that era, he wore Arab garb for the occasion, which he described in family letters. He saw "a review of thousands of camels; the feeding of thousands of poor who are fed daily from the King's kitchens—bedouins whose herds have died of starvation and thirst and disease, taking away the only means of livelihood; the King's falcons chained to a rick, the falcons he uses to hunt the sand grouse and bustards." He spent 45 minutes alone with the King, who "expressed satisfaction that someone who spoke the language had come not for an official visit but to see how the people live and what they lack." From Riyadh Eddy traveled on to Dhahran, on the Persian Gulf coast, all along the way seeing the carcasses and skeletons of livestock that had perished in the drought. That trip instilled in Eddy a sense of urgency in persuading Washington to provide assistance to the King, and marked the beginning of what grew into a strong friendship between himself and Abdul Aziz that would endure until the King's death in 1953. That friendship made it possible for Eddy to pull off the King's meeting with Roosevelt and the complicated negotiations over bilateral issues that grew out of that encounter.

There was more to Eddy's job than high-level bilateral relations. As chief of the U.S. diplomatic mission, he had to do what he could to make life easier and healthier for his family and his staff. Jeddah was by far the most advanced city in the Kingdom, but it was filthy, hot and primitive nonetheless. Only a few buildings had such basic amenities as running water, electricity and indoor plumbing. In a city where summer temperatures routinely reached 120 degrees and humidity was stifling, the bedrooms of the American legation had a form of air conditioning, but other buildings did not. Water was delivered by donkey cart. The city had no street lights other than a few kerosene lanterns, and no medical clinic or doctors. When Eddy's predecessor, James Moose, had a major dental problem, he had to cross the Red Sea to Asmara to be treated. In Jeddah there was not even a barber shop. Haircuts were provided by "an old Turk who was stranded in Jidda when Ibn Saud conquered the place," according to Clarence J. McIntosh, a young communications clerk who was one of the first staff members at the U.S. legation.

Flies and mosquitoes filled the fetid air. In the heat and dust, the few trucks and automobiles broke down. Refrigeration was scarce, making food hazardous. Office equipment wore out quickly. Because of the salty humidity, steel window screens could rust through in a week. Travel conditions were onerous—the vast kingdom had no cross-country roads and no airline. Jeddah had a rudimentary airport, but Saudi Arabia had no airplanes and there was no regular air service to Cairo or Beirut. A British-controlled radiotelegraph line to Sudan provided only limited communication with the outside world.

Eddy's early letters are filled with good-natured observations about the odd habits and folkways of the local people. He noted, for example, that they played chess without the bishop, for which they substituted an elephant, and without the queen, for which they substituted a "vizier." No Christians or women were going to be checkmating any king in Abdul Aziz's Saudi Arabia. But these upbeat notes made no effort to disguise the difficult conditions Mary would face once she joined him.

In fact, of all the foreign cities to which Bill Eddy might have been posted, probably none could have been worse for Mary than Jeddah in the 1940s. These were not auspicious conditions for a heat-averse woman whose health had already broken down once in Cairo, a far more sophisticated and congenial city than Jeddah. Mary had found even Princeton to be boring and flat; she was completely comfortable only during the Dartmouth years, when she could ski and hike in the hills of New Hampshire and Vermont, the polar opposite of Saudi Arabia. The State Department's Gordon Alling had alluded to this potential problem in the March 15, 1944, letter in which he offered Eddy the Saudi Arabia job: "I know, however, that you have some question in your mind about Mary's reaction to living in such a place as Jidda. You will, therefore, have to consider this angle thoroughly."

So difficult was travel in Saudi Arabia that the State Department tried to get Eddy his own airplane. An internal memo noted that "the area to which he is assigned is one third as large as the United States." It was 550 miles from Jeddah, the diplomatic capital, to Riyadh, and 800 miles to the oil community in Dhahran where 1100 Americans were working. "Not only are there no railroads or adequate roads connecting these communities, but there are no regular air services in the country," this memo noted—a particular hardship for the embassy staff who, to go on vacation, had to pay $165 each way to fly to Cairo, assuming there were any flights on planes operated by the military or the oil company.

To visit the handful of Americans working at a gold mine 240 miles deep in the interior, Eddy wrote in one letter, "I have to wait for regular trips made by commercial companies, or by government officials, as there is no private transport, no bus service, nothing on wheels to hire for love or money." On each of these trips at least three vehicles were required to travel in convoy because breakdowns and skids into the deep sand were inevitable. At the mining camp itself, he reported, there was little to eat because this was a time of deep privation in the Arabian hinterlands; no imports were available because of the war, and the Arab workers lived on camel milk, dates and millet gruel. On the other hand, he found, these undernourished workers took comfort in their religious faith, so that "there is no insanity (except among camels). What comes, must come."

The physical hardships were compounded by social isolation. There were only a few dozen Western residents in Jeddah, most of them male. Mary Eddy was the only American woman and there were perhaps half a dozen other foreign women; Anita Burleigh, wife of an oil company executive, lived in Jeddah before the war, but when the United States entered the war she went home, as did almost all the American women in the oil camp on the other side of the country.

So there was basically nothing for Mary Eddy to do aside from the amusements she could create for herself. ("It is pathetic," Bill Eddy wrote to the children about the foreign women. "There is absolutely nothing for them to do all day long.") Other than the weekly movie that Eddy arranged to show on the roof of the U.S. legation, the opportunities for recreation and socializing were very limited, although there were a few tennis courts that legation personnel could use. Across the country in Dhahran, CASOC built swimming pools and movie theaters for its American families; no such facilities existed in Jeddah, where there was no public entertainment of any kind. There was a bathing beach for foreigners on the Red Sea, but sharks lurked in the water; only after Eddy's departure did his successor obtain royal permission to construct a protective steel net to keep the sharks away.

Eventually the king authorized the Eddys to import Mary's piano, which he said was the first in "the Wahhabi blue-law Kingdom where musical instruments were prohibited along with painting and sculpture." Indeed, among the Arab population no music other than ceremonial drums was permitted, whether live or recorded.

In the same letter in which he recounted the trip to the gold mine, Eddy reported that he had finally learned to sleep through the muezzin's call to dawn prayer, which rose from a nearby mosque at about 4 A.M., but was now awakened instead by the braying of the donkey pulling the daily water delivery cart. The water itself he drank only after boiling, but even so, he said, "you will inevitably get ill from the ceremonial lemonade at some event . . . "

Those who did fall ill were in peril because of the lack of medical facilities. A true emergency required evacuation to Cairo, which was possible only if some oil company personnel or military group happened to be flying that way. One of Eddy's great administrative accomplishments was to persuade the State Department to put up $54,700—a considerable sum in those days—to create a medical clinic to be staffed by personnel from the hospital of the American University of Beirut; it would treat local people and pilgrims passing through Jeddah on their way to Mecca as well as Americans.

An internal State Department memo of November 6, 1945, gives an idea of what Eddy was dealing with in trying to run a diplomatic mission in that environment. The subject was typewriters.

"Typewriters at the Legation in Jidda, as well as all other mechanical equipment, are subject to very rapid deterioration because of the excess humidity—within a few months they become so rusted, corroded by salt air, and gummed, the operation is seriously impaired," it said. "When machines are allowed to remain in this condition for an extended time they reach a point where it is impossible to repair or recondition them. The factor of a depleted staff attempting to carry on essential work with almost inoperative machines also arises." To ship a typewriter to the United States for repairs took six months, the memo said. The writer recommended that Eddy be allowed to purchase standby machines beyond those in the budget, and to ship the ones that broke down to Cairo to be fixed rather than all the way to the United States.

In normal conditions the chief of a U.S. diplomatic mission would not concern himself with such matters, but the Eddys were not living and working in normal conditions. They were not complainers. They made the best of it, aided by their fluency in Arabic and the fact that the king liked them. According to R. Parker (Pete) Hart, a former student of Eddy's at Dartmouth who was now a young diplomat in Saudi Arabia and would later be ambassador to the Kingdom, Eddy's "total fluency in the king's mother tongue and his quick sense of humor made him instantly a most welcome guest." On many occasions Eddy was invited to accompany the ruler as he roamed the country camping with the tribes. These expeditions were the defining characteristic of the King's style of one-man rule. According to H. St. John Philby, a British adventurer who ingratiated himself with Abdul Aziz and was his longtime confidant and adviser, "It certainly stands to the credit of Ibn Saud that, at whatever cost of inconvenience to himself, he never ceased to be freely accessible to all his subjects, high and low, rich and poor alike, to hear and redress their grievances, and to help them over their difficulties." It was an honor for Eddy to be invited to join the King on these forays into the hinterlands, where they slept in tents among the bedouin, and it is regrettable that he said little about them in the family correspondence preserved with his papers.

"THE LIGHTS ARE ON"

On October 19, 1944, Eddy reported to his wife that "the generator works, the lights are on, and the refrigerator is working. The water runs in the faucets and baths, so the essentials are there." Mary Eddy arrived in Jeddah on October 31 after dropping off their youngest child, Carmen, at a school in Beirut. On her first night, she wrote a long chatty letter to the four Eddy children.

"Here I sit in a pleasant air-conditioned room looking out to the Red Sea, where some black fishermen are knee deep in water and dragging their nets, stopping now and then to club the fish to death," she wrote. "I have been transported so quickly into such a strange and different world that it is hard to know where to begin." (Many Saudi Arabs are dark-skinned because of centuries of commercial contact and slave trading across the Red Sea to Africa.)

At that time of year, she reported, the weather was tolerable except at mid-day. They had a houseboy, a cook, and a driver, as well as a mechanic assigned to keep the air conditioner running. The water delivered by donkey cart was pumped to the roof, where the sun heated it for bathing. "All native women are veiled," but pilgrims from other countries are not. Distances are measured in camel travel—"four days by camel." Time itself was a strange concept in Saudi Arabia: Whenever the sun set was 6 P.M., regardless of the season and regardless of where in the vast country one might be. To the bedouin, time was an irrelevant concept anyway, but many of the foreign residents kept their watches set to Greenwich Mean Time to avoid confusion.

In another letter Mary described a dinner party to which they invited all the Americans in town—about 15 of them, including geologists and engineers from the gold mining company, a few diplomats, one military man. On that occasion, "we sat in the light of a full moon, with a soft breeze blowing," but another social event was wiped out by a violent night-long storm that covered everything with sand.

One day a man arrived to do the laundry, but there was no water. Everything they needed had to be imported, and imports were expensive because of the war. Mostly they were comfortable when at home, she reported, but "you have no idea how complicated it is to live in a house that has no closets, no shelves, no cellar and no attic!"

The Eddys amused themselves by sailing and bird watching. They roamed the *souk*, or Arab market, and watched the pilgrims come and go. The family Pontiac was shipped out from the States, and Mary drove it around town herself, which, she reported, "astonished the native population."

In fact, much of what they did astonished the native population because they tested the limits of Saudi social taboos. Mary having been invited to tea with the three wives of Abdullah Sulaiman, the crafty old finance minister who had negotiated the first oil agreement a decade earlier, reciprocated with an invitation to tea at the Eddys' residence. There they were joined by three English women and the sole Dutch, Russian and French women in Jeddah. The wives of Sulaiman arrived fully veiled but uncovered once inside. No men could enter while they were present, of course; the house staff had to put the tea things down outside the door and go away. After tea, Mary wrote to the children, "At six o'clock we showed a movie, setting up the apparatus in the upstairs hall, with the operator, Merrit Grant of our legation, completely hidden in my bedroom where the machine was set up. He just had a crack of the door open, and in this way he could show the movie without being seen by the ladies. When the movie began they asked if other women of their household could come and of course I said yes, so they sent for mothers, mothers in law, cousins and several slave women who came with them including a little girl and her slave. Some had never seen a movie in their lives and you should have heard the chatter and remarks and ohs and ahs, which went on during the whole picture. Of course they could not understand the English, but the movie we showed, 'Two Girls and a Sailor,' did not need much interpreting. They loved it." This was the same early era of U.S.—Saudi relations when Pete Hart's wife Jane, living across the country in Dhahran, was introducing women of that region to such novelties as the brassière.

The Saudi prohibition against social interaction between men and women affected every decision about what sort of parties to give, what sort of events to promote and whom to invite. At a dinner party at the home of his Iraqi counterpart, Eddy reported, his host's wife presided, but that meant no Saudis could be invited "as they would be outraged to see a Muslim lady serving strange men." The wives of Muslim diplomats—including a Turkish woman who was a graduate of Wellesley—were not subject to the same rules as Saudi women, but under no circumstances could Saudi men and women be brought together in a non-Saudi home.

The social peculiarities of life in Jeddah and among the Arabs as a people provided a steady source of humorous commentary in Eddy's letters. One of his narratives from this period bore a title: "Tea, Whisky and a Cruise with King Farouk." The King of Egypt came down the Red Sea in his yacht, accompanied by his sister, the beautiful Princess Fawzia, whose unhappy marriage to the Shah of Iran had ended because she did not bear a male heir. The unannounced arrival of the Egyptian royal party, Eddy reported, caused great consternation in Jeddah because the Saudi King was hundreds of miles inland, in Riyadh, and nobody knew what protocol required in his absence: a king could not just drop by, there had to be ceremonies and banquets.

"When the yacht hove in sight, the deputy foreign minister and the minister of finance had a violent and public difference of opinion, loud and guttural curses rent the air at the Jidda port, as the two harassed officials disputed what to do," Eddy reported. The urbane and well-educated Farouk, however, was undisturbed. He "received the small delegation which came on board and said he and his grief-stricken sister wanted no fuss or ceremony. . . . He would come ashore once to pray in the Jidda mosque and attend one lunch."

Farouk invited the diplomats of the American and British legations to tea aboard the yacht. "The King was at his informal best" at this event, Eddy wrote, "chatting in his perfect English about his ship and his travels and his hobbies in the infectious man-to-man style with which in Cairo he often slipped away from his palace to join a picnic or to help cook waffles in an American officer's quarters. . . . A few minutes before six, Farouk suddenly said, 'the sun is over the yard arm; time for whisky and soda,' which were produced. All of us drank except the King, who said simply, 'I never touch alcohol,' a statement which, to his detractors, must seem incredible." Eddy never did meet Fawzia, because even the relatively cosmopolitan Egyptians excluded women from such occasions.

In "King Ibn Saud: Our Faith and Your Iron," a celebrated essay published in 1963, Eddy wrote that during his tenure many items of modern technology were brought into the Kingdom for the first time, such as the airplane, the piano, the kerosene-powered refrigerator and the freezer. (He was wrong about the airplane; the British provided four De Havilland biplanes for royal use as early as 1930, though because of the war these had been withdrawn by the time Eddy arrived.) The local people, who through no fault of their own were unfamiliar with these things, often viewed them with suspicion and even fear. When American agricultural technicians assisting the Saudis at a royal experimental farm imported a Servel kerosene-powered refrigerator, the Arabs wanted to know the purpose of this "heavy white box." When one of the Americans replied that "It makes ice," there ensued "a stir and a near riot. What is ice? A Syrian was found who swore on the Qur'an that ice exists and he had seen snow himself on Mount Hermon. A spokesman demanded that they be given a demonstration. [The American] replied that it would take some hours but he was ready to oblige. He got down on his knees and struck a match to light the pilot beneath the coils. 'Wait a minute,' yelled the spokesman. 'You are building a fire to make ice?'" When the answer was affirmative, "the Arab worker fled and did not return to work for several days."

There is no way to know, of course, what Eddy said to Arabs in face-to-face conversations, but it appears from the documentary record and accounts by friends that he told such tales not in a condescending manner but in a spirit of shared amusement, knowing that the Arab's sense of humor is as acute as his sensitivity to slight and insult.

In December 1944, King Abdul Aziz came to Hijaz, or western Saudi Arabia, for his annual visit to Mecca—where the Eddys as non-Muslims were not permitted to go—and then passed through Jeddah, which he rarely did because he was a man of the desert and disliked the steamy seaport. According to Clarence McIntosh, "his caravan consisted of some 5000 cars, all American make. His particular auto is a large red Packard equipped with all the latest innoventions [sic] and handrails on the outside for his guards to hang onto. . . . It takes 500 cars alone to move the Crown Prince. His wives and around 50 daughters also have a fleet of black curtain-drawn limousines and hundreds of attendants." Surely McIntosh was exaggerating for effect—but perhaps not. The King did live extravagantly, and it did require numerous vehicles to transport his retinue over the rutted tracks that passed for roads.

"I saw the old boy four times," Eddy reported in a letter to Bill Jr., "once at the reception for the Diplomatic Corps when I wore my Marine Corps white uniform, once alone on business, once to present fellow Americans, and once at a private audience for Mother [i.e. Mary] and Carmen," who was down from Beirut for Christmas. "To put it mildly it was certainly the first time the fierce old battle-scarred but essentially kind monarch had ever received a small American girl. The three of us paraded in past guards of honor, ante-chamber filled with desert sheikhs with scimitars and second son, Emir Faysal, with whom Mother and Cita [their nickname for their other daughter] had dinner in Washington. Carmen claims to have been scared but she didn't show it and carried herself very well. Mother sat on the King's right and conversed easily with him in fluent Arabic. The visit caused quite a flurry of curiosity and excitement among the King's retinue. I should add that we wear our own western clothes here, as this is the Christian 'reservation.' When visitors go to Riyadh they all wear Arabian dress." (The following summer, when Mary went home to New Hampshire for two months, Eddy wrote to his son, "It is becoming clear to me that mother was making altogether too much of a hit with the King and I did well by myself to take her afar off." It is hard to imagine exactly what actions of the king prompted this comment.)

As for Eddy's official duties, being envoy to Saudi Arabia was like no other job in the U.S. diplomatic service. In other countries the senior U.S. envoy would be expected to work with many cabinet officers and high-ranking government officials, and to cultivate the leaders of major non-governmental organizations and perhaps members of oposition groups. In the Saudi Arabia of 1944 there were no such people; the country had no real government, no functioning economy, and no political or educational organizations other than the mosques. There was no legislature; in fact, there was no constitution other than the Koran. The King answered only to the senior religious authorities, and even they had mostly been bent to his will. The King made all important decisions, and he consulted only a few of his favorite sons and two or three trusted advisers. To alienate any of them was to imperil the entire bilateral relationship, including the oil concession.

King Abdul Aziz was regarded by Americans who met him as wise, courageous and thoughtful—Eddy called him "one of the great men of the twentieth century"—but he was also prickly, sensitive to insult, and insistent upon being treated as an equal even when he brought nothing to the table. To make the task of cultivating him even more difficult, the King mostly stayed in Riyadh, his desert capital 550 miles inland. There were few telephone lines outside Jeddah, no roads, and no airports other than a few primitive landing strips, so that communication with him was as difficult as it was essential. Riyadh was a closed city to which foreigners could go only by royal invitation, and only clad in Arab garb. Not until the 1980s did foreign embassies in Saudi Arabia relocate to the royal capital.

Except on Eddy's forays with the King into the bedouin heartland, his contacts with local people were limited because much of the Arab population was hostile to outsiders and suspicious of technology; in the 1920s, the King had been forced to confront his own fanatical warriors on the battlefield to establish the principle that he was in charge and could invite foreigners into the country if development required their presence. By 1944, the entire non-Muslim population of the vast country still was no more than four hundred, mostly the diplomats in Jeddah and the hundred or so Americans who stuck out the war at their oil camp in Dhahran, on the other side of the country. It stretched the imagination to envision the "bonds of civilization" between Saudi Arabia and the United States that Roosevelt had talked about in his 1942 letter.

King Abdul Aziz liked Eddy and appreciated his fluency in Arabic, and he was charmed by Mary and by the Eddys' youngest daughter, Carmen. But Eddy still had only sporadic access to him. With these limitations, Eddy had only six months to establish trust and rapport before the fateful message arrived from Washington: The president wants to see the King, and very soon.

On February 3, 1945, acting Secretary of State Joseph C. Grew sent cables to Eddy and to his counterparts in Egypt and Ethiopia telling them that Roosevelt wanted to meet the leaders of those countries "on board a United States man of war at Ismailia about February 10"—that is, just a week later. For Egypt's King Farouk and Ethiopia's Emperor Haile Selassie, who were sophisticated and worldly, traveling on short notice to meet a foreign dignitary was relatively simple; for King Abdul Aziz, it was an unprecedented undertaking that would require frantic negotiations about logistics, lodging, diet, and every other detail. Each decision was complicated by the need to maintain secrecy, for security reasons, about Roosevelt's itinerary. The ensuing three weeks were the most grueling and intense days of Eddy's life, other than the Belleau Wood campaign. It was no wonder he had "a certain harassed look about him," as Mary wrote to the children.

The president would travel from the United States to the Mediterranean aboard a Navy cruiser, the USS *Quincy*, then fly from Malta to the Crimea for the conference at which he, Churchill and Stalin would negotiate the postwar world order and the creation of the United Nations. He would reboard the *Quincy* in Egyptian waters for his encounters with Farouk, Haile Selassie and Abdul

Aziz. The Navy's Destroyer Squadron 17, which had been on convoy duty in the Atlantic, was detached to escort the *Quincy*.

That was the easy part of the arrangements. The hard part was delivering King Abdul Aziz and his entourage, who knew no way of life other than their own and took for granted that their habits, diets and religious practices would travel with them. Roosevelt was a wealthy, educated patrician with a sophisticated knowledge of the world; Abdul Aziz was a semi-literate desert potentate whose people knew little of plumbing or electricity. Roosevelt was a politician; Abdul Aziz was a warrior who bore the scars of combat and had killed men with a sword. *TIME* magazine, in its account of their meeting, described them as "the Squire of Hyde Park, schooled at Groton and Harvard, [and] the Lord of Arabia, schooled in the Koran, the desert, the raid, the running horse, the harem." Yet the Saudis assumed—rightly, as it turned out—that the two leaders would meet on equal terms; Abdul Aziz would accept nothing less.

THE STRANGE VOYAGE OF THE USS *MURPHY*

The plan called for the King and his advisers to travel overland from Riyadh to Jeddah and board a U.S. Navy destroyer, the USS *Murphy*, for the voyage up the Red Sea to Egypt. Because of wartime security restrictions, the plan was kept secret from Jeddah's small diplomatic corps and from the Arab populace. Eddy accepted social invitations knowing he would not be attending the events, just as he had done in Tangier before Operation TORCH; the King put out the word that his caravan was heading for the holy sites at Mecca, about fifty miles inland from Jeddah. When instead he boarded the *Murphy* and sailed away, there was consternation and grief among the people, who feared he had abdicated or been kidnapped. Jeddah "was plunged into hysterical commotion," Eddy recalled. "The rumors which flew about like bolts of lightning cancelled each other out, leaving the people stunned and bewildered."

Knowing nothing about the King, his country or his habits, Captain John S. Keating, commander of Destroyer Squadron 17, and

the *Murphy*'s skipper, Commander Bernard A. Smith, were under-
standably nervous about protocol and worried about how their
crew would behave; because of the secrecy requirements, they had
not yet been told that Eddy would accompany the Arab party to
navigate these issues for them. Their only information came from
an encyclopedia, which informed them that the King had many
wives and scores of children, and that the consumption of alcohol
and tobacco was forbidden in his presence. The Americans knew
that Islam prohibited the consumption of pork and that the King
liked to eat lamb, but otherwise they knew nothing of his dietary
preferences. Their only chart of the Jeddah harbor dated to 1834;
no U.S. Navy ship had ever put in there.

The Saudis said the traveling party would consist of 200 people,
including some of the King's wives. Commander Smith said the
most the *Murphy* could accommodate was ten. Eddy negotiated the
number down to 20, but when the King and his party arrived at the
pier there were 48, including the King's brother Abdullah; two of
his sons, Mohammed and Mansour; his finance minister, Abdullah
Sulaiman; and the royal astrologer. As his companions and advisers
had told the Americans, the King also planned to bring along a wife
or two, as he always did when he traveled. It fell to Eddy to explain
why no women could make the voyage: there was no place aboard
the *Murphy* where they could be sequestered, and they would be
exposed to prying male eyes as they negotiated the gangways. More
cultural dissonance was soon to come.

"A few hours before the launches with the Arab party came
alongside the destroyer," Eddy wrote, "several large dhows also
arrived at the ship laden with tons of vegetables, sacks of grain
and rice, and one hundred of the best and fattest sheep. In other
words, the normal provision which the King would provide for an
extensive sojourn in the desert. He had given orders that everybody on the ship must eat of his bounty, including all the American sailors who had come to Saudi Arabia. The Saudi Minister of
Finance, Shaikh Abdullah Sulaiman, preceded the King on board
ship and told Commodore Keating that all these provisions and
the one hundred live sheep must be loaded at once by royal order
of His Majesty. The Commodore had quite contrary and standing

orders from the U.S. Navy, and he was fortunately able to stall until I arrived with the King on the pretext that he did not fully understand what was being asked of him through a very halting interpreter. I was immediately in the middle of a conflict, and I was destined to stay in the middle for a week. I explained to the King that the Commodore had 60-days' provisions in the lockers on board, adequate for all. The King replied that this made no difference—his American guests must eat from his table and from the produce of his country, and particularly they must eat the freshly slaughtered lamb every day. The Navy replied that their lockers also included frozen meat—more than enough for everybody. The King had not yet, however, had any experience with refrigeration in his country where meat spoils within twenty-four hours and he brushed aside this superstitious proposal that anyone could eat meat sixty days old, insisting that fresh sheep must be slaughtered daily on board. Finally he had to be told that the sailors would be put in prison if they disobeyed Navy regulations and ate anything except the Navy rations provided for them, and surely he did not wish all of these good sailors to be dishonored for life and imprisoned unnecessarily! He then compromised, shaking his head over the curious ways of the Unbeliever, but insisted that his Arabs as good Muslims must obey the ceremonial and dietary laws of their own land. No Saudi Muslim ever ate meat more than twenty-four hours old. Commodore Keating, with a couple of dirty looks at me, finally agreed to take seven live sheep on board out of one hundred. As Mrs. Eddy went out in a launch to lunch on the *Murphy*, she saw the other ninety-three returning to shore on their dhow, reprieved to live a little longer."

Once on board, Abdul Aziz spurned the cabin designated as his quarters; he and his 47 companions insisted on sleeping outdoors, bedding down where they could around the deck. Because of the King's foot and leg ailments, he could not walk easily on steel, so his retainers spread carpets around the desk, in a colorful panorama that contrasted with the standard Navy gray. The Arabs rejected the sturdy chairs from the *Murphy*'s wardroom as inadequate; aboard came the King's high-backed gilt throne, in which the King sat facing the bow at all times except the hours of prayer, when he and his party bowed toward Mecca—the location of which was plotted for them by the ship's navigators. Most of the Arabs had never before seen a motorized vessel or sailed outside coastal waters; many became seasick, but not the King.

Other Navy regulations were thrown overboard to accommodate the Arabs. To the consternation of the Americans, the Saudis built charcoal fires to brew coffee, including one next to an open ammunition storage room. When the King asked for names of all crew members, Eddy knew he was preparing to give gifts to all of them, and he persuaded Keating and Smith to accept this breach of the rules rather than offend the King by refusing. "Explain to your superiors that it couldn't be helped," Eddy said.

"Believe me, mine was a twenty-four hour job," Eddy reported in a letter to his son Jack, "mediating between the royal party and the U.S. Navy en route, and doing all the interpreting and fixing of minor arrangements from A to Z. I do not covet a job as a court flunkey permanently."

If any Americans were inclined to ridicule the Arabs or take the King lightly, they were overpowered by his commanding presence and by the determination of Eddy and Keating to deliver him to his meeting with Roosevelt in a positive frame of mind. When Abdul Aziz boarded the *Murphy*, Keating wrote, "The immediate impression was one of great majesty and dignity. One sensed the presence of extreme power."

The voyage of the *Murphy* lasted two nights and one full day, during which Abdul Aziz saw his country's Red Sea coastline for the first time. "The voyage was delightful," Eddy wrote later. "The weather for the most part was fine. The sailors were much more impressed and astonished by the Arabs and their ways than the Arabs were by life on the U.S. destroyer. Neither group had seen anything like their opposites before, but the difference is that any such violent break with tradition is news on board a U.S. destroyer; whereas wonders and improbable events are easily accepted by the Arab whether they occur in the Arabian Nights or in real life. The Arab is by nature a fatalist and accepts what comes as a matter of course and a gift from Allah."

The Americans entertained the King with displays of naval gunnery and navigational instruments, in which he displayed a lively interest. The King ate his first apple and discovered the delights of apple pie à la mode. The crew showed Abdul Aziz a documentary film about operations aboard an aircraft carrier. According to Eddy he enjoyed it, but said he was disinclined to allow movies in his country because they would give the people "an appetite for entertainment which might distract them from their religious duties."

Public movie theaters were unknown in Saudi Arabia, but in truth the King had installed a movie projector and screen at his Riyadh palace as early as 1942 and watched films for his own pleasure and the entertainment of his guests. He just did not want ordinary people to have access to them. His fears on this point would have been confirmed had he been aware of what was happening belowdecks, where others in the Arab party were delightedly watching American commercial films.

Showing movies seemed like an easy way to entertain guests with whom the American sailors had nothing in common, but even this presumably harmless diversion proved to be a cultural minefield.

"I said that a good time was had by all on the voyage, but a good time was had by all except me," Eddy wrote in a brief book about these events. "The matter of movies was a case in point. After the showing of the documentary films on the deck and after the King had retired for the night, the usual ship's movies were shown to the crew belowdecks. This secret leaked to the ears of the King's third son, Amir [Prince] Mohammed, who on the first morning on board took me aside by the rail and inquired quietly whether I would prefer to be destroyed all at once or to be chopped up in small pieces bit by bit. I asked him what was the matter, and he said Hollywood pictures were being shown belowdecks and that he was not invited. Abject with terror, I reminded him that his royal father would not approve of any Arab, much less one of his sons, attending these godless exhibitions of half-naked women, and I begged him to forget the matter. He said very little but what he said was emphatic—to the effect that either he would see these pictures or my children would soon be orphans, and he swore if I obeyed him he would keep my confidence and not tell his father.

To make a long story short, Amir Mohammed and Amir Mansour, his younger brother, were in the front row at the late showing for the crew that night of a movie which featured Lucille Ball loose in a college men's dormitory late at night, barely surviving escapades in which her dress is ripped off. The film was greeted by whistles and applauding whoops from the crew, an approval fully shared by the two princes."

Eddy's tone here is jocular, but in fact Prince Mohammed was not to be trifled with. For decades he had a reputation for cruelty and rapaciousness; it was he who arranged the execution of a grand-daughter for adultery in the notorious episode depicted in the 1980 British film *Death of a Princess*. Eddy, however, liked him; in a letter to his children a few years later he described Mohammed as "strikingly handsome, witty, and lots of fun," as well as "immensely popular with the people." When Eddy's brief book about these events was published in 1954, Prince Mohammed received number eight of the "author's copies" that went to people Eddy valued. Number one went to King Abdul Aziz, numbers two through six to Mary and the children, number seven to Prince Faisal, number nine to Admiral William Leahy, Roosevelt's naval aide, and number ten to Eleanor Roosevelt. Prince Mohammed was in elevated company.

Eddy was the only person on board who spoke both Arabic and English languages and cultural differences popped up everywhere. He said he had a "24-hour job interpreting and mediating. I had to keep Arabs out of the engine room and chart room," and he roamed the decks at prayer time to make sure that no sailor passed between any of the Arabs and holy city of Mecca during their devotions because, as he wrote later, "No unbeliever should cast his shadow between a praying Muslim and Mecca." And yet, "The Arabs and sailors fraternized without words with a success and friendliness which was really astonishing. The sailors showed the Arabs how they did their jobs and even permitted the Arabs to help them; in return the Arabs would permit the sailors to examine their garb and their daggers, and demonstrate by gestures how they are made and for what purposes. The Arabs were particularly puzzled by the Negro mess-boys on board who, they assumed, must be Arabs and to whom they insisted on speaking Arabic since the only Negroes whom they had ever known were those who had been brought to Arabia as slaves many years ago."

Throughout the voyage up the Red Sea and then through the Suez Canal to Egypt's Great Bitter Lake, Eddy shepherded American sailors past their differences with "these weird, courteous and fascinating Arab travelers." As the rendezvous with the *Quincy* approached, the King handed out gifts: Arab costumes and gold daggers to Keating and Smith, an Arab costume and a watch inscribed with the King's name to each of the other officers, and cash to the petty officers and enlisted men. At Eddy's suggestion, Keating and Smith gave the King "gifts of objects which he had already admired: two submachine guns and a pair of Navy field glasses."

THE PRESIDENT MEETS THE KING

With the cultural shoals safely navigated, the King was delivered to the *Quincy* at 10 A.M. on February 14, 1945. As the *Murphy* approached, everyone in President Roosevelt's party was mesmerized by the spectacle, at once majestic and bizarre. On a deck covered with colorful carpets and shaded by an enormous tent of brown canvas, a large black-bearded man in Arab robes, his headdress bound with golden cords, was seated on a gilded throne. Around him stood an entourage of fierce-looking, dark-skinned barefoot men in similar attire, each with a sword or dagger bound to his waist by a gold-encrusted belt. On the *Murphy*'s fantail, sheep grazed in a makeshift corral. It was, one American witness said, "a spectacle out of the ancient past on the deck of a modern man-of-war."

In preparation for this encounter, the State Department gave the president a briefing paper about the King. It described him as "a big man, well over six feet tall, and heavy. In all probability he resembles most desert Arabs in neither knowing nor caring about the date of his birth, but he must be sixty-odd years old. Careful use of dye keeps his beard black. Both his eyes are afflicted by cataracts; but he is still able to see fairly well with one of them.

Messages for him to read are written with special care in large characters. The King is lame in one leg as a result of old injuries"— an afflication that gave him and Eddy something in common.

"Like most Arabs, he has a good sense of humor," the briefing paper said. "To a visitor of Ministerial rank, he often makes the facetious offer of an Arab wife. . . . The King's three admitted delights in life are said to be in women, prayer and perfume"— which tastes, the paper said, were similar to those of the Prophet Muhammad. As a ruler, the paper said, the King exhibited "much personal charm and great force of character. His rise to power established order in a country having a tradition of uninterrupted lawlessness, and was partially based on astute policy and on well-publicized displays of generosity or severity, according to the occasion. Statesmanship contributed to his success to a greater extent probably than his ability as a desert warrior." Other than the brief reference to women, the paper omitted any mention of the King's prodigious, indeed insatiable, sexual appetite.

This laudatory assessment by a U.S. government agency of a man who had risen to power through conquest and whose style of rule was antithetical to the most basic American values reflected the views of the handful of American officials who had met him, including Hurley, Hoskins and especially Eddy, whose admiration for Abdul Aziz is reflected in all his diplomatic dispatches. American diplomatic correspondence of the time is virtually devoid of criticsm of the King or his style of rule. Americans in government, like those at CASOC, chose not to challenge or question Saudi Arabia's autocratic system, its harsh retributive justice or its religious intolerance. This "hands off" policy, dictated by the King as a condition of staying on good terms, prevailed for decades and was the key to maintaining a bilateral working alliance on strategic and economic issues.

Once the King was safely aboard the *Quincy,* he and Roosevelt almost immediately struck a personal rapport by focusing on what they had in common rather than on their obvious differences. Eddy, in his Marine Corps uniform, was the interpreter for the King as well as for Roosevelt, a unusual gesture by the King that reflected the trust he had already developed in Eddy. (In his letter

to Jack about this assignment, Eddy said he was present as a "necessary piece of furniture.") According to Eddy's narrative, "the
King spoke of being the 'twin' brother of the President, in years,
in responsiblity as Chief of State, and in physical disability. The
President said, 'but you are fortunate to still have the use of your
legs to take you wherever you choose to go.' The King replied, 'It is
you, Mr. President, who are fortunate. My legs grow feebler every
year; with your more reliable wheel-chair you are assured that you
will arrive.' The President then said, 'I have two of these chairs,
which are also twins. Would you accept one as a personal gift
from me?' The King said, 'Gratefully. I shall use it daily and always
recall affectionately the giver, my great and good friend.'"

The wheelchair donation may have been a spontaneous gesture
on the part of the president, but the question of what official gift
the president would bestow had been the subject of extensive discussion in Washington. The State Department's Wallace Murray recommended an automobile, preferably a Cadillac, but the King already
had a large fleet of motor vehicles. Someone else proposed a bronze
figure of a horse, with or without rider. That provoked a memo from
Murray's State Department colleague, Gordon Merriam, reminding the White House that "there are Moslem objections to 'graven
images' of any kind"—therefore no statues and no paintings. Meetings were held, memos were sent, diplomats in the field were consulted. The outcome was that Roosevelt bestowed upon the King a
gift that would have great long-term implications for the relationship
between the two countries: a DC-3 passenger airplane, which was
delivered to the Kingdom by an American pilot named Joe Grant,
who stayed in Saudi Arabia as the King's personal pilot.

That DC-3 became a flying symbol of the U.S.-Saudi relationship. It is said that the plane was specially outfitted with a rotating
throne that allowed the King always to face Mecca while airborne—
which he often was, given the size of his domain. It was not the
first airplane in which the King had flown, but ownership stimulated his desire to develop air travel within the Kingdom. Once
he acquired a larger plane some years later, the DC-3 given by
Roosevelt went into public service as the first aircraft in the fleet of
what would become—after decades of aviation and maintenance

training by Americans from Trans World Airlines—the modern Saudi Arabian Airlines. The pilot Joe Grant, still robust at the age of 99, was honored as a friend of Saudi Arabia at the Kingdom's embassy in Washington in 2007.

The King's gift to the president was a diamond-encrusted sword, emblematic of his power and his martial history.

After this exchange of gifts and pleasantries, the King joined the president for lunch. Following the instructions of Roosevelt's naval aide, William M. Rigdon, the mess stewards served grapefruit, curried lamb, rice and whatever they could scrounge up as condiments—eggs, coconut, chutney, almonds, raisins, green peppers, tomatoes, olives, and pickles. After some hestitation, "His Majesty fell to, taking several servings and eating with visible pleasure," Rigdon recalled.

When it was time for coffee, the King asked Roosevelt if his ceremonial coffee server could do the honors, to which request the president of course assented. The result was Roosevelt's first taste of the cardamom-scented brew served in tiny cups that is ubiquitous in the Arabian peninsula. He took two cups, with apparent enjoyment; only several days later did he tell the crew that he found it "godawful."

As they sipped their coffee, Eddy reported to the State Department afterward, "They talked as friends of the responsibilities of governing, of the encouraging progress of the Allies in the war, of compassion for the multitudes rendered destitute through oppression or famine. The King smiled in knowing assent to the President's jovial confidence about the English: 'We like the English, but we also know the English and the way they insist on doing good themselves. You and I want freedom and prosperity for our people and their neighbors after the war. How and by whose hand freedom and prosperity arrive concerns us but little. The English also work and sacrifice to bring freedom and prosperity to the world, but on the condition that it be brought by them and marked Made in Britain.' Later in the day the King told me, 'Never have I heard the English so accurately described.'"

So much did King Abdul Aziz enjoy his meal with the president that he stunned his host with an unexpected request: he wanted the cook for himself. "He said the meal was the first he had eaten in a long time that was not followed by digestive disturbance and he would like, if the President would be so generous, to have the cook as a gift," Rigdon wrote in a memoir, *White House Sailor*. The King meant this as a compliment, but there was consternation among the Americans when Eddy translated his request.

"FDR, always a skillful talker in a jam, explained that the cook on the *Quincy* was under obligation to serve a certain period of time and that the contract with the Navy, or something of the kind, could not be broken," Rigdon recalled. "He was complimented that His Majesty was pleased with the food and regretted so much that he could not grant his request. Perhaps His Majesty would allow us to train one of his cooks?"

After this exchange, the president and the King retired for a substantive conversation. They sat side by side in easy chairs, the King in his Arab garb at the president's right, Roosevelt in a tan suit with his famous cloak draped over his left shoulder and his battered fedora on a table next to him. Eddy, in his Marine Corps uniform, perched before them on one knee, so their faces were all at the same level.

That Roosevelt was able to engage the King in a lively back-and-forth exchange that went on for nearly four hours, always through Eddy's translations, was a tribute to the president's indefatigable will, because he was ill and exhausted. The arduous trip to Yalta and the equally arduous negotiations there had fatally undermined his already fragile health, and by the time he sat down with Abdul Aziz he was only two months from death.

"Throughout this meeting," Eddy observed, "President Roosevelt was in top form as a charming host [and] witty conversationalist, with the spark and light in his eyes and that gracious smile which always won people over to him whenever he talked with them as a friend. However, every now and then I could catch him off guard and see his face in repose. It was ashen in color; the lines were deep; the eyes would fade in helpless fatigue. He was living on his nerve."

THE PALESTINE QUESTION

The record of what the two leaders said is remarkably skimpy, considering the importance of the event. The meeting attracted little notice in the American press; Roosevelt described it only briefly in his comments to reporters afterward, and the president's report to Congress about the Yalta conference mentioned his post-Yalta meetings only in passing. The lack of interest in the press is not surprising, considering what else was happening in the world at the time. Measured against the climactic campaigns of the war in Europe and the Pacific, the president's brief encounter with an obscure potentate from a little-known desert country did not appear to be a compelling story. It was not immediately apparent that Roosevelt's meeting with the King of Saudi Arabia would have far-reaching and long-lasting consequences, and that it was thus very different from the meetings with Haile Selassie and Farouk, mere courtesy calls. Moreover, the participants decided that the delicate issues under discussion did not lend themselves to public ventilation, and they kept silent about the details. The U.S. government's official report on the meeting, published in the Department of State Bulletin of February 25, 1945, said only this: "The discussions were in line with the President's desire that the heads of governments throughout the world should get together whenever possible to talk as friends and exchange views in order better to understand the problems of one another." It did not say what views were exchanged.

Various American officials in Roosevelt's traveling party picked up bits and pieces of the conversation afterward, but most of what is known about it comes from two sources: *FDR Meets Ibn Saud*, a brief memoir by Eddy, who as interpreter for both sides was the only American other than the president who heard it all, and an official joint memorandum prepared at the time by Eddy and Yusuf Yassin, a Syrian-born royal adviser on foreign affairs, which became known to the public only when it was declassified 25 years later.

The president led the discussion; as his guest, Abdul Aziz initiated no topics of conversation, waiting to see what Roosevelt wished to discuss and then responding. Eddy's account emphasizes that the King asked for no economic assistance and the subject did not arise, even though Saudi Arabia at the time was suffering widespread hardship and food shortages because the war had cut off its sources of revenue.

Roosevelt came straight to the most urgent point: the plight of the Jews and the future of Palestine, where it was already apparent that the governing mandate bestowed upon Britain by the League of Nations twenty years earlier would come to an end after the war. After World War I and the Versailles conference, the League of Nations deferred a decision on the final status of Palestine by this maneuver to place it under British administration. By now, in 1945, the full scope of the horrors inflicted on Europe's Jews by the Nazis was becoming clear, and Zionists in Palestine, Britain and the United States were clamoring for Palestine to be handed over to the Jews as a refuge and national homeland. They were demanding that Britain deliver on the promise of the "Balfour Declaration" of 1917, when British Foreign Secretary Arthur Balfour had declared that "His Majesty's government view with favour the establishment in Palestine of a National Home for the Jewish people." The Zionists seldom mentioned the second half of Balfour's sentence: "It being clearly understood that nothing shall be done which may prejudice the civil and religious rights of existing non-Jewish communities in Palestine."

The King-Crane Commission had found the two parts of Balfour's policy to be incompatible, and now two decades later Roosevelt was confronting the same difficulty. "The President asked His Majesty for his advice regarding the problem of Jewish refugees driven from their homes in Europe," according to the joint memorandum by Eddy and Yassin. "His majesty replied that in his opinion the Jews should return to live in the lands from which they were driven. The Jews whose homes were completely destroyed and who have no chance of livelihood in their homelands should be given living space in the Axis countries which oppressed them."

Roosevelt said Jews were reluctant to go back to Germany and nurtured a "sentimental" desire to go to Palestine. But the King brushed aside the argument that Europe's surviving Jews might be fearful of returning to their homes: surely the allies were going to crush the Nazis, break them to the point where they would never again pose a threat, the King said—otherwise, what was the point of the war?

"Make the enemy and the oppressor pay; that is how we Arabs wage war," he said, according to the joint memorandum. "Amends should be made by the criminal, not by the innocent bystander. What injury have Arabs done to the Jews of Europe? It is the 'Christian' Germans who stole their homes and lives. Let the Germans pay."

The King—from whose land Jews had been expunged during the lifetime of the Prophet Muhammad twelve centuries earlier—said that "the Arabs and the Jews could never cooperate, neither in Palestine nor in any other country. His majesty called attention to the increasing threat to the existence of the Arabs and the crisis which has resulted from continued Jewish immigration and the purchase of land by the Jews. His Majesty further stated that the Arabs would choose to die rather than yield their land to the Jews." The public record contains no indication that the King saw any contradiction between his assertion that the Arabs of Palestine would rather die than give up their land and the fact that Palestinian Arabs had for years been selling land to Jewish buyers.

Charles E. Bohlen, a prominent American diplomat who was a member of Roosevelt's official party, wrote in his memoirs that the King also raised another point about Palestine that is not mentioned in Eddy's account or the joint memorandum. "Ibn Saud gave a long dissertation on the basic attitude of Arabs toward the Jews," Bohlen wrote in *Witness to History.* "He denied that there had ever been any conflict betweeen the two branches of the Semitic race in the Middle East. What changed the whole picture was the immigration from Eastern Europe of people who were technically and culturally on a higher level than the Arabs. As a result, King Ibn Saud said, the Arabs had greater difficulty in surviving economically. The fact that these energetic Europeans were Jewish was not the cause of the trouble, he said; it was their superior skills and culture."

Other American officials traveling with Roosevelt said in their various memoirs that the President seemed at first not to understand the rigidity of the King's opposition to further Jewish migration into Palestine, an incomprehension that seems inexplicable given what his briefing paper had told him: "Any relaxation of his steadfast opposition to Zionist aims for Palestine (about the only question on which the Moslem world shows unanimity) would violate his principles; it would cause him to lose the respect which he now commands from his co-religionists; it might threaten his influence with his intolerant Wahhabi subjects; and could even result in the overthrow of his dynasty. The possibility that the King can be persuaded to alter his position with regard to Palestine is, therefore, so remote as to be negligible." Roosevelt apparently thought he could charm the King into flexibility, and brought up the matter several more times, eliciting the same negative response. The President then raised an idea he said he had heard from Churchill—resettling the Jews in Libya, which was far larger than Palestine and thinly populated. Abdul Aziz rejected this notion as well, saying it would be unfair to the Muslims of North Africa.

"His Majesty stated that the hope of the Arabs is based upon the word of honor of the Allies and upon the well-known love of justice of the United States," the joint statement reported, "and upon the expectation the United States will support them."

In response to that, Roosevelt gave the King a promise that would become the cornerstone of U.S. policy on Palestine (or lack of it) for the next two and a half years: "The President replied that he wished to assure His Majesty that he would do nothing to assist the Jews against the Arabs and would make no move hostile to the Arab people," and that his government "would make no change in its basic policy in Palestine without full and prior consultation with both Jews and Arabs."

Here Roosevelt the politician was playing a double game. The previous October, he had committed himself in writing to the establishment of a "Jewish commonwealth" in Palestine. He wrote a letter to Senator Robert Wagner of New York, who was planning to speak at the annual convention of the Zionist Organization of America. In this "Dear Bob" missive, Roosevelt asked Wagner to convey to the delegates his "satisfaction" that his party, at its presidential nominating convention that summer, had included this plank in its platform: "We favor the opening of Palestine to unrestricted Jewish immigration and colonization, and such a policy as to result in the establishment there of a free and democratic Jewish commonwealth." The president promised to "help bring about" the realization of this aim if re-elected, saying it was supported by "the American people."

But after meeting Abdul Aziz, on April 5, just a week before his death, Roosevelt restated the "full consultation" promise in writing. He sent a letter to the King under the salutation "Great and Good Friend" reaffirming the "full consultation" formula and his promise that he "would take no action, in my capacity as Chief of the Executive Branch of this Government, which might prove hostile to the Arab people."

The King, steeped in the Arab tradition of face-to-face talk and handshake agreements, was gratified by Roosevelt's promise, but he also made too much of it. As Eddy noted at the time, Abdul Aziz took it as a commitment of the United States, rather than as a personal pledge from its current leader. "In the conversation the King never seemed to distinguish between F.D.R. as a person and as President of the U.S.A.," Eddy noted. "To an absolute as well as a benevolent monarch, the Chief and the State are the same." The King's failure to understand this distinction accounted for his outrage and disappointment when Roosevelt's successor, Harry S. Truman, endorsed the postwar partition of Palestine and recognized the new Jewish state there.

Upon his return to Washington, Roosevelt would tell Congress, "On the problem of Arabia, I learned more about that whole problem—the Moslem problem, the Jewish problem—by talking with Ibn Saud for five minutes than I could have learned in the exchange of two or three dozen letters," but he did not specify exactly what it was he had learned. As one of his senior aides observed sarcastically, "The only thing he learned was what everyone already knew—that the Arabs didn't want any more Jews in Palestine."

After giving the King his "full consultation" pledge, Roosevelt broached the idea of an Arab mission to Britain and the United

States to press the argument against Zionist aspirations because "many people in America and England are misinformed." The King, according to Eddy's account, replied that such a mission might be useful but "more important to him was what the President had just told him concerning his own policy toward the Arab people."

The conversation then turned to Syria and Lebanon, where the Arabs feared a liberated France would seek to reassert control after the war. Abdul Aziz asked what the U.S. position would be "in the event that France should continue to press intolerable demands upon Syria and the Lebanon." Roosevelt replied that France had given him written guarantees that Syria and Lebanon would be granted independence, and he intended to hold the French to their promise. "In the event that France should thwart the independence of Syria and the Lebanon," he told the King, "the United States Government would give to Syria and the Lebanon all possible support short of the use of force."

Then the president took the conversation in another direction entirely. He raised the possibility that Saudi Arabia could develop agriculturally with irrigation and proper farming techniques— the vision that had inspired his interest in the country during his flight over it after the Tehran summit conference in 1943.

The idea was not so far-fetched as it might have sounded at the time. Karl Twitchell's agricultural mission had identified areas of the country where irrigation was feasible, and a team dispatched by ARAMCO (as CASOC was renamed in 1944) was growing useful crops on the royal experimental farm in al-Kharj, southeast of Riyadh, where its pumps were pulling up large quantities of water from underground caverns.[2] "The President spoke of his great interest in farming, stating that he himself was a farmer," according to the joint memorandum. "He emphasized the need for developing water resources, to increase the land under cultivation as well as to turn the wheels which do the country's work. He expressed special interest in irrigation, tree planting and water

2. CASOC was renamed the Arabian American Oil Company, or ARAMCO, in 1944, after Exxon, Texaco and Mobil joined Standard of California as owners in a consortium. For convenience the name ARAMCO is used henceforth in this book.

power which he hoped would be developed after the war in many countries, including the Arab lands. Stating that he liked Arabs, he reminded His Majesty that to increase land under cultivation would decrease the desert and provide living for a larger population of Arabs."

"I am too old to be a farmer," the King replied. "I would be much interested to try it, if I wasn't too old to take it up." He thanked the president for his interest, but added that "He himself could not engage with any enthusiasm for the development of his country's agriculture and public works if this prosperity would be inherited by the Jews." This was little short of paranoia—there were no Jews in Saudi Arabia and none were proposing to go there. There is no record of what Roosevelt said in response, if anything.

VICTORY OVER CHURCHILL

It is evident from the accounts of participants and witnesses to this meeting that the American president and the Arabian King, as different as two men could be in language, religion, education and knowledge of the world, liked and admired each other and struck up a personal rapport. Their mutual esteem delivered to Roosevelt one of the most important and least expected outcomes of their encounter: a tactical and strategic victory over Churchill, who hoped to keep the Arabian peninsula within Britain's sphere of influence after the war.

The King had given the oil exploration contract to an American firm a decade earlier, rejecting a rival bid from a British enterprise for reasons that had as much to do with palace intrigue as they did with economics, and thus only the Americans were taking part in the economic development of Saudi Arabia. But the King had long-standing debts to the British, who had sent military units to help him consolidate his victory over rival tribes in the 1920s and had provided much-needed economic assistance in the early years of the war, and British influence was entrenched all around his realm, in Palestine, Iraq, Transjordan and Aden, in what is now Yemen.

In the Middle East, the United States and Britain were allies, but also rivals.

Churchill, according to American accounts, was surprised to learn at Yalta that Roosevelt planned to meet with Abdul Aziz after that conference, and in Eddy's words "burned up the wires to his diplomats" to set up a similar encounter for himself. He got his meeting—in a gloomy hotel in the Fayoum Oasis, south of Cairo—and arranged for the King to return to Saudi Arabia aboard a British ship rather than an American one, but the results were counter-productive because the King found Churchill arrogant and disrespectful, on matters great and small.

Whereas Roosevelt had abided by the King's wishes and refrained from smoking in his presence, Churchill did the opposite. As he wrote in his memoirs, "If it was the religion of His Majesty to deprive himself of smoking and alcohol, I must point out that my rule of life prescribed as an absolutely sacred rite smoking cigars and also drinking alcohol before, after, and if need be during all meals and in the intervals between them." He puffed cigar smoke in the King's face.

On his homeward voyage, the King found the British Navy's food unpalatable and its officers dull; they did not match the Americans' entertaining gunnery displays. And while he was delighted with Roosevelt's gift airplane, he was displeased by the Rolls-Royce automobile he received from Churchill because the steering wheel was on the right. That would have required the King to ride on the driver's left, a position of dishonor, and he never used the car. These were exactly the sorts of blunders in dealing with the King that the Americans had avoided thanks to Eddy's knowledge and diplomatic skill.

The British naturally have a different version of these encounters. British diplomatic files examined by the BBC in 2006 show that the King told the British envoy in Jeddah that he would feign illness and decline Roosevelt's invitation if he could not also see Churchill, and that Churchill—far from being surprised by news of the meeting—encouraged the King to travel to see Roosevelt. "I greatly desire you to meet the president of the United States," the British report quoted Churchill as saying. In addition, the British files say that the King personally handed to Churchill a detailed report about his meeting with Roosevelt.

Nevertheless, upon Eddy's return to Jeddah, the King summoned him to a private meeting at which, Eddy reported to the State Department, he praised Roosevelt and disparaged Churchill. "The contrast between the President and Mr. Churchill is very great," the King said. "Mr. Churchill speaks deviously, evades understanding [and] changes the subject to avoid commitment, forcing me repeatedly to bring him back to the point. "

Compare the King's estimation of Churchill with what he told Eddy about Roosevelt: "The President seeks understanding in conversations; his effort is to make the two minds meet, to dispel darkness and shed light upon this issue. I have never met the equal of the President in character, wisdom, and gentility."

In his report to the State Department, Eddy added an important detail about the King's meeting with Roosevelt that was omitted from his joint memorandum with Yassin. The King asked Roosevelt what he should say to Britons who argued that his country's future lay with them, not with the United States, because America's interest in the region was transitory and would dissipate after the war. Abdul Aziz said the British told him they would be responsible for security and international communications in the region and "based on the strength of this argument they seek a priority for Britain in Saudi Arabia. What am I to believe?"

The King was not being entirely forthright. In the two years before Roosevelt made Saudi Arabia eligible for U.S. assistance, the British had provided tens of millions of pounds in unrestricted financial aid when the King most needed it. Besides, the British had a point; at the time their influence prevailed throughout the Arabian Gulf region, and it was not unreasonable for them to expect that to continue. And it was possible that the Americans, having retired from the world stage after World War I, might do so again. But Roosevelt had a different vision for the post-war world in which there would be no place for this residual colonialism. He told the King that his "plans for the post-war world envisage a decline of spheres of influence in favor of the Open Door; that the United States hopes the door of Saudi Arabia will be open for her and for other nations, with no monopoly by anyone; for only by free exchange of goods, services and opportunities can prosperity circulate to the advantage of free peoples." That was much more to the King's liking than the British line, for his greatest fear as he opened his country to the foreign technical help he needed was encroachment on Saudi sovereignty, and he was suspicious of British designs.

In his audience with Eddy back in Jeddah the following week, the King again brought up his irritation with Churchill, who he said had tried to bully him about Palestine. In his report to Washington, Eddy gave this paraphrase of the King's remarks:

> Mr. Churchill opened the subject confidently wielding the big stick. Great Britain had supported and subsidized me for twenty years, and had made possible the stability of my reign by fending off potential enemies on my frontiers. Since Britain had seen me through difficult days, she is entitled now to request my assistance in the problem of Palestine where a strong Arab leader can restrain fanatical Arab elements, insist on moderation in Arab councils, and effect a realistic compromise with Zionism. Both sides must be prepared to make concessions and he looks to me to help prepare the Arab concessions.
>
> I replied that, as he well knows, I have made no secret of my friendship and gratitude to Great Britain, a friend I have always been ready to help and I shall always help her and the Allies against their enemies. I told him, however, that what he proposes is not help to Britain or the Allies, but an act of treachery to the Prophet and all believing Muslims which would wipe out my honor and destroy my soul. I could not acquiesce in a compromise with Zionism much less take any initiative. Furthermore, I pointed out, that even in the preposterous event that I were willing to do so, it would not be a favor to Britain, since promotion of Zionism from any quarter must indubitably bring bloodshed, wide-spread disorder in the Arab lands, with certainly no benefit to Britain or anyone else. By this time Mr. Churchill had laid the big stick down.
>
> In turn I requested assurance that Jewish immigration to Palestine would be stopped. This Mr. Churchill refused to promise,

though he assured me that he would oppose any plan of immigration which would drive the Arabs out of Palestine or deprive
them of the means of livelihood there. I reminded him that
the British and their Allies would be making their own choice
between (1) a friendly and peaceful Arab world, and (2) a struggle to the death between Arab and Jew if unreasonable immigration of Jews to Palestine is renewed. In any case, the formula
must be one arrived at by and with Arab consent.

However accurate the King's forecast may have been, it was
destined to have little impact on events in Palestine, because a
few months later Roosevelt was dead and Churchill had been
voted out of office. It would be left to others to decide the fate
of Palestine. If anything, the King's entreaties to Roosevelt on
this subject had negative results for him, because the president's
comments back home about how much he had learned from the
King stimulated influential American Zionists to redouble their
efforts.

Neither the joint memorandum nor Eddy's book *F.D.R. Meets
Ibn Saud* mentions any specific agreements or commitments by
the United States or by Saudi Arabia, yet the impact of the two
leaders' afternoon together was far-reaching.

Eddy saw it as a world-historical moment that offered the
opportunity for a grand moral alliance between the Christian
world and the Muslims, such as the one he believed had been
forged centuries earlier by Richard Lion-heart and Saladin. Eddy,
who knew the Arabs probably better than any other American
of his generation, was exultant that "The Guardian of the Holy
Places of Islam, and the nearest we have to a successor to the
Caliphs, the Defender of the Muslim Faith and of the Holy Cities of three hundred million people, cemented a friendship with
the head of a great Western and Christian nation. This meeting marks the high point of Muslim alliance with the West," he
wrote. The people of the Near East, Eddy added, "have hoped and
longed for a direct dealing with the U.S.A. without any intervention of a third party. The habits of the past which led us to
regard North Africa and the Near East as preserves of Europe

were broken at one blow by Mr. Roosevelt when he met the three Kings in the Suez Canal in 1945."

Two weeks after he met the president, King Abdul Aziz declared war against the Axis powers. Roosevelt and Churchill had told him that doing so was the price of his country's admission to the new United Nations organization that was being formed, but it was not an easy decision for the King. According to H. St. John Philby, his longtime British adviser and confidant, "Ibn Saud shrank from the unseemliness, not to say the absurdity, of declaring war on Powers already doomed, with whom his country had no quarrel. Yet in the end he yielded to the diplomatic pressure of his friends; and Saudi Arabia joined the ranks of the belligerent nations in name, if not in fact." Improbable as it seemed, the Kingdom of Saudi Arabia was now an ally of the United States.

Bill Eddy's task for the next year was to work with the King to translate that alliance into concrete arrangements and agreements that would bring practical benefits to both countries. But first he had to navigate through one last crisis related to the two leaders' meeting. The morning after the meeting, at the Mena House hotel in Cairo, he was summoned to the lobby to see King Abdul Aziz's personal physician, Dr. Rashid Pharaon, who was "in a sweat and state of jitters such as I had never seen in any mortal man." The doctor had left the King's medicines aboard the *Murphy*, which had sailed away, and feared for his life if the King found out. "On his knees, and wringing his hands, he begged me to get these medicines back immediately," Eddy wrote.

This was no easy task, because the ship was at sea, and under radio silence for security reasons. Eddy told Pharaon it might be several days before it would be in a port where the medicines could be retrieved. Meanwhile, the desperate doctor wanted to duplicate the medications from pharmacies in Cairo or from U.S. military supplies; the list was forwarded to American military doctors.

"Within half an hour the Chief Medical Officer of the U.S. Army in the Near East reappeared to tell [the commanding general] that the list of medicines could not be duplicated. Of the 240 items on the list, no less than 210 were aphrodisiacs, half of which were obsolete and many of which were certainly entirely phony,"

Eddy reported. "Even ignoring the phony items, medicines which could be recognized as alleged aphrodisiacs were mostly of German or Turkish origin and certainly not to be found in the stores of the Army Medical Corps."

Happily for the doctor, the crew of the *Murphy* found the medicines on board before the ship left Egyptian waters and put them ashore at Port Said, where the American vice consul put the package on a train to Cairo. They were delivered to Pharaon before the King knew they were missing. Dr. Pharaon survived to become Saudi Arabia's ambassador to France.

Chapter 6

SAUDI ARABIA, PART TWO

*O*ne immediate result of the King's meeting with the president was a growing stream of visitors from the United States who came to inspect this little-known country that seemed to be taking on such importance. They strained the very limited facilities and appropriate guest quarters that Bill Eddy could muster, and they invariably sought an audience with the king. As Pete Hart put it, "'Sword collectors' was the term Eddy used in protesting to the Department of State the gathering wave of officials with dubious job descriptions who had wired ahead for arrangements to 'pay respects.' It was getting to be more than the relationship could bear, and in no uncertain terms Eddy had demanded a screening of such visitors in Washington or he would do it arbitrarily from Jeddah." Eddy could limit the number of people from the executive branch of government and the military who wanted to drop in because ambassadors traditionally have had the power to veto visits by other U.S. government officials, but congressional delegations had to be accommodated.

These visitors may have been a nuisance, but their presence reflected official Washington's growing interest in the Kingdom. After the King's meeting with Roosevelt, the administrative and logistical matters that occupied so much of Eddy's time in the early months gave way to negotiations and consultations on a much higher level, involving issues of economic aid and development, investment and strategic commitment. Many of these arrangements would require Congressional approval, for which reason Congressional delegations that desired to visit could not be turned away. Here Bill Eddy was the point man for an evolving American policy of engagement with, and commitment to, a country that had not even been on the radar screen five years earlier.

THE DHAHRAN AIRFIELD

In this new climate, Eddy's most important professional accomplishment was probably the negotiation of an agreement by which the U.S. Army Air Corps constructed a strategic air base at Dhahran, among the oil fields on the Kingdom's eastern coast. Just as the oil industry was the foundation of the commercial partnership between the United States and Saudi Arabia, the airfield was the foundation of the strategic partnership. Throughout the Cold War, Saudi Arabia would be the stronghold of American security interests in the Arab World.

From the point of view of the U.S. military, the need for such a base in 1944 was self-evident. The armed forces were fighting a major war in Asia as well as Europe and were committed to the defense of an asset—the Saudi oil fields—that had been bombed by the Italians early in the conflict (although probably by mistake). Moreover, the British, ever sensitive to their own presumed prerogatives in the region, took the position that their air base on nearby Bahrain could not accommodate heavy transport aircraft and thus was not available for use by American transport planes. British reluctance to let their American allies use the bases they controlled on Bahrain or across the Gulf in Abadan did not translate into a willingness to see the Americans build their own in Dhahran. On the contrary, Britain strenuously opposed the Dhahran plan, and the King vacillated.

This argument was not just about one airfield in one remote country. The British were trying to protect what had been a virtual worldwide monopoly on air travel between Europe and all the outposts of empire in Africa and Asia. The United States, a rising global power which almost alone in the industrialized world still had the capacity to produce large fleets of aircraft, was promoting an international policy of open skies and rights of cabotage for foreign carriers, which would mostly mean American carriers. (This was the so-called Fifth Freedom, which the United States was trying to sell to a reluctant world as the end of the war came into sight.) A U.S.-controlled base in Dhahran was central to this policy, and Washington adopted tough negotiating tactics, with both the British and the King, to bring it into existence. At one point London's chief representative in Saudi Arabia complained of American "diplomatic gangsterism in the service of an unscrupulous economic imperialism."

Nor were the politics of the airfield entirely clear-cut in Washington. The War Department viewed the airfield project only as a military venture useful in conducting the war. The State Department and other agencies saw it as a way of pumping money into a destitute country without the direct authorization of Congress, an objective the War Department did not endorse, as well as a way to promote American commercial aviation.

In February 1945, a week after Roosevelt met the King, his "State-War-Navy Coordinating Committee" (SWNCC) circulated a paper with the title "Recommended Procedure for the Extension of Financial Assistance to Saudi Arabia." This paper provided the policy framework for the negotiations that followed.

The Lend-Lease assistance program that had helped to sustain a destitute Saudi Arabia in 1943 and 1944 would end with the war (although President Truman extended it briefly for Saudi

Arabia), but the Kingdom's need for assistance would not. The State Department believed it would be five years before the Kingdom became self-supporting. The basic problem confronting the Kingdom, the SWNCC paper observed, was that its oil industry, almost shut down by the war, was not yet sufficiently developed to provide enough revenue to cover the budget. Eventually this gap would close, but "as of the end of 1945, it is expected that production will reach a level where oil royalties approximate 7½ millions of dollars; whereas the King's annual requirements from oil royalties, as distinct from and exclusive of all of his non-oil revenues such as the pilgrim traffic, are approximately double this amount."

Throughout these months of late 1944 and early 1945, before and after Roosevelt's meeting with the King, Eddy peppered Washington from his post in Jeddah with reports of varying degrees of urgency emphasizing the extent of the Kingdom's penury and the need for prompt additional American aid. "Stability of Saudi economy admits of no prolonged gap in arrival of food and other necessities," he said in a typical message. "In view of current distrust of US Near East policy [because of Palestine] early conclusion of loan is urgent for political reasons also."

Palestine was the leitmotif of every conversation Eddy had with the King and the senior princes. In one typical conversation, Eddy reported to Washington, Prince Faisal told him that "it would be useless to discuss specific lines of cooperation so long as the atmosphere is clouded by grave distrust of the basic USA policy in the Middle East. I personally still hope that your Gov't will not sacrifice the good will and the considerable investment of the American people in the Middle East in favor of Zionism." Faisal even personalized the argument. "If I, one of the few Arabians who know and love America, am disillusioned, imagine the state of mind of my fellow countrymen who do not know the USA," he told Eddy. "Yet as matters stand, I would not wish to return to the USA, where the friendship for which I worked there, as you have worked here, appears to be held in contempt."

Eddy was a sympathetic listener to all such outbursts. In fact, on the crucial subjects—financial aid and Palestine policy—the

King could not have asked for a more forceful advocate within the U.S. government. When Washington instructed Eddy to counsel the King to be patient on the matter of U.S. government loans because they required congressional approval, which could take six months, Eddy responded, "he *has* waited six months, and obviously must wait as many months as may be. The question is whether *we* can afford to wait," because U.S. interests were in jeopardy. Eddy's advocacy was matched in persistence and urgency only by that of the ARAMCO oil consortium. In general terms the White House—first under Roosevelt, who by 1943 no longer believed Saudi Arabia was "a little far afield for us," and then under Truman—accepted the arguments of Eddy and the oil interests about the King's need for financial aid; the issue was not whether to help the King, but how.

The paper delivered by a SWNCC subcommittee assigned to address that question on February 22, 1945, a week after Roosevelt's meeting with Abdul Aziz, said that a direct request to Congress for an appropriation of cash should be considered only as a last resort. The White House wanted to avoid such a request because the mood in Congress was not receptive; as the war neared an end, Congress faced more compelling demands abroad and long-neglected needs at home. The SWNCC document, though hardly a model of clarity, merits quoting at length because it summarizes the policy debate that was going on in Washington at the time and Eddy's role in it:

> The most important economic fact in connection with Saudi Arabia is the presence in that country of rich oil resources presently under concession to American companies. Although the War Department has an interest in Saudi Arabia because of its geographical location athwart the most direct air route to the East, it is the oil of Saudi Arabia which makes that country of particular interest to the armed services. It is the wartime inability to develop the existing oil concessions in a normal commercial fashion which is the main source of the present budgetary deficits. It has been recognized from the begining that, in addition to the extension of self-liquidating loans for projects by an

agency such as Export-Import Bank, a solution not available for the moment, the channels of possible assistance to Saudi Arabia divide broadly into two:

(a) The immediate and interim, although indirect, assistance which can be furnished by the War Department through (1) the construction of military air fields, (2) the improvement of roads, and (3) the dispatching of a military mission; and

(b) The longer range and much more important direct assistance which may conceivably be supplied through arrangements relating to the oil resources.

The Sub-Committee's consideration has been given to both of these avenues of approach. In the case of the former, on February 7, 1945, SWNCC referred to the Sub-Committee a paper, SWNCC 19, consisting of a report to the Assistant Secretary of War [John J. McCloy] from the Army Deputy Chief of Staff reciting the projects which the War Department is prepared to embark upon immediately. They are: (a) the establishment of a military [training] mission, (b) the improvement of certain roads, and (c) the construction of an airport at Dhahran. The first two are not regarded by the War Department as necessary to the prosecution of the present war and will be proceeded with only upon the State Department's assurance that they are advisable and in the national interest in order to assist in the accomplishment of other important objectives. The construction of the Dhahran field is, on the other hand, considered by the War Department to be necessary for the prosecution of the present war.

The State Department member of the Sub-Committee reports that the State Department is ready to extend the formal assurances required with respect to the military mission and road improvement projects. The State Department also strongly favors the third project but, on the basis of information received by it, is of the opinion that permission to construct the Dhahran field cannot be obtained from King Ibn Saud until after British consent is procured, which, in this instance, involves concurrence by the British members of the Combined Chiefs of Staff. In the case of all three of the War Department projects there is, of course, the need for prior discussion and negotiations with Ibn Saud in order that he shall have been fully informed, and shall have approved in advance, of everything this is proposed to be done. Assuming the fact of British consent to the proposed air field, it is the recommendation of the State Department that a War Department representative be sent immediately to Saudi Arabia to meet with Colonel Eddy, the American Minister, to discuss the presentation to King Ibn Saud of the plans for the three War Department projects. It will be for Colonel Eddy, in consultation with the War Department representative, to recommend whether or not the military mission and the road improvement projects are to be presented to the King as matters on which the War Department is prepared to proceed immediately and irrespective of the construction of the air field; or whether the three projects are to be taken up simultaneously on the basis that Saudi Arabian consent to the air field is a *sine qua non* of this Government's decision to provide the other two.

Allowing any foreign power to build a military facility in the Kingdom was not an easy decision for the King. The extremely conservative religious establishment and tribal sheikhs who formed his constituency were opposed to any infidel presence on the holy soil of Arabia. With the oil concession of 1933, the King had established the principle that it was acceptable to bring in foreigners if necessary for the development of the country, but a military airfield was not in the same category. Abdul Aziz had reluctantly consented to the U.S. request to open a consulate, or embassy branch, in Dhahran to serve the growing American community there. Now he was being asked to allow an even more provocative American presence. For that reason, he drove a hard bargain. Most of all, he wanted to avoid any arrangement that could be portrayed as a diminution of Saudi sovereignty.

On paper, negotiations between the United States and Saudi Arabia might have looked like a walkover for the Americans, who were as powerful and sophisticated as the Saudis were weak and limited, but the Saudis were shrewd and skillful negotiators who knew that the Americans wanted the airfield more than they did and bargained accordingly. Moreover, they had an advantage in that the chief negotiator on the American side, Bill Eddy, basically wanted their interests to be served.

The principal negotiator on the Saudi side was Yusuf Yassin, the same sharp-tongued Syrian with whom Eddy had written the joint memorandum recounting President Roosevelt's conversation with the King aboard the *Quincy*. Yassin was a prominent figure among a small but influential cadre of exiles from other Arab countries who found new lives in Saudi Arabia by providing skills that the King's own subjects lacked. According to Robert Lacey, "It had long been Yussuf Yassin's special skill—and one key to his influence—to secure ever more luscious concubines for his master, and in the quest for rejuvenation the Syrian drove their ages lower and lower, on the ancient theory that some transfer of vitality can be sparked by contact with the flesh of barely nubile little girls."

In the bargaining with the Americans, the King sought material benefits, including money and equipment, but he also wanted arrangements that would keep the American presence to a minimum and shelter him from domestic criticism of his deals with infidels. He wanted, in effect, to be a little bit pregnant. His concern over appearances led him and his negotiators to haggle over every detail, including which flag would fly over the installation.

On May 3, 1945, just a few weeks after Roosevelt's death, the State Department sent Eddy a list of terms that were to form the U.S. position in the negotiations. A U.S. military team would construct the airfield and a 300-mile road from Dhahran to Riyadh. (The Saudis wanted the paved road to go all the way across the country to Jeddah, but the War Department declined to make that commitment because there would be no military justification.) U.S. commercial airlines would have exclusive landing and transit rights—a provision that would come as a shock to the British when they learned of it. If military landing rights were terminated a year after the end of the war, as envisioned, American airline companies would still have commercial rights if any foreign companies did. These provisions for commercial service by an American company were for the benefit of

Transcontinental and Western Air Co., or TWA, the airline created by Howard Hughes. In 1945 the U.S. Civil Aeronautics Board, which then regulated U.S. airlines, granted TWA a certificate to fly extensive international routes, including Cairo-Bombay. The airline wanted a safe, reliable refueling and maintenance base along the way. Thus the airfield project had many supporters and, on the U.S. side, no serious opponents. But getting from that point to an operational flight line proved to be an enormously vexing assignment, in which Eddy had to negotiate not only with the Saudis but with the Truman administration back home.

Upon receipt of the State Department's instructions, Eddy traveled overland on the difficult unpaved track to Riyadh to convey the terms to the King, who accepted them subject to certain provisos, which Eddy listed in a cable to Washington:

1. King Abdul Aziz grants permission for construction of airfield at Dhahran provided field and fixed installations pass to Saudi government immediately war ends.

2. King grants use of field by US forces for period of 3 years after end of war, and most-favored-nation terms for US commercial airlines when field is open to civil aviation.

3. King is grateful for offer to build road but wishes engineer and survey team be sent now to determine with him location and type of road from Riyadh to Persian Gulf before construction is planned. He holds strong views on route to be chosen.

4. King wishes a week or more to consider with advisors other services offered with military mission. His desire for aviation school was obvious as well as need for medical and health services but his reply on services requested of mission will follow later.

As he did with ARAMCO, the King intended to use his bargaining power with the U.S. military to acquire training programs, health care and other services for the people of Saudi Arabia that he could not otherwise afford.

But not so fast. By early summer the war in Europe had ended, and it was apparent that the war in the Pacific would be over by the end of the year. The War Department decided it no longer wanted to spend money on a new airfield in Saudi Arabia. That change of heart made sense from a short-term military perspective, but Eddy and his State Department colleagues were by now envisioning Saudi Arabia as a long-term strategic asset that should be cultivated. They argued that the U.S. had made a promise to the King and that the base would be valuable even in peacetime. The War Department "feels expenditure of funds for construction of airfield on basis of military necessity would be of doubtful legal validity," the State Department's Joseph C. Grew cabled Eddy on June 25. "It is generally agreed however among interested departments that airfield would be in American national interest. These interested departments have recommended that matter be presented to President on national interest basis. If President approves presumably military airfield will be constructed at Dhahran. . . . No action will be taken until his decision is made."

The following day, Grew laid out the case in a memo to the president, or rather, the State Department laid out the case in a memo that bore Grew's signature because he was acting secretary of state. Grew was a classic example of the blue-blood types who dominated the diplomatic service in that era: son of a Boston banker, educated at Groton and Harvard, married to a granddaughter of Commodore Matthew Perry. He rose rapidly in the diplomatic service, becoming ambassador to Denmark at the age of 40, then to Turkey, Switzerland and Japan, where he was serving at the time of Pearl Harbor and was briefly held captive by the Japanese. In a cover story about him in 1934, *Time* magazine said he and the president, "old Grotonians," called each other "Frank" and "Joe."

The Saudi oil fields, Grew's memo said, would be increasingly important economically and strategically in a few years. "The manifestation of American interests in Saudi Arabia, in addition to oil, will tend to strengthen the political integrity of Saudi Arabia externally and, hence, to provide conditions under which an early expansion of the costly development of the oil concession can be proceeded with. The immediate construction by this country of an airfield at Dhahran, to be used for military purposes initially but destined for an ultimate civil utilization, would be a strong showing of American interest," Grew wrote. He said the Secretaries of War and the Navy concurred with State that construction was in the national interest and recommended that Truman concur. It took only two days for the president to give the go-ahead to the three-part package.

Now it was up to Eddy to negotiate the details. There was probably no other person in U.S. government service at the time who could have brought those negotiations to a successful conclusion. His position was that the airfield should be constructed by the Army at "the expediture of the very best (and not the easiest or cheapest) services, namely the establishment of a well-equipped air mission, and the building of a first-class highway etc. [The Army's] resources should be used to the utmost to establish impressive monuments to American technical skill and enduring goodwill." But complicated haggling lay ahead, especially because it turned out that the question of Britain's role was still unresolved in the mind of the King.

On July 4, Eddy cabled home the news that the King "has declined the service of a U.S. Army military mission." Senior officials in Washington were surprised, but it appears that the King was disappointed in the work of a small U.S. military training mission with twelve American officers already in place in the city of Taif. In April an Army officer, Major Harry R. Snyder, had written a secret memorandum after inspecting the training mission, which said that after the current class of Saudi trainees graduated on May 1, "the question of the disposition of the mission becomes pressing" because of "many urgent problems" arising from the Saudi government's doubts about the advisability of continuing it. Eddy was briefed on these unspecified problems, Snyder's memo said, but decided that it would be "unwise" to raise the issue with the King "when the U.S. has not yet decided other issues raised by Saudi Govt. Thus matters have reached a stalemate that must soon be broken if governmental relations are not to be prejudiced."

It is not clear what "urgent problems" Snyder was talking about. Eddy, in fact, had given the Taif mission a rave review. In a May 4 memo to Washington, he wrote that he had attended the graduation ceremony of the third class of ninety Saudi cadets, and concluded that "No one who attended the exercises could have any doubt of the professional success of the U.S. Army Military Mission of Instruction, nor of the gratitude and goodwill they have earned for themselves, for the U.S. Army, and for the United States." Nevertheless, the Taif mission folded its tents in July.

In his notice to Washington that the King had declined the offer of a new, more extensive training mission, Eddy said nothing about problems at Taif. He attributed the King's decision to three factors: "(1) Criticism by fanatical reactionary subjects, (2) abuse from his Hashemite enemies who proclaim him a puppet under foreign military control and (3) objection by British to a military mission in which they do not share at least equally."

The term "Hashemite enemies" referred to the Banu Hashem clan, an old and noble family that had been prominent in the Arabian peninsula since before the time of the Prophet Muhammad. The Banu Hashem had ruled the western part of the country, known as the Hijaz, before Abdul Aziz overthrew them and seized the Hijaz as he unified the country early in the twentieth century. Because the Hashemites had supported Britain against the Turks in World War I (in the famous campaign led by T.E. Lawrence), after the war the British gave them what were in effect two consolation prizes, the thrones of Iraq and Transjordan. Throughout his reign, Abdul Aziz feared that his old rivals were plotting their return.

Eddy told Washington that the King was "sincere and correct in anticipating violent criticism from reactionaries and fanatics if a substantial foreign military mission engaged in extensive services in the interior of his country." If those were indeed the King's reasons for declining the new training mission, his apprehension about the reaction among his subjects was well founded. Even many decades later, when the country was modernized and long accustomed to foreigners, hostility to a large foreign military presence inspired furious conservative opposition to the U.S. deployment for Operation Desert Storm. But the King's arguments were also specious—he did eventually allow construction of a U.S. military airfield that was much more visible to his subjects than any training mission in Taif would have been, and he did so despite British objections that were withdrawn only at the very end of negotiations. This was the kind of twist and turn in Kingly argumentation that Eddy faced on virtually every one of the issues he was required to negotiate with Abdul Aziz, and only someone with his deep understanding of the king and his country could have succeeded.

In fact, the "violent criticism from reactionaries and fanatics" about Abdul Aziz's efforts to modernize his country to which Eddy referred was a constant feature of the King's long reign. In his essay "King Ibn Saud: Our Faith and Your Iron," Eddy described the King's philosophy: "Ibn Saud explained to me his simple rule of thumb in dealing with our godless, materialistic West: 'we Muslims have the one, true faith, but Allah gave you the iron, which is inanimate, amoral, neither prohibited nor mentioned in the Qur'an. We will use your iron, but leave our faith alone.' Ibn Saud spelled this out in conversation," Eddy wrote. "The Qur'an regulated (from the cradle to the Resurrection) all matters of faith, family, education, marriage, inheritance, property and home, which must not be touched by unbelievers. Our patriarchal authority and the veiling of women are none of your business. On the other hand you have much which we need and will accept: radio, airplanes, pumps, oil-drilling rigs and technical know-how. This acceptance of technology was far in advance of his people, and the King had to fight many battles with bigots to win support for his suspected friendship with Christian governments and his cordial partnership with the Arabian American Oil Company."

Writing this in the early 1960s, Eddy was succinctly describing the fundamental internal conflict that still defines Saudi Arabian life today, between the forces of what we in the West would call progress—technological, economic and social—and the deeply conservative, entrenched anti-Western elements opposed to all change, especially if imported. "Fortunately for the old King's peace of mind," Eddy wrote, "he died [in 1953] before learning that his 'Faith and Iron' could not coexist insulated from each

other for long. With the machine comes the educated machin-
ist, and with the engine the enlightened engineer, who wants the
more abundant life to which we were raised, freedom and education for his wife and daughters, the rights to raise his voice in politics, religion, and sex—the three topics of every campus."

In truth, unrest among the Arab workers in the oil fields, dis-
satisfied with housing conditions and unequal pay, long predated
the death of King Abdul Aziz. As early as 1945, during Eddy's tenure, ARAMCO's Arab workers went on strike, alleging what one
diplomatic report called "discrimination in wages, in housing and
quality of food." While still in Jeddah Eddy himself was warning ARAMCO that Arab discontent with worker housing could
threaten the oil company's concession.

As for the King's expressed concerns about Britain's views of
the proposed military training mission, Eddy took the occasion
to put the subject into the much larger context of the overall U.S.
commitment to the King and his Kingdom—a matter which in
the King's mind was evidently not settled at his conference with
Roosevelt.

"This past winter," Eddy wrote to Washington, "there were
plenty of signs that the King was prepared to free himself of British censorship and deal independently with us provided, of course,
that he would be assured of continued economic stability and supply of elemental needs. However, more recently the King seems to
be reverting to the belief that, however powerful and friendly the
United States may be, Britain continues to dominate the Middle
East, to act where others concur. . . . Whether under British tute-
lage or not, the Saudi government seems to be presently persuaded
of the return of regionalism, of a future British sphere of influence
in the Middle East, similar to her past position and similar to our
Monroe Doctrine. I do not believe I am exaggerating the abrupt
revival of Brtish prestige."

The King was not naive about Britain's capabilities, which by
this time were hardly comparable to those of the United States.
"To be sure," Eddy noted in his cable, "the King stated to me
frankly that Britain would be bankrupt and vanquished without
the United States." The King, he added, was aware that "Britain

is not outbidding us in offers of economic assistance; quite the contrary. However, she does guarantee his political and national security from aggression, and she holds potential economic sanctions we do not by virtue of her control of commodities and foreign exchange. . . . Only when we find a way to match Britain as an effective guarantor of Saudi Arabian economy can we hope to eliminate, once and for all, this British veto on United States proposals in Saudi Arabia."

In response, the State Department's Grew said grumpily that "the King's fear of adverse reaction within his country is appreciated but not considered sufficient reason [to decline the U.S. military mission] inasmuch as the King has for over 2 years pressed this Govt to have the US Army provide services that he now rejects. Furthermore since Army is only American agency equipped to render these services free of charge the King is in effect turning down American aid. This is reversal of policy that apparently can be explained only in terms of British pressure."

This exchange amply illustrates the difficulties Eddy faced as he tried to come to terms with the King about the airfield. What is missing is any sense, on either the Saudi or the American side, that British influence in the region was about to evaporate rather than reassert itself. Exhausted by two world wars, Britain was soon to yield most of its empire; with the independence of India in 1947, the entire Persian Gulf region declined in importance to Britain. With the 1956 takeover of the Suez Canal by Egypt's charismatic president Gamal Abdel Nasser and the rise of Arab nationalism of which Nasser was the emblematic leader, Britain would cease in a decade or so to be a serious player in the region. At the time of Eddy's negotiations with the King, everyone was respectful of British concerns out of habit, but in truth the empire was running on fumes. It is never clear from the documentary record whether King Abdul Aziz understood that; if he did, he was even more clever than he appears in playing London and Washington against each other. The same could be said about Eddy as he used fear of British influence as a tool to badger Washington into giving the King what he wanted.

In addition to the geostrategic issues, the airfield negotiations required reaching an understanding about how many Americans and other foreigners would be involved in the project and the terms on which they would live in Saudi Arabia. The King had bludgeoned the most conservative religious elements among his subjects into grudging acceptance of imported technology and the infidels needed to develop the oil fields. The American presence in the Kingdom's Eastern Province had already swelled to the point that the King had allowed the establishment of the U.S. consulate there. Now he was being asked to allow the entry of American military personnel who, like the oilmen in their self-contained town nearby, would want recreation facilities forbidden to the Saudi people and who would not be subject to Saudi law while on their base. The Americans would also import hundreds of other foreigners to do the construction work that local Arab people did not know how to do. As Eddy wrote in a letter to Yusuf Yassin, the U.S. military wanted "to import into Saudi Arabia, during the construction period, approximately 500 Americans, 1500 Italians, 500 Iraqis and Iranians, 1000 from Aden protectorate [in Yemen] and 25 Egyptians of European descent for the construction work on the airbase."

When complete, Eddy informed Yassin, the airfield would cover 25 square miles. It would have two runways and a troop capacity of 500, expandable up to 2,000 men if the United States wished. For the duration of the war, "the land for the Dhahran airbase will be reserved for the exclusive use of the United States Government and the installations thereon will be at the disposition of the United States Government who will use, operate, control and maintain same." After the war, the Saudis would exercise nominal control, but the United States would have the right to continue using the base and its equipment for three years.

The King was eager to develop aviation in Saudi Arabia, but these requirements for obtaining it made him all the more determined to emphasize his ultimate sovereignty. It took Eddy another month to finalize the agreement. When complete, it was a masterpiece of bargaining in which both sides got pretty much what they wanted.

By mid-1945, it was clear to the British that they were not going to be able to match what the Americans could offer the King to build and operate the airfield, in terms of money, equipment or personnel, and they reluctantly got out of the way, removing the final obstacle. Under an agreement signed on August 5, 1945, the Americans would construct an airfield at Dhahran—not an air "base," out of deference to Saudi sensitivity about the sovereignty issue. The Americans would be allowed to use it at will for the duration of the war against Japan (which turned out to be only a few weeks, because later that month Truman ordered the atomic bomb dropped on Hiroshima and Nagasaki) and for three years after that. The Saudi flag would fly over outlying navigation stations and the emergency landing field, even though the technicians there would be Americans.

"The agreement includes all the concessions we were able to secure and more than I expected we would carry away," Eddy informed Washington. "Several points on which I expected debate and compromise, such as he numbers of foreign workers to be imported and their nationality, were accepted without question. . . . Reservations and objections raised by the King were almost exclusively concerned with preserving the appearance of as well as the reality of his sovereignty and jurisdiction; he insisted that the Saudi flag should fly over the inland posts, the emergency landing field and isolated stations where navigational aids are to be located. The operation and control of technical services at these posts will belong to the United States Army. As a matter of fact I am convinced that this will promote the security and efficiency of these posts, as the untamed tribesmen near these inaccessible posts will respect a station which belongs to the King and will not consider the presence of isolated United States Army personnel as an 'invasion.'"

On the crucial question of recreational facilities and religious worship for the American personnel, Eddy said, "I had expected possible objection to pagan dramatics or Christian worship, neither of which was mentioned. The only query was to whether the clause would be abused to import prostitutes. Oral assurances to the contrary were accepted."

Eddy the scholar of literature added a personal note to the end of this cable from Eddy the diplomat: "In conclusion I would add a word of apology for the execrable style which mars portions of this agreement: awkward phraseology, nonsequiturs, repetitions, and lamentable incoherence. Hurried attempts at joint revision of phraseology, both at Jidda and at Riyadh, during a few crowded hours, are partly to blame; but the original reason is the attempt to cover in the English text elaborations and explications coined in Arabic by the Saudis and inserted at points which, however eloquent they may be in classical Arabic, disfigure the English text."

Without Eddy's facility in Arabic, there is no telling how long the negotiations might have gone on. Instead, construction began in September, even though three more months of haggling remained over the issues of Fifth Freedom rights and the operation of the airfield after the departure of the military. The Americans insisted on the designation of "an American company approved by the the United States government," namely TWA, "to operate the airfield for the Saudi Arabian government until January 1, 1956, or until such time as the SAG [Saudi Arabian government] has available trained technicians competent to operate the airfield," as Loy Henderson put it in a memo to Dean Acheson. Finally, on December 27, Henderson wrote, "Colonel Eddy, the American Minister to Saudi Arabia, telegraphed that the Foreign Minister had told him the King will probably grant the United States Fifth Freedom privileges so long as these rights do not conflict with the welfare of that country." With that message, Henderson wrote, "the long struggle over the Dhahran airport will be drawing to a successful conclusion."

The base would be an important strategic asset for the U.S. Air Force for years to come. And Saudi Arabia, having nominally joined the Allied war effort and given permission for the U.S. military to establish itself in the Kingdom, became a long-term ally of the United States, with arrangements that would endure after the war, even though the two countries did not have and never would have a mutual defense treaty. And at the King's insistence, TWA— as the price for its exclusive landing rights—embarked on a long-term program to create a Saudi national airline and train its crews. TWA personnel were in Saudi Arabia for decades afterward, doing for Saudi aviation what Chevron and ARAMCO had done for the Saudi oil industry.

And yet, according to "A Summary of Views on United States Relations with Saudi Arabia," a fascinating 14-page, single-spaced document written in 1947 by Nils E. Lind upon completion of a tour as U.S. cultural attaché in Jeddah, "American friendship in the eyes of the King was not enhanced by this whole affair of the airfield" because of the way Washington insisted on setting up the arrangements.

Lind said the airfield package ought to have been presented as a straightforward and temporary proposition based on military need, which the King could have understood. Instead, by including the proposed Dhahran-Riyadh road "over the most impassable sands of Saudi Arabia" and a hospital as part of the package, the Americans confused the issue and reinforced the King's suspicions about their intentions. "The King said he could not deny his allies any facilities for ending the war but he could not accept Army personnel in uniform for the constructing of it. His ignorant people, he claimed, would become unduly alarmed and suspect a military occupation of their country." He wanted civilian contractors, but the Army had engineers and technicians already on duty and wanted them to do the work, saving the money that outside contractors would have charged. According to Lind, "there was no conceivable reason to the King's way of thinking why Americans could not take off their uniforms while constructing the work, whereas to his people there remained all the difference in the world between men in uniform and ordinary workmen." Then, after the war ended, the road and hospital components of the package were dropped for budgetary reasons, leaving the Saudis disappointed and skeptical about the American commitment.

BREAKING THE BRITISH CABLE MONOPOLY

As the negotiations over the airfield were being conducted, Eddy also took on the task of breaking the British monopoly over the Kingdom's external communications. Cable & Wireless, the global British telecommunications conglomerate, had held the franchise since 1926 through its Eastern Telegraph unit. Cable & Wireless would not transmit encrypted messages, which forced Eddy

and his small staff to travel all the way to Cairo when they needed
to communicate privately with Washington. For the same reason
ARAMCO chartered a boat with a transmitter and anchored it outside Saudi territorial waters.

Loy Henderson summarized the U.S. objections to this arrangement in a memo on April 27, 1945: "With the prospective establishment of an American military air base at Dhahran, the completion
of the [ARAMCO] refinery at Ras Tanura and the prospective establishment of an American controlled shipping company in Saudi Arabia, the obstructive tactics of the Eastern Telegraph Company will
be even more troublesome and may become almost intolerable. The
Arabian American Oil Company has had to resort to the device of
mounting a radio transmitter on a tugboat whence company radio
messages are sent from a point in the Persian Gulf outside the three
mile limit directly to New York." The Saudis, Henderson observed,
took the position that it was up to the United States to persuade
Britain to accept an end to the Cable & Wireless monopoly.

The Americans disputed the King's interpretation of his 1926
agreement with Britain. They noted that the agreement was due to
expire on June 1, 1945; it would automatically be extended to December 1, 1949, unless the King decided to modify it. This was the opening for a pressure campaign, waged mostly by Eddy, in which the
Americans kept reminding the King of how much they were doing
for him—including the fact that the United States was now providing
the silver and minting the coins that paid the salaries of the King's
workers. This was one of the few occasions on which Eddy could be
said to have achieved results by bullying the King rather than cajoling and flattering him. On October 10, 1946, the Saudis signed an
agreement with an American firm, Mackay Radio and Telegraph Co.
(later a subsidiary of ITT), to build and operate a radiotelegraph station in Jeddah. With ARAMCO and TWA already in place and Mackay now joining them, corporate America was forging into the Saudi
Arabia gold rush, from which trillions of dollars would flow into
American balance sheets over the next half century. In their excellent book about modern Saudi Arabia, *The House of Saud*, the British
journalists David Holden and Richard Johns titled the chapter about
these years "America Takes Over."

CROSSING JORDAN

For many months these negotiations were complicated by Eddy's personal animosity toward his British counterpart, Stanley R. Jordan, who Eddy believed was trying to undermine American interests in Saudi Arabia for the purpose of bolstering what remained of British influence. According to Robert Lacey, Jordan was "a breezy Australian who had served as vice-consul in Jeddah in the final days of Hashimite rule in the Hijaz, and, arriving back in Jeddah in August 1943, he felt qualified, as an old Arabian hand, to speak his mind."

Jordan's malign input was summarized in Nils Lind's paper. The King, Lind wrote, wanted friendly relations with both Britain and the United States, and regarded their rivalry in his country as an unfortunate family quarrel that would be resolved in mutual accord. But as long as Jordan remained there, "all attempts at finding a harmonious working plan failed. He not only found fault with American methods of assistance, but he attempted to block every American effort which was sincerely believed to be in the best interests of Saudi Arabia." During Jordan's tenure, according to Lind, "the counter measures of the British were no more than crude hostility without cleverness or their usual subtlety."

This view was fully shared by Eddy's superiors in Washington. They complained that Jordan had persuaded the King to remove some pro-American officials and appoint a British economic adviser, and they sometimes instructed Eddy not to inform Jordan about what he was up to. The maneuvering between Eddy and Jordan—in which Eddy prevailed when Jordan was recalled—was another chapter in the same story of one-upmanship that had unfolded with Churchill during the summit meetings in Egypt the previous year and in the rivalry over aviation. It might appear petty, but at the time the stakes seemed quite large: the British were still hoping for a piece of the oil action in Saudi Arabia, and were still telling the King that his future would be more prosperous and secure in partnership with them than with the Americans. The King was still vacillating, or trying to maximize his gains by playing London against Washington, or both.

The replacement of Jordan by Laurence Grafftey-Smith put an end to the personal animosity that had made Eddy's life difficult, but according to Lind, Grafftey-Smith turned out to be an even more formidable rival because he was better at his job. "Whereas the former Minister had minimized the King's importance, looking upon him as no more than a desert chieftain, the new Minister treated him as the ruler of a sovereign state. Within three months of his arrival British prestige had not only been restored but he had succeeded, also, in winning the King's confidence into the acceptance of British guidance in most of the foreign policies affecting Saudi Arabia. An astute politician had arrived with far more ability than the American Minister was able to cope with."

In his memoir *Bright Levant*, Grafftey-Smith recalled that "Surprisingly, and regrettably, our relations with the American Legation were a little precarious. Colonel William Eddy, the Minister, was an admirable choice for the post. . . . We were on most friendly terms. But in those closing months of the war America was becoming convincedly aware of her imperial destiny. Until then, non-involvement in Middle East affairs had well suited America's mood." But by the mid-1940s, in his view, the United States had come to think of itself as the rising power in a region where the forces of colonialism had spent themselves. The Americans believed that if they replaced the colonialists, "old hostilities must surely fade for lack of cause" and goodwill would spring from the desert sands. (American complaints eventually got rid of Grafftey-Smith, too; he was recalled before completing his tour of duty.)

This push-pull between the United States and Britain was a constant theme of Eddy's many conversations with the King. Aside from his passionate opposition to Jewish immigration into Palestine, no external issue concerned the King more than his fear that his old rivals, the Hashemites, would return with open or covert British support to challenge his rule.

In a conversation on New Year's Eve 1945, Eddy reported to Washington, the King said that "certain members of the Hashemite family are heads of state in Iraq and Transjordan. In bitter and ancient enmity they work against me and my country. I desire always to improve my relations with neighboring countries to keep my Kingdom at peace but I must also be able to fend off aggression if it should occur. I have never had any reason to believe that my good friends the British would connive at such aggression nor tolerate it. On the other hand, the rivalry that exists between the Americans and British in the Near East and especially in [that] which concerns my country may have led the British to avert their eyes from threats on my frontiers, willing to let those threats grow to emphasize my dependence on British support and help. I trust no aggression will take place, but if it should, what would be the opinion of the US Govt?" The King asked that Washington tell the British, without quoting him, that the "integrity, security and defense of Saudi Arabia is of great concern to the US Govt which would not acquiesce or stand by in case of aggression against Saudi Arabia. . . ."

The King would make many such requests for security guarantees from Washington throughout the remaining seven-plus years of his life. At the time of this conversation, which took place before the creation of the North Atlantic Treaty Organization, the United States had no permanent international defense commitments with any country, let alone a remote principality on the Arabian Peninsula; most of the time, and in this case, Washington responded with bland language intended to reassure the King without actually promising to do anything. In this case it didn't quite work.

In a top-secret cable on March 21, 1946, Eddy reported that he had delivered Washington's response to Abdul Aziz. "He expressed appreciation of the message and showed genuine satisfaction at learning of the U.S. interest in Saudi security and territorial integrity. The King spoke with heat of the recent slanders published by the Amir Abdullah of Transjordan and repeated his resentment against the British for keeping Abdullah supplied with trained troops and arms [in the form of Glubb Pasha's renowned Arab Legion] while at the same time keeping Saudi Arabia unarmed. The audience only confirmed to me the oriental, complicated and unsatisfactory foreign relations of the King. Increasingly a vassal of Britain, he nevertheless confides to the US Govt his dissatisfactions with the British to be in our confidence also."

That was one of the few occasions on which Eddy let his frustration with the King's maddening tactics show in his memos to Washington.

THE ARAMCO CHALLENGE

The departure of Jordan from Saudi Arabia and his replacement by Grafftey-Smith made Eddy's life more pleasant, but it did nothing to help Eddy with another problem he faced throughout his tenure, which was the role played by ARAMCO in matters that would not normally be of concern to a corporation.

The intimacy that Eddy cultivated with the King was not entirely welcome to the Americans of the oil consortium at Dhahran. ARAMCO wanted and needed a credible advocate of its interests within the U.S. government, but it also had grown accustomed over a decade to being the only representative of American interests in the Kingdom and to having exclusive access to the King. In his papers and the State Department files documenting Eddy's tenure in Saudi Arabia, there are only occasional hints of tension between him and the oil company—in one dispatch he said he had "come confidentially into possession of evidence that ARAMCO does not believe it has much to expect from our government except trouble"—but according to Eddy's successor, J. Rives Childs, ARAMCO was a constant irritant and "shows no signs of abatement."

In a dispatch to Washington in February 1947, Childs said he and Eddy had discussed this issue at length. "Unfortunately, the Arabian American Oil Company was in Saudi Arabia before the Legation at Jidda or the Consulate at Dhahran," Childs wrote. "The King and his ministers, few of whom are familiar with normal diplomatic procedure, as practiced by countries which have a settled tradition of diplomatic intercourse, became accustomed, in the absence of American official representation, to dealing with ARAMCO as they would with representatives of a foreign government. By the time that a Legation and consulate had been established in Saudi Arabia, the affairs of ARAMCO and of Saudi Arabia had become so intermingled that it was natural that the Saudi Arabian Government should continue to deal with the company on its old footing and, equally as natural, for reasons of prestige among others, that the company should continue to perform diplomatic functions. It is for these reasons that the task of the Legation in Jidda and the Consulate in Dhahran in persuading the Company to confine itself to purely commercial affairs has been so difficult."

ARAMCO deferred to the diplomats when convenient—the oil executives always said they had nothing to do with policy on Palestine, that was up to the State Department—but otherwise stayed close to the King. ARAMCO had a resident staff in Riyadh, the isolated royal capital, for years before the U.S. government was allowed to have a representative there. As late as 1955, the CIA operative Wilbur Crane Eveland wrote in his controversial book *Ropes of Sand*, ARAMCO offered him a job as a respresentative in Riyadh. "As I understood it," he wrote, "I'd set up in a large villa at the desert capital and maintain a kind of open house to receive the royal princes and senior government officials. . . . Lobbying and pressure tactics would be proscribed, yet my mere presence would provide better opportunities for gaining the confidence of government officials than those available to the U.S ambassador in Jidda." Not until 1966 was there any official U.S. government presence in the royal capital.

And yet for all its efforts to cultivate the King, ARAMCO even during Eddy's tenure as U.S. minister was falling into royal disfavor because of worker unrest in the oil camp and the loud complaints of Arab employees that the company was treating them unfairly, in contravention of the concession agreement. Lind, in his assessment of U.S.-Saudi relations, observed that "It is easy to assume that our commercial concessions are helping to improve the standard of living and, as the oil company officials argue, the Arabs in their employ have never lived better or seen so much money in their lives. That is simply the old method of placating labor and hushing up grievances. The 'ungrateful' Arab does not see it in this light and he has resorted to industrial strikes which are a complete novelty in Arabia. . . . Even the King has been swayed by the workers' demands and taken sides against the company." Eventually ARAMCO would recruit Bill Eddy to help deal with this problem.

MARY EDDY'S ILLNESS

The ability of Eddy and Childs to put pressure on the oil company was limited by the fact that until the late 1940s the U.S. diplomatic missions in Jeddah and Dhahran were dependent upon ARAMCO for logistical support. For Mary Eddy, living in squalid Jeddah without benefit of the air conditioned amusements of the oil camp in Dhahran, the hardships soon proved too much; in December 1945, she suffered a breakdown.

Eddy's papers at Princeton University have been purged of almost all references to this family crisis, and his daughter said in an interview that it was never discussed within the family. State Department records preserved in the National Archives, however, leave no doubt about what happened.

On December 29, 1945, a department official named George V. Allen wrote a high-priority administrative memorandum: "This office recommends urgently that money from the Department's emergency fund be allotted to defray expenses for the return to the United States of Mrs. Mary A. Eddy, wife of our Minister in Jidda. Mrs. Eddy has had a nervous breakdown and must be returned to the United States immediately. Colonel Eddy has telegraphed his resignation to the President, but in view of the very great national interest involved in negotiations which Colonel Eddy is now conducting in Jidda, he has expressed willingness to return to Saudi Arabia for a brief period after he brings his wife to this country and obtains care for her here." The official date of the resignation was July 1, 1946.

Another memo two weeks later, signed by Gordon Merriam and classified "secret," said that Mary Eddy "suffered a serious mental and nervous breakdown. She has been brought from Jidda to Egypt where physicians have stated that she must leave the Near East in the immediate future." Bill Eddy informed Washington that his wife was being cared for at the "Psychiatric Hospital of the Suez Canal Zone" until she could sail for the United States aboard the *Gripsholm* on January 28. He would accompany her, and planned to take her to the Shepherd Pratt Hospital in Baltimore where she could be treated in "a restful environment . . . which would allow exercise, constant attendance and treatment by a psychiatrist."

Thus the apprehension that Gordon Alling had expressed about sending Mary Eddy to Saudi Arabia in the first place proved to be well founded. This episode was apparently a reprise of a similar breakdown that had struck Mary years before in Cairo, but no details about either incident or about the exact nature of her illness are in the Eddy family papers. When Bill Eddy published *F.D.R. Meets Ibn Saud* in 1954, his dedication to Mary and Carmen said they "cheerfully shared" the hardships of wartime Jeddah.

Pete Hart, who was U.S. consul in Dhahran at the time of Eddy's departure (and later became ambassador to Saudi Arabia himself), wrote years later that Eddy resigned "giving no public reason for his action, other than the health of his wife (which was excellent). But he explained to me what had prompted his departure: it was the position taken by Truman with regard to Palestine. Truman was about to issue an open appeal to Britain to immediately admit 100,000 refugee Jews into Palestine (in the face of the known attitude of Ibn Saud). Truman's public appeal came over the airwaves shortly after Eddy's resignation. Eddy probably knew in advance of Truman's plan and at once concluded that his own credibility with Ibn Saud was thereby undermined. The two had enjoyed an informal, open, fraternal relationship—insofar as one could use that expression between a king and a foreign diplomat—and it was now gone. As for Truman, Eddy told me privately that he could not feel the same personal loyalty to Truman as before, but would find other than policy grounds for use with the public in order not to disparage his chief, the president, whom as a Marine and a Minister, he felt honor-bound to respect, even after resigning."

This account, with its reference to Mary Eddy's "excellent" health, confuses rather than enlightens. When examined along with the lack of reference to her illness in the family papers and with Eddy's next career moves, it gives a strong indication of what happened: Eddy was so anxious to protect his wife's reputation that he limited disclosure of details about Mary's mental condition even as he cited her general health as a reason for his resignation, while among colleagues he concocted a plausible, policy-related pretext for his abrupt departure from Saudi Arabia. If Eddy had indeed quit because he could not accept the pro-Zionist drift he perceived in Truman's White House, it is unlikely that he would have remained in government service, let alone take on the assignments the State Department gave him next, as a special envoy to Yemen and then as the department's chief intelligence officer. It is accepted among family members and has been written by some historians that Eddy quit his post in Jeddah, and later resigned from the State Department, over the Palestine issue. It may be true, but the documentary record does not back it up in either case.

Chapter 7

YEMEN

*B*y the time Bill Eddy left Saudi Arabia, the foundation and building blocks of the strategic and economic partnership that would join the United States and Saudi Arabia for the next seven decades were in place, in great part because of his negotiating skills and his commitment to the King and his country. The entire strategic and economic balance of the Middle East had shifted, and the odd new alliance of Saudi Arabia and the United States was the keystone of economic development and resistance to communism.

As Richard H. Sanger of the State Department's Bureau of Near East Affairs put it in a memo of November 6, 1946, "If our relations with Saudi Arabia continue to be satisfactory that nation is in a fair way to becoming a new American frontier where large amounts of United States capital and substantial numbers of skilled United States citizens will find employment. Moreover, such an American-assisted modernization of Saudi Arabia would be an example to the entire Near and Middle East and one which would fundamentally affect the attitudes of not only the United States but also of Great Britain, France and Russia toward that area." The only cloud on this otherwise sunny horizon, Sanger said, was U.S. policy toward Palestine.

Another internal State Department memorandum of that period noted with satisfaction that "Probably no part of the world has witnessed a more rapid expansion of American interest and activity in the last fifteen years than has the Arabian Peninsula. . . . In 1930 except for a few scattered missionaries and merchants there were virtually no Americans in this area and American affairs could easily be handled by a single small consulate at Aden." Now in mid-1946, the memo noted, Americans and American companies were deeply involved, especially in Saudi Arabia; it gave a long list of examples, beginning with the oil arrangments:

> The Arabian-American Oil Company has obtained a concession for most of Saudi Arabia, has drilled a number of wells on the Persian Gulf side of the country and tapped the largest single oil reserve in the world, a series of fields which apparently contains as much oil as all of the United States. Over 1000 Americans are at work drilling wells, laying pipelines, operating a large modern refinery and expanding their activities so fast that Saudi Arabia has already become the fifth largest oil producing country in the world. American investment in Saudi Arabia is over $100,000,000 and it is expected that this figure will be doubled within two years. A tanker a day is now being filled on the oil coast, a stretch of desolate gulf shore virtually unknown fifteen years ago.
>
> A first-class landing field and airport has been constructed and is being operated by the U.S. Army at Dhahran on the oil coast of Saudi Arabia, complete with over fifty buildings including an administration building, a restaurant, a hospital, a movie theater, and quarters for 500 persons, all air-cooled.
>
> Dhahran's airport has become a stop on the TWA New York-Cairo-India service and promises to become a great center for around the world air traffic.

The government of Saudi Arabia has purchased five American transport planes and has requested assistance from TWA in organizing a Saudi Arabian airline [which after thirty years of operational and technical assistance from TWA would become the region's largest airline by the end of the century].

The Saudi Arabian Government has asked the Mackay Radio Company to erect and operate a radio sending and receiving station at Dammam near Dhahran, capable of communicating with the United States. . . . "

The memo went on at considerable length to summarize the growing and increasingly important economic and political arrangements between the United States and Saudi Arabia. Americans, it said, were installing urban water systems, planning to build a railroad and electricity generating plants, runnning the gold mine that Eddy had visited and the royal experimental farm southeast of Riyadh, and operating Jeddah's only modern medical clinic. That clinic was in addition to the medical facilities built and operated by ARAMCO, across the country in Dhahran, which treated Arabs as well as Americans.

That same memo reported the beginnings of an economic relationship with Yemen, Saudi Arabia's neighbor to the south, where the ruler was beginning to import American transportation equipment and was looking for American help in medicine and agriculture. Those stirrings of bilateral commerce with a country even more remote and less developed than Saudi Arabia had been were also in large part the work of Bill Eddy.

THE LAST ARABIAN FRONTIER

In the late 1940s Yemen, at the southwestern corner of the Arabian peninsula, was more isolated and impoverished than Saudi Arabia had been when the American oilmen arrived in 1933. The land that became Saudi Arabia had for centuries interacted with the rest of the world through its stewardship of the annual pilgrimage to Mecca, or *hajj*, which drew visitors from many parts of the globe. Yemen, mountainous, tribal and feudal, was almost entirely cut off from the outside world, despite a rich and colorful history that earned it the appellation "Arabia Felix." Its ruler, fearful of all progress, kept his domain closed to outsiders, and thus closed to development and education.

After centuries in which the Ottoman Turks exercised nominal rule but true control rested in the millennium-old al-Rassi dynasty, Yemen became formally independent upon the dissolution of the Ottoman Empire after World War I. It had had only one ruler ever since, the Imam Yahya bin Muhammad Hamid al-Din, whose fanatic fear of foreign domination led him to seal off his country—in 1945 there were hardly any foreign diplomats in Yemen, let alone foreign businesses or armies. Its principal export was telegraph poles cut from trees in the mountains. Yemen was a founding member of the League of Arab States in 1945, but was a complete political backwater.

The southern region of what is today the country of Yemen, the territory then known as the Protectorate of Aden, was under

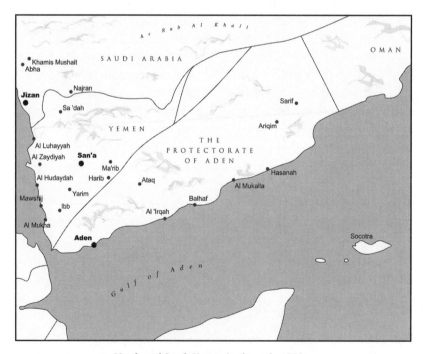

North and South Yemen in the early 1950s.

British rule and for that reason relatively modern and open. The rest of Yemen was controlled by Imam Yahya, a Shiite Muslim of the Zaidi sect. As spiritual leader of his people as well as temporal ruler, Yahya was determined to keep the colonialists away from his door. He was the opposite of King Abdul Aziz, his neighbor to the north, who sought help from foreigners because his country lacked the resources to develop itself. Yahya excluded foreigners, with a few exceptions, and his country remained much the same as it had always been.

In his book *The Arabs*, Peter Mansfield wrote this about Yemen and its government: "The Imam's system of rule ensured that the country remained in a medieval condition. In his extreme autocracy, every item of government business depended on his personal decisions and all outside influences were excluded as far as possible. He managed the tribes through a system of alliances and the hallowed Yemeni tradition of taking hostages, whereby one or more of the relations of the heads of important tribes would be held in a prison school maintained by the Imam as a guarantee of the tribe's good behavior."

Yet even this octogenarian autocrat was preparing to look outside for assistance in shoring up his rule. He knew about Americans because of the visits to his country before the war by Charles C. Crane, the Chicago philanthropist of the King-Crane Commission, who developed a lifelong interest in the Arabs and had been instrumental in opening Saudi Arabia to oil exploration. Crane had sent to Yemen the engineer Karl Twitchell, who had established mining projects and constructed the only steel-truss bridge on the Arabian peninsula; these were apparently the only foreign-sponsored economic activities on Yemeni territory during Yahya's rule. Through them Yahya, like Abdul Aziz, came to believe that Americans could be helpful without trying to take over. In the spring of 1944, he sent an agent to the U.S. mission in Cairo to ask that the United States intervene in a dispute with Britain over the border with Aden.

This request, from a country that had been entirely off Washington's radar screen, would probably have been ignored or rejected if it had come a couple of years earlier, in the period when President Roosevelt was dismissing Saudi Arabia as "a little far afield for us." But by 1944 the Arabian peninsula had taken on new importance, and the State Department reacted with alacrity.

At the time even the Department's career Arab world specialists were unfamiliar with Yemen; according to the State Department, only seven Americans had ever visited the country before 1946. Now, if the Americans were to take on a mission there, they wanted to know something about the territory involved. The Department assigned Harlan P. Clark, the U.S. consul in British-ruled Aden, on Yemen's southern seacoast, to travel to Sana'a, Yemen's remote capital, to test the waters.

Clark journeyed overland early in 1945. He was accompanied by a U.S. Navy doctor, Alfred Palmer, who at every stop was called upon to minister to the health needs of the local population, to whom modern medical care was unavailable. Upon reaching Sana'a, they met the Imam, and Clark cabled this report to Washington:

> On my informal visit to the Yemen I was given courtesies and facilities such as they have not before accorded a foreigner and was received with great cordiality by the Imam and the royal princes. They frankly said they had known for many years that Yemen has vast natural resources to be developed but had so feared the imperialistic designs of the great powers who offered help that they preferred to remain backward and isolated. They had long believed that the only nation they could rely on for disinterested help was the United States and now that its world leadership to maintain the rights of small nations was assured they would welcome such economic and cultural assistance as it could give. They wished first to enter into a standard treaty of friendship and commerce with the United States and to employ sufficient American technicians to assist in developing the country.

Clark said he had been told that Yemen held commercial quantities of iron, lead, copper, mica, and asbestos, as well as oil.

Considering all the foreign policy issues confronting the United States as Truman succeeded Roosevelt, this initiative moved through government channels with remarkable speed because, as the State Department's Sanger noted, "the United States now had a direct interest in the Arabian peninsula." President Truman agreed to extend formal recognition to the Imam's government and to open diplomatic relations if the Yemenis were willing.

A presidential decision to recognize, however, was not the same as a decision about what would actually happen on the ground to construct a bilateral relationship where none had existed. It was not as if there were an existing U.S. embassy that would simply be accredited to a new government and continue to function, as sometimes happened after coups d'état or revolutions. In an internal memo, Sanger noted that "active steps must be taken taken to: a) arrange a message of recognition which might be telegraphed in code to Aden or in clear to Sanaa; b) organize a mission to go to Sanaa, possibly to be headed by Mr. [James] Moose with Mr. Clark as a member; c) obtain the medical items desired by the Imam and arrange about having an American doctor, perhaps from the Rockefeller Foundation, stationed in Sanaa; d) the recognition Mission should either be made permanent, or else US advisers should be attached to the Government of the Yemen; e) the question of surveying the oil resources and mineral and agricultural possibilities of the Yemen must be worked out; f) the British must be notified of our intention so that we do not appear to be going in behind their backs."

On November 19, the president wrote to the Imam to propose sending a special envoy to conclude the treaty the Yeminis sought. The Imam accepted, and on March 4, 1946, the president wrote him a letter carrying the same salutation Roosevelt had addressed to Abdul Aziz: "Great and Good Friend."

"I take pleasure in informing Your Majesty," Truman wrote, "that the Government of the United States recognizes the absolute and complete independence of the Yemen and by this letter makes known its intent to accord you and Your Majesty's Government the privileges of such recognition and endeavor to promote friendly relations between our two countries." The Imam had told Washington that he did not want foreign diplomats to take up residence in Yemen. Accepting that decision, Truman told Yahya that he would send a special one-time diplomatic mission to negotiate commerce and friendship agreements.

"I have selected the Honorable William A. Eddy, in whom I repose special trust and confidence, to be my representative" on that mission, Truman wrote. By late March, Eddy and his team, which included Clark, Sanger, a medical unit directed by a Dr. Hedley, and a communications team, were on their way. They carried with them food, medicine, tents and radio equipment, because in those days any voyage to the Yemeni interior was arduous and uncomfortable and reqired camping under the stars along the route from the Red Sea port of Hodeida to the capital.

When the Americans sailed into the harbor of Hodeida aboard a U.S. Navy destroyer, the *Ernest G. Small,* Yemenis insisted upon welcoming them with a 21-gun salute, which took quite some time because their old Turkish cannon could be fired only once every six minutes. The 100-mile journey on horseback to Sana'a, which is at an altitude of 7,200 feet, took about three weeks. (The paved road was not completed until 1961.)

As is customary on such occasions, the Americans brought a gift for their host. A truck convoy that struggled up the mountain trails in the wake of the diplomatic travelers carried a complete mobile radio station, with transmitter, power unit, antennae and accessories, which could be set up wherever the Imam wanted it. This was a modest but important U.S. contribution to the modernization of the country.

THE "MOST MEDIEVAL THEOCRACY"

Our knowledge of what happened on this voyage comes mostly from accounts that Eddy and Sanger wrote some time afterward. Sanger's is a straightforward narrative that he incorporated into a book about Arabia. Eddy's, never published, is a sardonic commentary on what he found during his mission to what he called "the most medieval theocracy on earth." Notes that he took en route are also preserved among his papers.

As they traveled, Eddy scribbled random jottings and observations:

"Friendly, smiling natives. Congregate at sundown."

"Wild baboons, in troops across road."

"Schools: Gymnastics. Pupils chained for tardiness."

"Women mostly unveiled. Much prettier than in
     S.A. [Saudi Arabia]"

On April 14, in the capital, he met the Imam Yahya and delivered Truman's letter recognizing the country. The Imam, Eddy noted in his account, "never returned the compliment by recognizing the 'absolute and complete independence of the USA,' although such courtesies are usually reciprocal: Perhaps it was just his congenital wariness of signing anything which might involve his hidden kingdom in world affairs; perhaps he doubted our sovereignty, having heard that the Seminoles in Florida still hold out against the invader."

In his notebook, Eddy jotted down some of what the Imam had to say in this first encounter, including his disavowal of reports that he had previously signed a friendship treaty with Nazi Germany.

"No treaty with Germany," the Imam said, according to Eddy's notes. "We gave [indecipherable] to get arms. Refused treaty."

"Germany puffed up with pride, fell. Only mutual respect can be basis of friendship, not 'superiority.'"

"The Mikado [that is, the emperor of Japan] blasphemously made himself a God, and Allah more than the hands of the Americans struck him down." The use of the term Mikado must have been Eddy's invention; it is unlikely that the Imam Yahya was familiar with Gilbert and Sullivan.

Eddy described Yahya as "a short, peppery, rotund man of 81, quick witted and quick tempered. He dressed, like a Pope, all in white, skull-cap, robe and sandals. He seldom left the capital, and then only for short drives to country estates. He had never left the plateau of the High Yemen nor ever seen the Red Sea nor the Tihama, the western province of his country."

It turned out that making the voyage to Sana'a and presenting the president's letter to Yahya was the easy part of Eddy's mission, contrary to what the Americans expected. The friendship treaty that the United States proposed to sign with Yemen consisted largely of boilerplate language that had been used in similar treaties with other countries and was therefore non-controversial, or so the Americans thought. They were wrong, for three reasons: the unique nature of the Imam's rule created an unfathomable decision-making process, the Imam and his negotiators did not understand basic legal and diplomatic terms that the Americans took for granted, and a power struggle erupted among the Imam's sons and other members of his entourage, some of whom were opposed to any treaty with an outside power. Working through these issues to a successful conclusion was yet another test of Eddy's skills at understanding his Arab interlocutors and cajoling them into agreement.

By comparison with Saudi Arabia, Eddy found Yemen fertile and verdant, but also very backward. "Saudi Arabia is very advanced," he wrote, "compared to these people who punish offenders brutally without trial and put in chains schoolchildren who are tardy or do not know their lessons." Yemeni justice, he observed, was arbitrary and cruel: "People disappear without anyone knowing why or daring to ask any questions." Even two of the Imam's thirteen sons were in prison, and the rest were "constantly suspected by their father of scheming for power (sometimes with reason.). . . . Distrust of the foreigner was no greater than distrust of brother and son." (Arbitrary justice and horrifying cruelty were and still are characteristic of Saudi Arabia as well, but Eddy's affection for King Abdul Aziz and his country evidently led him to overlook such unpleasant facts. His letters and dispatches from the Kingdom have little to say on that subject.)

As for Yemen's ruler, Eddy wrote, "Surprising as it may seem, this absolute monarch, unlike so many dissolute Turkish Sultans, was a very hard working king. He had no deputy, no Council of Ministers, no parliament, no civil service; only an army and municipal officials. Every subject had direct access to him as High Priest, Judge, Jury, Pardoner or Executioner rolled into one. . . .

"The Imam had no written laws or constitution; he governed by oral edict, which could be revised, and he distrusted the typewriter. I treasure several personal holograph notes from him, the ink dried with Islamic-red dust and royal seal he alone could use. He was too holy to be photographed."

Under the Imam's rule, Eddy noted, "no foreigner could immigrate to The Yemen, not even a brother Muslim from an Arab country." Because of that, he discovered, the entire concept of immigration was unknown to the Imam's negotiators, and they could not understand why there should be any reference to it in the proposed treaty. They responded with similar bafflement to language in the U.S. draft related to trade and tariffs on goods exported to Cuba or the Panama Canal Zone, about which they knew nothing.

"Our political work goes very slowly," Eddy wrote a week after negotiations began, "partly because this government is still in the dark ages and knows nothing of modern western ways. Even the simplest phrase needs to be explained," a process that was of course complicated by the need to explain in Arabic. The U.S. draft, for example, used the word "qawaneen" to mean "regulations." The Imam thought this was a reference to the "laws" of Islam. Muhammad Raghib Bey, the Imam's Turkish-born foreign minister, spoke Arabic and French but not English.

It was not even clear what the Imam really wanted.

"Recognition of his sovereign independence was no doubt important to the Imam, but the public health section of our Mission was our guarantee of welcome," Eddy recounted. "The Imam suffered from arthritis and Allah alone knows how many other ailments of age and effects of chewing Qat," a mildly narcotic leaf habitually chewed throughout Yemen. "Dr. Hedley examined and prescribed daily; when the Imam felt better our stock went up; when he felt worse, we felt feverish. Dr. Hedley begged me for God's sake to conclude the negotiation of the treaty and get the hell out of these mountain fastnesses before the Imam died of old age and we were accused of killing him. This was easier wished than done. Not only did the negotiations drag out as the Yemenis scrutinized strange and suspicious phrases like 'privileges commonly accorded under civilized law,' but the Imam did not wish to lose his medical guests in a hurry. I have said that no foreigners could take up residence in the Yemen [except, obviously, Raghib Bey]. True, but we found there in Sana'a two unwilling and permanent guests of the Imam, two Italian doctors stranded and impounded from the war days when the Italians sent them over from Eritrea to treat the Imam. The war was now over and they wanted to return to Italy and their families and homes, but the hospitable Imam would not hear of it. Dr. Hedley anxiously inquired daily as to the progress of our negotiations, but his interest was not in diplomacy."

According to Sanger, the negotiations proceeded cordially, if painstakingly, for two weeks, but were disrupted when Raghib Bey was suddenly replaced as chief negotiator by "small, wiry Prince Hussein, the third son of the Imam. Although he had traveled more than any of his brothers and had a sharp mind and beaming personality when he chose to exert it, all progress came to an end as soon as he joined the negotiations."

It was soon apparent that Prince Hussein's negotiating tactics arose from his desire to torpedo the entire undertaking: he wanted no treaty at all.

Hussein haggled over every article of the text. Some of the changes he demanded were beyond Eddy's authority to grant and had to be referrred to Washington, a time-consuming process. The biggest sticking point, according to Sanger, was the standard language of such treaties saying that citizens of Yemen in the United States and citizens of the United States in Yemen "shall be received and treated in accordance with the generally recognized international law."

Hussein drew the line at this apparently anodyne language. He argued that the only law Yemen recognized was the law of the Koran. "He felt," Sanger wrote, "that any recognition of Western law in Yemen would be the first step in breaking down the religious and social patterns of his country."

The stalemate continued until at last Eddy felt the time had come to call the Yemenis' bluff. He sent word to the Imam that the negotiations had failed, and asked for permission to pay a farewell courtesy call before departing. At that meeting, on April 23, the Imam asked what the sticking point was in the negotiations. He was told that a memo outlining the problem had been sent to him two days earlier. He had not received it; Prince Hussein had intercepted it.

In Sanger's account, which Eddy said was accurate, a melo-dramatic scene ensued. The Imam asked Eddy to postpone his departure, and once again assigned Raghib Bey to conduct the negotiations. At that Raghib Bey offered his resignation as foreign minister, unleasing an emotional tirade in which he said, "Just as I was about to conclude this international masterpiece, the work was taken out of my hands, and I was kicked out of your palace like a dog. In my place your unskilled son, Hussein, took over the negotiations. He dropped the masterpiece that I had made upon the floor of the guesthouse, where it was broken into a thousand pieces. All progress came to a halt. When it is clear that something must be done, you call me back like a sweeper to pick up the broken pieces and reconstruct something worthwhile from the wreck which your son has made. I will not be pushed about like a slave of the palace. I resign as your majesty's foreign minister." He asked permission to leave Yemen after 30 years and return to his native Turkey.

Instead of flying into a rage, the Imam heard him out and suggested gently that he needed a rest: "You will feel better soon." Again he asked Eddy to stay and resume the negotiations. "We will be at the guest house one hour," Eddy replied. "If you have any messages to send to me or my government, I shall receive them there."

Eddy, Sanger and their colleagues waited at the guest house while the Imam, Hussein and other princes, and Raghib Bey fought it out. Hussein continued to oppose the treaty, arguing that it would lead to the end of Muslim life and culture in Yemen, but the Imam finally overruled him. Just as the hour allotted by Eddy was about to expire, a courier arrived from the palace with news that the Imam had agreed to the jurisdictional language, and thus the deal was done at last. It had taken more than three weeks to negotiate a four-page agreement in which no provision was precedent-setting or controversial.

The American delegation did not linger in Sana'a. Eddy and his team set off for Aden "each of us on a litter borne by four gigantic Sudanese," Eddy wrote. At the coast they climbed into a sort of native canoe pushed by men wading in the water out to a waiting British vessel, "a neat motor launch onto which we clambered to find ourselves in deck chairs, being offered whisky-and-soda by a uniformed butler—from the Bronze Age to the British Empire in sixty minutes."

The following year, J. Rives Childs, Eddy's successor as minister in Jiddah (and his old boss in Tangier) arrived in Sana'a to present his credentials as the first American minister to that country, and Yemen with American support joined the United Nations.

By that time it was clear that the Imam had more on his mind than a friendship treaty when he agreed to receive the Eddy mission. State Department memos show that he wanted American assistance in developing a deep-water port at Hodeida, roadbuilding help, agricultural consultants and irrigation projects, $1 million worth of textile-making machinery, and permission to purchase "substantial quantities" of American trucks, automobiles, refrigeration equipment and "even four airplanes." It seems the Saudi model worked for the Imam.

Yet in the history of the modern Arab world, Eddy's achievement in Yemen turned out to be a minor development—unlike his work in Saudi Arabia—because Yemen remained a poor country, plagued by violence and political upheaval, and a relatively unimportant voice in regional affairs. The Imam was killed in an abortive coup attempt in 1948. His son Prince Ahmad succeeded him but proved a clumsy player in the turbulent Arab politics of the 1950s.

That was not surprising, considering the sort of person Ahmad was and his reputation among the population. He was, according to the left-wing British writer Fred Halliday, "a notoriously cruel [military] commander who had a terrifying appearance because his eyes seemed to pop out of his head; such was his reputation that it was believed by many Yemenis he had deliberately cultivated this appearance as a young man by continuously throttling himself with a rope." Ahmad was known as the most accomplished practitioner of the Yemeni art of hostage-taking; at one point he was reported to hold about 4,000 such unfortunates.

Ahmad, chronically ill and, according to Halliday, foggy in the head from overdoses of morphine, died in September 1961; his son, Badr, fled into the tribal hinterlands after a military coup in

1962, and the 1,064-year rule of the Imam's al-Rassi dynasty came to an end.

In the civil war that ensued, the military's new republican government in Sana'a was supported by Egypt's great nationalist leader, Gamal Abdel Nasser. Saudi Arabia supported forces loyal to the old Imamate, one monarchy coming to the aid of another. But neither Egypt nor Saudi Arabia was interested in Yemen for its own sake; the war was a Cold War proxy struggle between the Soviet Union, supporting the republican side, and the United States, backing the anticommunist monarchies. As Miles Copeland put it in his cynical classic *The Game of Nations*, "It should be recorded that Nasser's view of Yemen, in itself, was similar to our own—to wit, the human race would not be seriously inconvenienced if the whole country were to slide quietly into the Indian Ocean. . . . Nasser was not interested in Yemen, he was interested in the whole Arabian Peninsula. Yemen was only a foothold. Similarly, the United States government was not interested in Yemen—or shouldn't have been—but in having an orderly situation in Aden, and in eliminating any 'wave of the future' which might prematurely overrun King Feisal [of Iraq], the ruling family of Kuwait, and other Gulf Sheikhdoms."

Yemen's history since the 1960s has been complicated and violent, but its importance in world affairs is not much greater today than it was when Bill Eddy planted the American flag there in 1946. The British are long gone from Aden, and Yemen has been a unified republic since 1990. To Americans it is probably best known as the native land of Muhammad bin Laden, father of Osama, and as the country where terrorists affiliated with al-Qaeda attacked the USS *Cole*, a Navy destroyer, killing seventeen sailors in October 2000. And the country is still poor; Yemenis seeking better lives migrate to jobs in Saudi Arabia, legally or otherwise, much as Mexicans seeking better jobs migrate to the economically powerful neighbor to their north.

Chapter 8

WASHINGTON

After the Battle of Tarawa in November 1943 and the Allied landings in Normandy in June 1944, the eventual outcome of the war was no longer in question, and government leaders in Washington began to think about what would follow the end of combat. One big question was what to do with Wild Bill Donovan's OSS, which by D-Day had grown to 13,000 operatives.

The United States had no tradition of intelligence gathering or espionage in peacetime, and many officials of both parties, including Vice President Harry S. Truman, were opposed to the creation of a permanent spy agency. President Roosevelt and some of his senior advisers, on the other hand, were already beginning to envision the global power struggle with the Soviet Union that was to come—the Cold War, it would be called—and to understand the potential value of an effective intelligence service.

On October 31, 1944, Roosevelt asked Donovan for a memo on this subject. Donovan's response, classified "secret," was delivered on November 18.

"In the early days of the war, when the demands upon intelligence services were mainly in and for military operations, the OSS was placed under the direction of the JCS [Joint Chiefs of Staff]. Once our enemies are defeated the demand will be equally pressing for information that will aid us in solving the problems of peace," the OSS chief wrote. "This will require two things:

1. That intelligence control be returned to the supervision of the President.

2. The establishment of a central authority reporting directly to you, with responsibility to frame intelligence objectives and to collect and coordinate the intelligence material required by the Executive Branch in planning and carrying out national policy and strategy."

Donovan told the president that the country was entering "a period of transition which, before we are aware, will take us into the tumult of rehabilitation. An adequate and orderly intelligence system will contribute to informed decisions. We have now in the Government the trained and specialized personnel needed for this task. This talent should not be dispersed."

He attached a proposed Executive Order which, upon signature by the president, would create a "central intelligence service," under a director appointed by the president, which would have ultimate responsibility for all intelligence policy, all intelligence gathering by military and civilian agencies, and the "final evaluation, synthesis and dissemination within the government of the intelligence required to enable the Government to determine policies with respect to national planning and security in peace and war . . ." This office would also control recruitment and training of intelligence personnel.

That memo was the opening salvo of a bureaucratic war that would rage in Washington for almost three years—a war in which Bill Eddy would become an influential combatant. In many ways the contest in the mid-1940s was similar to the struggle over reconstructing the nation's intelligence apparatus that was precipitated by the terrorist attacks on New York and Washington in 2001. In 1945, the issues were two: would there be a peacetime intelligence apparatus at all, and if so, who would control it? The War Department had well-established intelligence capabilities within the armed services and wished to retain them. J. Edgar Hoover's FBI, which was the principal intelligence gathering agency in Latin America during the war, wanted to retain that responsibility and perhaps take over the global operation. Many officials shared Donovan's view that the government's intelligence assets were too valuable to dismantle but should be controlled by an independent agency reporting directly to the White House.

In the months between receiving Donovan's memo and his death the following April, Roosevelt took no action. It is not entirely clear why not, but OSS and CIA historians have advanced three main probable reasons. First, the surprise German offensive in the Ardennes in December, the Battle of the Bulge, showed that the end of the war was not imminent. Then in February Donovan's memo was leaked to the press—apparently by Hoover—and ignited a political storm as critics accused Donovan of advocating the establishment of a "Gestapo." By that time Roosevelt was engaged with the Yalta conference and his post-Yalta meetings. And the war in the Pacific, a theater of operations where the OSS had seven major stations, was still raging when Roosevelt died, leaving the issue unresolved.

Truman, however, wasted little time after the atomic bombs on Hiroshima and Nagasaki persuaded Japan to surrender in August. Donovan precipitated a decision with memos dated August 25, 1945, which are reproduced in the official declassified history of the OSS that was edited by Kermit Roosevelt.

Donovan informed the White House that the OSS was in effect working on its own liquidation, which he estimated would be completed by the following January. He restated his view, however, that the end of the OSS should not be the end of the intelligence story.

"I wish to return to private life," he wrote. "Therefore, in considering the disposition to be made of the assets created by OSS, I speak as a private citizen concerned with the future of his country. In our Government today there is no permanent agency to take over the functions which OSS will have then ceased to perform. These functions, while carried on as incident to the war, are in reality essential in the effective discharge by this nation of its responsibilities in the organization and maintenance of the peace. Since last November I have pointed out the immediate necessity of setting up such an agency to take over the valuable assets created by OSS. Among these assets was the establishment for the first time in our nation's history of a foreign secret intelligence service which reported information as seen through American eyes." Such an agency would now be essential in the post-war period, he wrote, but it should be restricted to gathering intellegence overseas—there must be no clandestine activity or surveillance of citizens within the United States.

Donovan sent a copy of that memo to Judge Samuel Rosenman, who had been Roosevelt's White House counsel and stayed on for the first ten months of Truman's presidency, with a personal note. "I understand that there has been talk of attempting to allocate different segments of the organization to different departments [of the government]. This would be an absurd and unsatisfactory thing to do. The organization was set up as an entity, every function supporting and supplementing the other. It's time for us to grow up, Sam, and realize that the new responsibilities we have assumed require an adequate intelligence system," he wrote.

In reality, there was no way the assets of the OSS could be retained in a single functioning organization after the war. Most of its agents were eager to return to their lives as scholars, scientists, writers or bankers. Some of them, upon returning home, were distressed by the infighting that centered on Donovan and his memo; some of them truly believed that their work should go on. But most of them, Stewart Alsop and Tom Braden wrote in *Sub Rosa*, "did not bother their heads about the matter. The war was over, and their had their terminal leave. They did not look back on OSS with the same pride as the Marines for example look back upon the Marine Corps, or men of the First Division look back to their unit."

By mid-September, Truman had made up his mind. On September 20, he signed Executive Order 9621, "Termination of the Office of Strategic Services and Disposition of Its Functions."

Under its terms, the OSS would cease to exist at the end of the business day on September 30. The next morning, its "research and analysis" functions would be taken over by a new Interim Research and Intelligence Service to be created within the State Department. This agency in turn would cease to exist as of December 31. After that, Truman directed Secretary of State James F. Byrnes to distribute whatever research and analytical functions he chose to maintain to other units of the State Department and eliminate those he decided the department could do without. Byrnes was also directed to take the lead in developing "a comprehensive and coordinated foreign intelligence program." All other functions of the OSS were transferred to the War Department. With that the OSS, a unique institution created almost overnight under the highest possible pressure, vaporized. Many of its agents and operatives would later become stars of the intelligence firmament in the Cold War spy agency that Congress would soon create, but at the end of 1945 it appeared that the "great game" of international spying and espionage, like the war itself, had come to an end.

It took Truman less than four months to realize that he had created a vacuum that would have to be filled. Byrnes, with whom Truman rapidly became disenchanted after appointing him against Sam Rosenman's advice, failed to produce the reorganization within the State Department that Truman had ordered or to develop the alternative program that Truman had assigned him to devise. At the same time, Secretary of the Navy James Forrestal was prodding the president to establish a new, comprehensive national intelligence service, and was lobbying for this outcome within the cabinet.

"The situation was ridiculous," intelligence historian Sherman Kent wrote in a secret internal narrative. "For more than a year and half the State Department had not been able to establish its own new unified intelligence office. Secondly, never had the Department evidenced any serious interest in 'taking the lead' in developing any government-wide coordination of foreign intelligence activity. Finally, all it did have for such coordination were the rec-ommendations of administrative and management specialists in the Bureau of the Budget. Nevertheless, State was in charge."

This phase of the interagency maneuvering came to an end on January 22, 1946, when the president signed a "Presidential Direc-tive on Coordination of Foreign Intelligence Activities." It took the form of an order to the secretaries of State, War and the Navy.

"It is my desire, and I hereby direct," Truman wrote, "that all Federal foreign intelligence activities be planned, developed and coordinated so as to assure the most effective accomplishment of the intelligence mission related to the national security. I hereby desig-nate you, together with another person to be named by me as my personal representative, as the National Intelligence Authority to accomplish this purpose." Truman ordered that "within the limits of available appropriations, you shall each from time to time assign per-sons and facilities from your respective Departments, which persons shall collectively form a Central Intelligence Group and shall, under the direction of a Director of Central Intelligence, assist the National Intelligence Authority. The Director of Central Intelligence shall be designated by me, shall be responsible to the National Intelligence Authority, and shall sit as a nonvoting member thereof."

It would be the responsibility of the Director of Central Intelli-gence to "accomplish the correlation and evaluation of intelligence relating to the national security, and the appropriate dissemination within the Government of the resulting strategic and national pol-icy intelligence. In so doing, full use shall be made of the staff and facilities of the intelligence agencies of your Departments." It would also be up to the Director to "plan for the coordination of such of the activities of the intelligence agencies of your Departments as relate to the national security and recommend to the National Intelligence Authority the establishment of such over-all policies and objectives as will assure the most effective accomplishment of the national intelligence mission."

Within whatever overall structure emerged from this process, Truman directed, "The existing intelligence agencies of your Depart-ments shall continue to collect, evaluate, correlate and disseminate departmental intelligence."

Despite its bureaucratic language, this directive had the virtue of clarity on two crucial points: there would be a centralized national intelligence organization, and Hoover's FBI was excluded from participating in it. Otherwise the directive raised as many questions as it answered because of its vagueness about lines of authority and funding: which Department's budget was going to pay for this? Those questions would have be answered by the new National Intelligence Authority, and that group's decisions would have to be codified into law by Congress.

The State Department's official history of "The Emergence of the Intelligence Establishment" makes clear how many matters remained to be resolved. With the signing of Truman's directive, it says:

> A peacetime national intelligence system was finally established. In fact, however, it existed only on paper. OSS had been broken up and dissolved. The Strategic Services Unit remained in the War Department as a potential nucleus of a clandestine intelligence capability, but at that point no one was certain of how or even whether it would be absorbed into the new national intelligence structure. A mechanism for producing 'strategic and national policy intelligence' had yet to be devised, and there was not yet even a common definition of the term. Beyond the generalities, there was no agreed view of how the new system should operate or even of what it should do. President Truman had his own idea of what the new arrangements could do for him, reflecting mainly his concern to be kept informed in a way that ensured that all of the relevant information was put together in a single package. Apart from this, his interest in the intelligence set-up seemed to be limited. The armed forces had been the prime movers of the effort to set up a centralized intelligence capability but they would soon begin to show signs of alarm that the new system was becoming too independent. The Department of State wanted to exert major influence on the Central Intelligence Group but seemed uncertain about how to do so, perhaps because it was still in the middle of its own bruising battle over intelligence. Secretary of State Byrnes feared that the new arrangements would enhance Admiral Leahy's role in foreign policy, to the

detriment of the Department's." (Admiral William Leahy had been Roosevelt's personal military adviser and was still at the White House, where Truman had appointed him as his representative on the National Intelligence Authority.)

Now the departments of State, War and the Navy began the work of sorting out these matters. This was the kind of process that is common in Washington but seems mystifying to ordinary citizens outside the capital. Whether the issue is agricultural subsidies, a free-trade agreement, taxation, storage of nuclear waste, or any other involving multiple interests and large amounts of money, development of a national policy that can gain public support and be approved by Congress involves months of meetings and arguments among the interested parties. Sometimes a high-profile person is in overall charge, as Hillary Rodham Clinton was with health care and Dick Cheney with energy, but each government agency and each Congressional committee involved in the process will have a senior representative. Most of the time that person will be of sufficiently high rank to be credible in meetings but not so high as to be well known to the public. So it was in the 1940s with the debate over intelligence.

The State Department's point man was Bill Eddy, who on August 1, 1946, took up the post of Special Assistant to the Secretary of State for Research and Intelligence. What would emerge from the group's deliberations, coordinated first by Admiral Sidney Souers as Truman's Director of Central Intelligence for the first five months, then by Lieutenant General Hoyt S. Vandenberg, would lead to the adoption by Congress of the National Security Act of 1947, which created the modern CIA and the president's National Security Council. This seems straightforward: the president decided on a course of action, designated senior officials to carry it out, and signed off on their product. In the reality of Washington, where everyone has turf to protect and ideas to promote, such proceedings are often protracted, tedious, politically charged and emotionally exhausting. It was just the sort of work environment that had so frustrated Eddy at Hobart College, but this time the stakes were so high that they validated the struggle.

THE FUDGE FACTORY

The Eddy family took up residence in a handsome house on Carvel Road in the Westmoreland Hills neighborhood of Bethesda, Maryland, a leafy suburb of winding streets and cul-de-sacs just a twenty-minute drive from downtown Washington. Out of uniform and back in suit and tie, Eddy ventured inside the closed circle of senior officials at the department known as the "fudge factory."

Obviously this was an entirely different professional setting for the freelancing operative of Tangier and Jeddah; government agencies have their own ways of doing things, and the inter-agency process requires constant negotiation as each participating department presses its case and often each participating individual does so as well. As Eddy began his new assignment, the State Department was in the midst of its own internal struggle over the deployment of the analysts and research specialists it had inherited from the OSS. In essence, the argument was whether to adopt the "McCormack plan," named for Colonel Alfred McCormack, a Princeton graduate and New York lawyer with intelligence experience who was Eddy's predecessor as Special Assistant to the Secretary for Intelligence and Research, or the "Russell plan," named for Donald Russell, assistant secretary of state for administration.

The McCormack plan called for the establishment of a permanent separate unit within the State Department that would carry out whatever intelligence functions emerged from the interagency deliberations—as the departmental historian put it, "a set of geographic and functional research offices that would roughly parallel the policy offices, working closely with them but remaining independent of their control and steering clear of involvement in policy." That is, within the intelligence unit, there would be specialists on the Middle East, Latin America, Africa and the other regions of the globe covered by the department's various bureaus. These intelligence analysts would work and share information with, but not be part of, the policymaking geographic bureaus, such as Near Eastern Affairs, or NEA.

The Russell plan called for splitting up the analysts and researchers among those existing geographic and functional bureaus, rather than creating a separate unit. Russell argued that "if the research personnel is retained in a central organization, a difficulty more serious than wasted talent is likely to result. To retain able research men, they must be given a voice in recommending policy. Those now being brought into the Department should be given such a voice. But the policy recommendations of a research unit which is not organizationally integrated with operations are very likely to be theoretical judgments with little basis in reality. Policy, to be sound, must be based on the closest contact between day-to-day operations and good basic research." This argument was supported by most of the department's senior career officers—but not by Dean Acheson, then undersecretary, who disliked Russell—and it complied with the recommendations of the White House budget office, which had tried to establish a government-wide principle that intelligence staff and policy staff should work side by side, not in separate functional units. Russell's position could not be reconciled with McCormack's, which was "That an intelligence organization must be free of operations or policy involvements is fundamental. That such freedom could exist in the 20-odd Divisions of the Geographic Offices is unthinkable."

After hesitating for months, ignoring the deadlines laid down in Truman's executive order, Byrnes adopted the Russell plan. McCormack resigned. Thus the decentralized system was being implemented, haltingly, when Eddy arrived to fill the position that McCormack had left. Eddy was in the peculiar position of being assigned to carry out the Russell plan when his personal views coincided with those of McCormack; he believed firmly that intelligence gathering and analysis must be insulated from policy.

This may sound like the kind of bureaucratic argument that takes place within large institutions such as universities and government departments and makes no difference to anyone except the participants. In the State Department case, though, the matter attracted attention in the press and was the subject of a column by the influential Arthur Krock of the *New York Times* on August 2, 1946, the day after Eddy started his new job.

The brilliant and daring work of Col. William A. Eddy in preparing for our invasion of North Africa comes into review with the notice today of his appointment as head of the intelligence unit of the Department of State," Krock wrote. "The nature and quality of his work in Africa, under the direction of Maj. Gen. William J. Donovan, and what later became the Office of Strategic Services, was far removed from the atmosphere of diplomacy that must now envelop and possibly stifle Colonel Eddy's great capacity for secret service of the type at which the British are especially adept. But if intelligence service, as he knows and has practiced it, belongs in the State Department—which this correspondent and many others do not believe—Colonel Eddy is admirably equipped to perform it.

Under a reorganization scheme the chiefs and operatives of the OSS, who helped so importantly to win the war, have either been retired to private life or scattered through the State, War, and Navy Departments, with Lieut. Gen. Hoyt S. Vandenberg as the coordinator of their efforts. In the State Department the new intelligence unit was distributed among what are called the 'geographic desks,' a very promising means to make it ineffective by subjecting its activities to the direction of career diplomats. Since their training and tendencies and those of intelligence workers are wholly at variance, the department's new unit may come to nothing—which may be desirable, because diplomacy and intelligence don't mix and there is a risk in trying to mix them. But if anything constructive can be done in this quarter, Colonel Eddy is the man to do it.

Despite the apparent conclusiveness of Byrnes's decision to adopt the Russell plan, the department's internal structure on intelligence matters remained unsettled for many months of 1946. Questions arose about funding, about recruitment, about lines of responsibility, even about office assignments and seating arrangements. Meanwhile, for unrelated reasons, Truman was rapidly becoming disenchanted with Byrnes. The president knew that Byrnes had expected to be chosen as Roosevelt's running mate in 1944 and thus believed that he, rather than Truman, should now be president; Truman thought this attitude showed through in Byrnes's dealings with him, and he thought the secretary was insubordinate.

Byrnes was in effect a lame duck anyway because he had tendered his resignation to Truman in April 1946 over a policy dispute with Henry A. Wallace, the former vice president who was now the Secretary of Commerce, and he remained in office only because the president wanted him to complete work on important postwar treaties. All that summer and fall Acheson, knowing that Byrnes was vulnerable, continued to agitate against the Russell plan, which in his memoir *Present at the Creation* he called "deplorable."

Byrnes finally left on January 21, 1947, to be succeeded by General George C. Marshall. Russell departed the day before Byrnes. Acheson, the most vocal opponent of the Russell plan, became Marshall's senior deputy as Undersecretary of State for Political Affairs. Eddy seized the opportunity. Ten days after Byrnes left, after a round of discussions with colleagues whom protocol required that he consult, Eddy recommended to a receptive Acheson that the Russell plan be scrapped.

"The Research and Intelligence organzation has operated since July 1, 1946, under the 'Russell Plan,'" Eddy's memo said. "The principal feature of that plan is the division between the Special Assistant and the Geographic Offices of authority over the basic research activities of the organization. The effective operation of an intelligence organization under such conditions has proved unworkable and impracticable." He recommended that the "geographic research divisions" be taken back out of the regional policy units and regrouped in a centralized intelligence and analysis staff that would report to him as Special Assistant. With his memo he submitted a proposed staffing chart showing the new setup.

In Washington such a memo often arouses suspicion and invites skepticism because it can be read as one official's effort to grab more power at the expense of others. In this case, however, Eddy knew he was on firm ground because Acheson already agreed with him, and it was clear that Marshall would follow whatever course Acheson recommended.

"General Marshall understood what G-2 was in the Army Staff and needed no long explanation of what should be done," Acheson wrote in his memoirs. "The necessary departmental order was, he directed, to be prepared at once. It went into effect on February 6, centering 'the administration of all research and intelligence units, including the regional research divisions . . . in the Office of the Special Assistant to the Secretary of State.' Thus a year too late my recommendation to Secretary Byrnes was put into effect and his own unhappy action of the preceding April undone."

Thus Eddy and Acheson, by outlasting Russell and Byrnes, created what is today the State Department's well-respected Bureau of Intelligence and Research (INR), a separate unit within the department headed by an assistant secretary of state, who is equal in rank to the assistant secretaries in the geographic bureaus and the functional bureaus such as Democracy, Human Rights and Labor. It is not unusual for the analysts in INR to draw different conclusions from those drawn by their counterparts in the CIA and the military intelligence staffs, and INR has a reputation for being right more often than not, a durable legacy of Eddy's handiwork. On its web site, the State Department gives this description of what INR does: "Drawing on all-source intelligence, [INR] provides value-added independent analysis of events to Department policymakers; ensures that intelligence activities support foreign policy and national security purposes; and serves as the focal point in the Department for ensuring policy review of sensitive counterintelligence and law enforcement activities. INR's primary mission is to harness intelligence to serve U.S. diplomacy."

Eddy himself would have found that language troubling because of the statement that "intelligence activities support foreign policy." He would have preferred "intelligence activities inform foreign policy"—that is, intelligence in whatever form must be policy-neutral as it is gathered, analyzed and disseminated; it must not be modified to comply with policy. The policy should be based on the facts, not the other way around. As the State Department representative in the interagency deliberations over the creation of the Central Intelligence Agency, Eddy was a vigorous and largely successful advocate of this principle, which is why he wanted the director to be a politically independent civilian rather than a military officer.

CONGRESS ACTS

Truman's executive order had created the basic structure of a peacetime intelligence apparatus, but the need for legislative action was clear to all the participants. Without it, General Vandenberg's fledgling organization would have no authority to spend money, and in any case Congress had previously ordered that no agency created by presidential directive alone could operate for more than a year. Therefore the members of the National Intelligence Authority took up the task of drafting legislation that all its members could accept and Truman could forward to Congress for legislative approval. Eddy's job was to craft the State Department's position in these deliberations and advocate it in the interagency process.

Vandenberg wanted legislation that would establish clear lines of authority for his central intelligence group and give it its own budget. The military services argued for retention of their long-established intelligence capabilities. Truman's White House counsel, the legendary Clark Clifford, was finicky about how "intelligence" would be defined in any proposed legislation. In one memorandum to Vandenberg, Clifford complained about "the failure of the [proposed] bill to define in clear terms the sense in which the word 'intelligence' is used. For example, 'intelligence,' 'foreign intelligence,' 'intelligence relating to the national security,' 'strategic and national policy intelligence,' 'the national intelligence mission,' and 'intelligence affecting the national security,' are used indiscriminately as though they were synonymous." Secretary of State Marshall, on Eddy's advice, insisted that the State Department retain the assets it had inherited from the OSS. "The Foreign Service of the Department of State is the only collection agency of the government which covers the whole world," he argued, using language drafted by Eddy, "and we should be very slow to subject the collection and evaluation of this foreign intelligence to other establishments, especially during times of peace."

FDR meets Abdul Aziz—Suez Canal, February 14, 1945.

TOP: *Aboard the U.S.S.* Murphy.
BOTTOM: *Left to right: Admiral Leahy, Col. Eddy, Abdul Aziz and FDR.*

TOP: *ARAMCO's James Terry Duce and Yusuf Yassin—ca. late 1950s.* CENTER: *Parker Hart and Mohammed al-Madhi—ca. late 1950s.* BOTTOM: *Princes Faisal and Khalid—San Francisco, 1943.*

Courtesy of T.C. Barger Collection

TOP LEFT: *Eddy with General Naguib of Egypt—1953.*
TOP RIGHT: *King Saud arrives in Dhahran—1954.*

BOTTOM: *Eddy, at far left, with Lebanese President Bishara al Khouri, at head of table, Premer Riad al Solh, at Khouri's left, and other Lebanese politicians—Sidon, 1947.*

TOP: *U.S. Mission to Yemen—San'a, 1946.*
BOTTOM: *Mary Eddy meets Prince Faisal—1944.*

A neighbor came to Goha and said, "Lend me your donkey for I have to go on a sudden journey." Goha, who had no great confidence in the man's integrity, replied, "I would willingly lend it to you, but alas, yesterday I sold my donkey and have it no more." Just then, the donkey which was in a rear room of the house, set up an interminable and deafening braying. The man said, "but your donkey is here." Goha replied angrily, "If you would take the word of an ass instead of that of a wise man, you are a fool, and I do not wish to ever see you again."

Jest one of The 50 and One Jests of Goha.

TOP: *Eddy Reunion—Hanover, N.H., 1959.*
BOTTOM: *40th Anniversary—Jerusalem, October 16, 1957.*

The personal correspondence in Eddy's papers at Princeton contains little about his work during this time, but the governmental documentary record makes clear that his principal concern in the interagency debate was to protect the integrity of the intelligence—to shield it from political or personal considerations. With the support of Marshall and Acheson, whose public statements and Congressional testimony usually incorporated language drafted for them by Eddy, he clung stubbornly to the view that those making policy should do so on the basis of accurate intelligence, and those gathering the intelligence should do so without regard to policy.

In one notable example, Eddy refused to give Vandenberg access to the State Department's internal policy documents. In a letter to Vandenberg on November 4, 1946, Eddy said, "I am writing in reply to your letter of October 24, 1946, in which you request that the Department of State reconsider its position of not releasing Policy Statements to serve as a basis for intelligence requirements. Our desire to cooperate fully with the Central Intelligence Group has led to a very thorough study of your request. The problem has been taken up on the highest level where the position of the Department has been reaffirmed, namely that it would be unwise for the Department to furnish its Policy Statements to serve as a basis for either Departmental or national intelligence.

"Briefly, the Department's position with regard to its own Policy Statements is that intelligence information should be available to influence Department policy, but that current Department Policy Statements should not be available to influence intelligence information."

This was not a trivial matter. The insulation of intelligence gathering and intelligence evaluation from political manipulation, as Eddy bluntly pointed out, is crucial to intelligence work; the product loses its value if tailored to fit preconceived notions. This fundamental principle of effective intelligence, established by Eddy and his allies at the dawn of the CIA, accounts for the furor that surrounded the use and interpretation of intelligence in the preparations for the U.S. invasion of Iraq in 2003: Did senior officials in the administration of President George W. Bush try to manipulate intelligence about Iraq's weapons in order to justify a policy decision that had already been made?

Eddy knew better than most people about the value to the armed services of their operational intelligence capabilities, and he did not argue that these should be stripped from them. But his concern for the integrity of intelligence led him to argue— successfully—that the peacetime process should be directed by an independent agency and that clandestine activities overseas should be undertaken by civilians working for that agency, not by military personnel. In a memo to Marshall on February 15, 1947, he said that "under-cover intelligence and espionage which should not compromise the official representatives of the United States of America . . . and which involves the employment of unofficial agents, both American and foreign, should be operated by an agency outside the Departments [of State and War] with funds not subject to departmental accounting."

He was less successful in advocating that the post of Director of Central Intelligence should be occupied by a career civilian. He stated his concerns in a memo to Acheson on February 28, 1947, about the possibility that Truman was going to name Rear Admiral Roscoe H. Hillenkoetter to succeed Vandenberg, a general, who himself had succeeded Souers, another admiral.

"The nature of the Central Intelligence Group requires that its director be, as far as possible, untouched by any departmental bias or influence," Eddy wrote. "Under such circumstances a Service director will always and inevitably be torn between absolute objectivity and natural allegiance to his own Service. Continuity and objectivity of leadership can best be assured by a director drawn from civilian ranks and not subject to demand from or allegiance to any single Department."

Given Marshall's military background, Eddy was unlikely to prevail on this point, and he did not; Hillenkoetter, who was supported by Admiral Leahy, got the job. (The senior career people at State favored a lifelong civilian, Allen Dulles, another Princeton graduate and OSS veteran. Dulles eventually became the first civilian director of the CIA when he was appointed to the post in 1953 by President Dwight D. Eisenhower, himself a renowned former general. From Dulles's time until the position of Director of Central Intelligence was abolished in the reorganization of 2006, only two of the fifteen men who held the job were career military officers.)

In April, Acheson was called to represent the State Department at Congressional hearings on the National Security Act and in preparation asked Eddy for a briefing paper on the subject. Eddy's forceful memo is worth quoting in its entirety:

> In connection with the hearings on national intelligence to which you have instructed me to accompany you Monday, April 21, I enclose a copy of the [pending] National Security Act of 1947, wherein Title II, Section 202, sets forth the plan for the Central Intelligence agency, concerning which I submit the following comments:
>
> 1. It is my conviction that the proposals in Title II, Section 202, would render more difficult the promotion of peaceful foreign relations by subordinating the political and economic intelligence activities of the Department of State to a Central Intelligence Agency completely dominated by the Armed Forces; and that it would further have the ultimate, if not the immediate, effect of placing the reporting activities of the Foreign Service under military control in time of peace as well as in time of war.
>
> 2. The National Intelligence Authority would be abolished and replaced by the National Security Council (Section 202 (c) (1)) Whereas the Secretary of State is at present Chairman of the NIA composed of four members, he would be reduced on the National Security Council to an equality with one of the three subdivisions of the Armed Forces establishment, and civilian political intelligence would, therefore, have one representative out of six or more (see Title II, Section 201 (a)).

3. The Central Intelligence Group would be abolished
    and would be replaced by the Central Intelligence
    Agency (Section 202 (c)(2)). This CIA would be
    dominated by the military, with no indication that
    a representative of the Secretary of State would be
    accredited even as an adviser to the new Director of
    Central Intelligence, to whom it is proposed to give
    the salary and prerequisites [sic] of a 4-star general.
    The extended discussion of his right to retain his
    military salary and allowances, together with a sup-
    plement to bring the total to $14,000, makes it quite
    clear that there is an expectation to appoint to this
    elevated office an officer on active duty in the armed
    forces who will serve the primary interests of the five
    military members of the National Security Council
    rather than the civilian and peacetime interests of
    the Department of State.

4. In this connection it should be pointed out that
    the Foreign Service is the only collection agency of
    the U.S. Government which effectively covers the
    world. For every Military or Naval Attaché's office
    abroad, there are dozens of Foreign Service Officers
    and specialists, and for every Embassy or Mission
    with a Military or Naval Attaché there are many
    Consulates General, Consulates or Vice Consul-
    ates with no military or naval staff. It is, therefore,
    clear that at present our Government is served with
    foreign intelligence chiefly by the Foreign Service
    trained to preserve political and economic good
    relations with the rest of the world. Under the pro-
    posed act this world-wide coverage and personnel
    would be forced into the service of the military,
    directly or indirectly, with a consequent damage to
    our peace-time policy that would be difficult to esti-
    mate. The provisions of this act might have merit
    if made effective upon the declaration of war, but
    in time of peace the National Intelligence Service

should be under genuinely civilian control and
its estimates of political and economic situations
abroad should be subject, as at present, to preview
by the Department of State, which has the responsibility for foreign policy.

Acheson and Marshall agreed with Eddy, but the haggling over
these issues went on for many weeks, both within the Truman
administration and between the administration and the Congress.
As can be expected in such a process, the State Deartment prevailed
on some points but not all. The House of Representatives, for example, approved a version of the legislation that would require the
Director of Central Intelligence be appointed "from civilian life."
But the Senate, at the urging of Hillenkoeter, decided the director
could be military or civilian, and this view prevailed in conference.
The law as passed stipulated that the director was to have two deputies; only one of these three top positions could be filled by a career
military officer, whether retired or on active duty.

In the end, the 1947 act was a historic piece of legislation
that created the modern-day defense and intelligence apparatus
of the United States. It created the Central Intelligence Agency
to be the nation's principal spy agency and intelligence clearing-
house, independent of the military. It created the White House
National Security Council, and established the Air Force as a separate branch of the military. It created the position of Secretary
of Defense, although the Defense Department itself came into
existence two years later. The law established on a permanent
basis the position of Director of Central Intelligence and specified that the person in that job was primarily responsible for the
country's intelligence-gathering and espionage activities. (It did
not specifically authorize covert operations of the kind the OSS
had conducted during the war, but neither did it prohibit them
except inside the United States, which was specifically excluded
from the CIA's arena of activity.) It elevated the post occupied by
Eddy to assistant secretary of state, equal in rank to the chiefs of
the geographic bureaus, but left intact the operational intelligence
units of the Armed Forces. The text contained extensive language

intended to ensure that overseas intelligence gathered under the new setup, by whichever agency and by whatever means, would be insulated from self-serving alterations or amendments in the interests of one department or another, and that information be distributed in a timely manner to authorized recipients who might need it—all points on which Eddy had been insistent and on which he had gained the support of Marshall.

After Truman signed the measure into law, it fell to Eddy to instruct the State Department's posts around the world about its implementation and the new procedures, including the need to cooperate with other agencies and the military. Here again, what shows most strikingly in the implementing memo he circulated is his concern for the integrity of the intelligence: "Nothing in this instruction shall be interpreted as authorizing any officer to delay, suppress or make substantive changes in any intelligence report without the concurrence of the officer submitting the report. Intelligence information and material which may have no significance to field representatives in a single area or which may appear to be at complete variance with the overall trend may have great significance and form a definite part of a picture being developed by the Departments or the Central Intelligence Group. Any dissenting opinion or commentary will either be incorporated in the report, or be submitted separately as promptly as possible." In other words, if some U.S. ambassador didn't like what an intelligence officer in his embassy was reporting, he could not quash the reports; he was required to forward them to Washington, with a separate dissenting note if he wished.

The 1947 act was not quite Congress's final word on this subject. The remaining step was to appropriate funds to operate the new system it had created, and from this process the State Department emerged a bureaucratic loser. As recommended by the president's Bureau of the Budget, congressional appropriators took the view that assets should be centralized as much as possible, and thus transferred to the new CIA many of the positions that State had inherited with the breakup of the OSS. Overall, according to the State Department's official history, some 600 positions were shifted, leaving the department "with a skeleton analytic group, thus limiting its mission to providing intelligence support only to the policymakers within the Department of State."

Eddy's rank was now higher, but his dominion much smaller. Government officials hate it when that happens, and Eddy was no exception, but this was not the only cause of his rapid disenchantment with life in the U.S. government.

THE PALESTINE QUESTION

As a senior official of the State Department with extensive experience in the Arab world, Eddy was inevitably drawn during this period into the ferocious argument raging within the Truman administration over the future of Palestine and the fate of Europe's traumatized Jewish survivors. This was, of course, the same issue that brought President Roosevelt and King Abdul Aziz to an impasse in their meeting aboard the *Quincy*, as Eddy knew better than anyone else.

The literature about this issue is voluminous, but in brief it came down to this: after the breakup of the Ottoman Empire, the territory known as Palestine came into the custody of the League of Nations, which gave a mandate to administer it to Britain. This was an obvious choice given Britain's interests and influence in the region, but also a controversial choice because of the Balfour Declaration. By the end of World War II, Britain was ready to surrender the mandate; Palestine had become virtually ungovernable because of the same conflict that plagues the area today: the Jews and the Arabs both wanted it and were prepared to fight for it.

The Jews already in Palestine, prewar Zionist pioneers reinforced by refugees from Nazi-dominated Europe, had taken up guerrilla warfare against the British authorities. (In the most famous incident, the Jewish underground force known as Irgun blew up the King David Hotel in Jerusalem, the site of British headquarters, in July 1946.) Unwilling to accede to postwar Jewish demands for unlimited immigration because of Arab opposition, the British were in an untenable position and were determined to extricate themselves from it. The new United Nations would have to decide what to do with the land, and the position taken by the United States would be crucial, perhaps decisive, in that discussion.

Truman, who had minimal foreign policy experience, was ambivalent. He was under severe and growing pressure from American Jewish groups and Zionist organizations to support creation of a new Jewish state in Palestine. This position was reinforced by the natural tendency of Americans, horrified by revelations about the Holocaust, to sympathize with Jewish refugees who had nowhere to go. The president was a regular guest at gatherings hosted by retired Supreme Court justice Louis D. Brandeis, who was Jewish and pro-Zionist; and the president had close Jewish friends, especially Eddie Jacobson, who had been his partner in a failed Kansas City haberdashery, but he also kept his distance— he did not invite these Jews to his home. He sympathized with the victims of Nazism, but he was disdainful of American political Zionists, whom he regarded as pushy and arrogant. As a U.S. senator he had delivered a few stirring, passionate speeches about the plight of the Jews in Europe, but he did not actually try to do anything about it. After he became the vice presidential nominee in 1944 he, like most American officials, was constrained by the war-first policy: the first and only priority was to win the war and obliterate the Axis, and it would undermine that cause to turn it into a war for or about Jews, which is how Hitler characterized it.

Within the State Department, where the foreign policy professionals worked, and in particular in the Near East bureau, the prevailing view and indeed the entire culture were strongly anti-Zionist and pro-Arab. The diplomats argued that yielding to the Zionists' entreaties would break faith with the Arabs, betray the commitments Roosevelt had made to Abdul Aziz, endanger American econonmic and strategic interests throughout the Middle East, and violate American values by creating a state based on a single religion. These positions were not obviously wrong, and it appears that they were sincerely held—that is, they derived from genuine assessments of American national interests, not from anti-Semitism, although there was plenty of that. But it also appears that these views were nurtured by the peculiarly insular, upper-crust atmosphere of the State Department. Like Eddy, most of the senior career diplomats responsible for Middle Eastern affairs were graduates of elite universities where Jews were scarce, and their social environments did not cater to Jews. They were the Arabists: their careers included long tours of duty in the Middle East, where they cultivated Arab and Turkish friends, and to a large extent they took on the coloration of their environment.

In his seminal study of the State Department in this period, *The Department of State in the Middle East, 1919-1945*, Philip J. Baram examined the backgrounds and biographies of the senior State Department officials who were involved in the Palestine issue and concluded that they were "all career officers of very similar social and intellectual background. When World War II began they were, moreover, in the prime of life, confident of themselves, their values and their understanding of the American national interest in the Middle East. The negative corollary, however, of all this otherwise admirable permanence and esprit de corps was that the men of NEA were all of like mind. Additionally, their collective mindset, despite individual differences in temperament, was already nearly completely and imperviously made up before the war with respect to positions the Department should or should not take on basic Middle Eastern questions."

As Baram noted, the Arabists were generally ignorant or contemptuous of domestic political considerations, which they believed should be excluded from foreign policy. "These men had difficulty coping with American political life," he wrote. "Insulated and inbred, elitist and of the upper middle class, the officers and colleagues of NEA viewed Congress and public opinion in general (and the growing public approval of the idea of a Jewish state in Palestine) with consistent disdain. This negativism toward the American hoi polloi is paradoxical, because abroad . . . the Department was usually beating the drums for anti-imperialism, majority self-rule and other democratic principles. Thus when the Arabs agitated or clamored for some issue or cause, when the sentiment on the 'Arab street' could be discerned, these men tended to accept it as legitimate vox populi. However, if American public opinion seemed to clamor for some object, NEA's instinctive reaction was to turn a politically attentive but deaf ear." The fact that

Jewish votes and Zionist opinion would be important in the 1946 congressional elections and in Truman's probable tough reelection campaign in 1948 was not, in the opinion of the Arabists, sufficient grounds for favoring the Jews over the Arabs.

Moreover, the Arabists and other senior career officials at the State Department were contemptuous of Truman, an ill-educated haberdasher from the hinterlands who had no college degree, let alone one from Princeton or Dartmouth. The department's memos to him in the first months after he succeeded Roosevelt reek of condescension. In one classic example, Edward R. Stettinius, who was secretary of state before Truman gave the job to Byrnes, wrote a memo to Truman on the subject of Palestine just a few days after Truman assumed the presidency. Stettinius warned the president that he could expect pressure from American Zionists to issue a statement of support for their cause and offered this advice: "The question of Palestine is, however, a highly complex one and involves questions which go far beyond the plight of the Jews of Europe. If this question shall come up, therefore, before you in the form of a request to make a public statement on this matter, I believe you would probably want to call for full and detailed information on the subject before taking any particular position"—as if Truman, an experienced politician, would not know enough to do that. Years later Truman, in an interview with the author Merle Miller, referred scornfully to this "communication from the striped-pants boys, warning me . . . in effect telling me to watch my step, that I didn't really understand what was going on over there and I ought to leave it to the experts."

During his tenure in Saudi Arabia and as go-between at President Roosevelt's meeting with Abdul Aziz, Eddy had heard plenty about the subject of Palestine and had formed strong views that were virtually identical to those of the career Arabists in the State Department. He believed that accession to Zionist aspirations, partition of Palestine, and creation of a Jewish state would inflame Arab sentiment against the United States, threaten American oil concessions and other economic interests, open a door to Soviet influence among the Arabs, and lead inevitably to war in the Middle East. As the U.S. envoy in Saudi Arabia he faithfully reported to Washington the passionate views on this subject expressed by King Abduz Aziz and his influential son Prince Faisal, the foreign minister. His memos about the king's sentiments are generally devoid of critical commentary—it is clear that he was not only relaying the opinion of Abdul Aziz and Faisal but that he also agreed with it.

THE AMBASSADORS MEET THE PRESIDENT

In the fall of 1945, while still posted to Jeddah, Eddy had his first opportunity to participate directly in the debate on this subject in Washington. He and three other U.S. envoys to the Arab world were summoned to Washington to brief President Truman on what Eddy called "the deterioration of American political interests in the Near East." The other three were George Wadsworth, minister to Syria; S. Pinckney Tuck, minister to Egypt; and Lowell C. Pinkerton, consul general in Jerusalem. (Even today the U.S. consulate in Jerusalem is in effect the U.S. diplomatic mission to the Palestinians. Diplomatic business with Israel itself is handled through the U.S. embassy, which has remained in Tel Aviv in deference to the Arab position that Jerusalem's status as Israel's capital is still open to negotiation.)

According to Eddy's account, published in 1954, the four diplomats were scheduled to meet with Truman on October 10 but "were kept idle in Washington for four weeks, away from their posts and with no duties whatsoever, because the White House advisors, including David K. Niles, persuaded the president that it would be impolitic to see his Ministers to Arab countries, no matter how briefly, prior to the November Congressional elections." In that assertion Eddy was uncharacteristically wrong about the facts; there were no congressional elections in 1945. The only election in which the Palestine question could possibly have been a factor was the mayoral election in New York. It is true, however, that the president did not see them until November 10, after that election was over. (The Democrat won.)

In preparation for the meeting with Truman, Eddy sent a memo on October 26 to Loy Henderson, then chief of the State

Department's Near East bureau. It is worth quoting in its entirely because it conveys Eddy's view on the Palestine question in the style he favored: he reports that he is relaying the views of the King and senior princes, but by doing so without any dissenting notes or critical commentary, he makes clear that he shares the opinions he is reporting.

> I wish to reaffirm in writing the adverse effect on United States interests in Saudi Arabia caused by the uncertainty of U.S. policy regarding Palestine, a subject on which I have heard the King speak frequently, and as recently as October 2, 1945.
>
> 1. The Saudi Arabian Government cannot reconcile the promise of prior consultation with Arabs and [the] reported proposal by the United States that 100,000 Jews should be admitted to Palestine now without prior consultation. I was given definitely to understand on October 2 that any such decision effected without participation by Arab leaders would constitute definite proof to the Saudi Arabian Government that the Government of the United States in its policy regarding Palestine is neither consistent nor friendly to the Arabs.
>
> 2. The Saudi Arabian Government believes that the publication of the letter from President Roosevelt to the King dated April 5, 1945 [in which the "full consultation" pledge delivered aboard the Quincy was reaffirmed in writing] would clarify U.S. policy and put an end to the Zionist demand for unilateral action. If unilateral action should nevertheless take place to affect the basic situation in Palestine, we shall be accused of bad faith, and our prestige with the Saudi Arabian Government will be liquidated. The King believes that the independence and survival of the Arab state of Palestine is a more legitimate concern of the surrounding Arab countries in the Near East than it is of Americans 5,000 miles

away, whether those Americans are Jew or Gentile,
and he consequently is determined that the Arab
Governments shall have not less but more to say
about the future of Palestine than Zionists living at
a great distance.

3.   If the growing suspicion should be confirmed that
the U.S. government is flirting with a Palestine policy friendly to political Zionism and therefore (in
Arab opinion) hostile to the Arabs, United States
enterprises in Saudi Arabia will be seriously handi-
capped. For example, our military airfield at Dhahran and its military personnel, whose presence
is suspect in any case by the more fanatic Arabs,
would appear increasingly to constitute a base for
political aggression and foreign occupation. While
the King has never mentioned to me the possibility of sanctions against the Arabian-American oil
concession (which has been rumored in the press)
he has stated that he will never permit any airplane
carrying a Zionist to Palestine to land in Saudi Arabia. The Deputy Foreign Minister has also intimated
to me unofficially that the King would not agree
to have the oil from his country carried in a pipeline which terminates in Jewish controlled areas,
thereby making his country contribute to the livelihood and prosperity of Zionists. These small straws
in the wind are indications of the attitude which
the Saudi Arabian government may be expected to
take in the event of any pro-Zionist move by the
United States government.

4.   The Saudi Arabian government takes the position
that Palestine is protected by the United Nations
Charter in the right to have its future settled by
international agreement. It is certain that they
expect consultation with Arabs to precede any set-
tlement of the future of Palestine, and unless such

consultation takes place in the very near future the
political climate of Saudi Arabia may well prove
hostile to United States interests.

Note that he raises a straw man of alarm: the possibility that
the King would revoke the ARAMCO concession. It was true that
this was ARAMCO's great fear, and that Eddy heard about it all
the time while he was in Saudi Arabia, but as his memo notes
the King had made no such threat—it had been "rumored in the
press." Unless Eddy knew that those rumors had been planted by
the King or Prince Faisal, this was duplicitous—one of the few
times in Eddy's life that such a thing could be said about him, and
a measure of the personal urgency he felt about this issue.

Henderson sent a note to Brigadier General H.H. Vaughan,
President Truman's military adviser, in which he offered "a little
background information which might be helpful" to the president
when he finally met with the four envoys. He said that Eddy and
his colleagues were anxious to know the direction that U.S. policy
in the region would follow now that the war was over. Henderson said the Arabs were disappointed and disillusioned when the
United States failed to stay engaged in the region after the first war
and left the Arabs to the machinations of France and Britain. Since
1939, Henderson informed Vaughan, the United States had been
developing a new policy of promoting independence for the countries of the region, "supporting them in their refusal to accord
a special position to any foreign power or any group of foreign
powers. . . . It is clear that during the next few years the people of
the Near East will move forward rapidly politically, economically
and socially, and it is felt that it is important that this movement
should be in the direction of Western democracies rather than
in the direction of some form of autocracy or totalitarianism . . .
We have been supporting the policy of the open door in the Near
East with regard to investments and commerce." This note too
reflected the arrogance of the State Department's attitude about
Truman—as if the president and his advisers had no idea what
U.S. policy had been since 1939, as if Vaughan would not ask for a
briefing if he or the president felt it necessary.

When they finally met the president, the four envoys designated Wadsworth, a career diplomat and a committed anti-Zionist, to do the talking.

Wadsworth was a prototypical diplomatic "Arabist" of the breed Truman found irritating. A graduate of Union College, he taught at the American University of Beirut during World War I. Joining the U.S. Foreign Service after the war, he rose to become ambassador to Syria, Saudi Arabia, Iraq, Yemen and Turkey. His great passion in life was golf; throughout his career he raised money to create golf courses in the Middle East.

No transcript of the envoys' meeting with the president exists, but the State Department prepared a "summary of remarks." It says Wadsworth began by telling Truman, "We believe the countries of the Arab world, especially if taken as a whole, will warrant a more important place in our positive postwar foreign-policy thinking than is normally given them as a simple counterpoise to Zionist ambitions or because they lie at the strategic center of the British Empire or because they happen to contain the two cradles of civilization and the greatest known undeveloped oil resources of the world. All these we feel are important, but to us it seems vital to recognize that the whole Arab world is in ferment, that its peoples are on the threshold of a new renaissance, that each one of them wants forthrightly to run its own show, as the countries of the Western Hemisphere run theirs, without imperialistic interference, be it British or French, in their internal affairs."

"I know that," the president interjected. Undeterred, Wadsworth rolled on.

"Our moral leadership is recognized today," he said. "The governments to which we are accredited want most of all to know whether we are going to implement that leadership, whether we are going to follow through after our great victory or leave the field, as we did at the end of the last war, to others. In the latter event, the governments to which we are accredited know from bitter experience and present trends that Britain and France will make every effort to consolidate their pre-war spheres of influence; they look specially to us to support them in their efforts to block any such development. If the United States fails them, they will turn to Russia and will be lost to our civilization; of that we feel certain."

Any Arab who knew how to read would have laughed at the idea that the Arabs could be "lost to our civilization," as if they were people with no civilization of their own who needed some outside civilization to which they could attach themselves. But in fairness to Wadsworth, Eddy and their colleagues, they truly believed that the Arab people, as they gained independence, would face a choice of external loyalties and that it would be far preferable for them to align themselves with the United States than with the looming great rival, the Soviet Union. Wadsworth's phrasing was infelicitous, but he believed what he was saying. A few years later, Eddy would reveal a vision grander still of U.S.-Arab relations.

Wadsworth said the heads of state in the envoys' respective capitals had turned to the American diplomats as friends and counselors, and wanted them to return from Washington bearing honest advice and straightforward answers to four questions:

1. Is the United States prepared to sign with the newly independent Arab states the "standard treaty of friendship and commerce" that it had with other countries?

2. Will their requests for technical assistance be considered favorably?

3. Will the president be prepared to receive the king of Egypt and the presidents of Syria and Lebanon as he had received Prince Faisal of Saudi Arabia?

4. What is the American policy toward "political Zionism"?

According to the State Department summary of the conversation, the envoys did not presume to recommend to Truman what the answer to question four should be, but given all that had gone before he could have had no doubt about their opinion. The president answered the questions in order. To the first, "You may tell them that." To the second, "You may tell them that too." To the third, "Yes." But when he got to question four, "the President smiled and said, 'That IS the sixty-four dollar question.' He said

it is the kind of question that he simply couldn't answer at the present time. The question had been causing him and Mr. Byrnes more trouble than almost any other question which is facing the United States."

When the envoys said the Arabs feared they would be blind-sided by some proposal about which they had not been briefed, "The President replied that both President Roosevelt and he had given assurances that the Palestine problem would not be disposed of without full prior consultation. He added that, of course, the final solution might not be agreeable to everybody, but that at least all would have an opportunity to state their side of the case."

Truman was nobody's fool. He immediately grasped what the Arabs and their advocates in the American diplomatic corps did not: that Roosevelt's promise of "consultation" was empty because in the end a decision would have to be made and one side or the other would not like it. It was not a promise to give either side what it wanted. Consultations, like a trial in a courtroom, would come to an end and a verdict would be issued; one side would win, the other would lose. Jews would flood into Palestine and achieve their Zionist dream, or they would be largely excluded from Palestine and the Arabs would have it. Truman suggested that allowing more Jewish refugees to migrate to the Holy Land without reference to the question of sovereignty would alleviate the humanitarian crisis in Europe, but at this point he offered no political solution. His inability to devise a compromise that both sides would accept was no reflection on him; sixty years and many presidents later, that compromise has still not been found.

The State Department record of this meeting ends with a prediction from the president that Palestine would be an issue in the 1948 presidential election campaign because it would not be resolved in the two intervening years. Eddy, in a brief postscript written several years later, said Truman had one last comment as the session ended: "I'm sorry, gentlemen, but I have to answer to hundreds of thousands who are anxious for the success of Zionism; I do not have hundreds of thousands of Arabs among my constituents."

That quotation has entered diplomatic lore, and has appeared in many books and articles over the past half century, but Eddy's brief narrative appears to be the only source for it; no one else who was present recorded it. It was obviously true, but whether the president actually said it or it reflects Eddy's thoughts about his attitude is an open question. According to Evan M. Wilson, who was the State Department's Palestine "desk officer" for most of the 1940s, "Truman kept on his desk for a whole year the pro forma resignation of these same envoys, before deciding to continue them in office." There was no point in accepting the resignations. Had these envoys been replaced by other Middle East experts from the State Department, these new men would have had the same attitude, as Truman knew perfectly well.

If Eddy's account of the White House session is accurate, the anguished public and private debate about Palestine throughout 1946 and 1947 meant little because the president had made up his mind two years before the United Nations General Assembly took up the matter. As far as the public knew, Truman was caught between the irresistible force of Jewish demands and humanitarian impulses and the immovable object represented by Arab opposition, and would not finally make up his mind until the virtual eve of the U.N. General Assembly's vote in November 1947.

Throughout his tenure in Jeddah, Eddy sent messages to Washington saying that King Abdul Aziz and other Arab leaders were inflexibly opposed to Jewish immigration into Palestine, let alone the creation of a Jewish state, and making clear that he agreed with them. Thus Eddy's views about the Palestine question were well known within the State Department when he took up his intelligence post in Washington in the summer of 1946, several months after the four envoys' meeting with the president. He fit right in with the State Department climate of opinion.

"Eddy was probably the closest thing the United States had to a Lawrence of Arabia," Philip Baram wrote. "He was *the* great and personal friend of the Arabs and expressed their point of view, especially Ibn Saud's, with unceasing advocacy, the premise being of course that American and Arab interests were one and the same."

The subject of Palestine was not part of his official portfolio of duties, but in the State Department of that era there was no escaping it. Within Truman's administration, it was the State

Department and the newly formed Central Intelligence Agency where the relatively few Americans opposed to the creation of Israel found a sympathetic response.

When some prominent Jews such as Lessing Rosenwald, chairman of Sears Roebuck & Co., and *New York Times* publisher Arthur Hays Sulzberger opposed the creation of a Jewish state because they feared an anti-Semitic backlash in the United States, the State Department encouraged them to organize and to take a public position, which they did with the formation of the anti-Zionist American Jewish Committee and the American Council for Judaism (ACJ). As the historian Michael Cohen wrote, "For State, these two groups were useful because the department could argue that the Zionists did not speak for all American Jews; it was respectable, and not anti-Semitic, to oppose creation of a Jewish state."

The ACJ's point man on this subject was George J. Levison, member of a prominent German Jewish family in San Francisco, whose contacts in the State Department and the intelligence community illustrate how the web of like-minded officials interacted and supported each other. During the war Levison had been posted to Cairo, where he shared an apartment with Kermit Roosevelt, grandson of Theodore, who was an architect of the OSS and after the war became a Middle East specialist at the CIA. From his time in government service, Levison also became friendly with Acheson and Henderson. Thus when Levison went to Washington in February 1947, he was received at State by Acheson, Henderson, Roosevelt and Eddy. According to the definitive account by Thomas A. Kolsky, "they not only expressed respect for the Council's work but also gave him the impression that constructive suggestions from the ACJ would receive sympathetic consideration."

The State Department thrashed about here and there, looking for alternatives to Zionism and a Jewish state. One senior department official proposed sending the refugees to Angola; another favored repatriation to a Europe purged of anti-Semitism. These improbable ideas were not much different from the idea President Roosevelt had floated aboard the *Quincy* of resettling the Jews in Libya. By this time, however, the tide of public opinion in the United States was running irreversibly in favor of the Zionist program. Revelations of the full scale of the atrocities perpetrated against the Jews during the war, news accounts of the desperation of the survivors, the natural tendency of Americans to root for the underdog, skillful lobbying by American Zionists and the absence of Arabs from the American political scene combined to decide the issue, just as Eddy had told King Abdul Aziz they would. (Virtually the only person of any stature outside the State Department, the military, and the CIA arguing for the Arab side in the U.S. deliberations was James Terry Duce, the Washington representative of ARAMCO. He and other oil industry lobbyists, who all favored the Arab side for obvious reasons, were always welcome at the State Department and especially in Eddy's office.)

TRUMAN'S FRUSTRATION

By the summer of 1947 Truman was fed up with both sides and frustrated by the inability of all parties—American, British and Arab—to devise a workable compromise. He had sought a middle ground by asking for the immediate admission of 100,000 Jewish refugees to Palestine, far above the number permitted by the British, without committing himself as to Palestine's sovereignty or political future. Like all other proposals of the time, this satisfied nobody, leaving Truman with the same quandary he had faced since he assumed the presidency. Now he essentially took the easy way out. He sided with the people who could vote for him, the people who had the sympathy of the world in their favor, the people who had persuasive advocates inside the White House—and the people who showed just enough flexibility to merit his consideration. These were the international Zionists, who dropped their demand for a Jewish state in the whole of Palestine and agreed to accept partition, in which part of Palestine would be given to the Jews, the rest to the Arabs. The Arabs, by clinging to their absolutist position and refusing to yield any land to the Zionists, forfeited the political high ground, to their lasting detriment. The idea of partition was developed as a possible compromise that would resolve the issue without conflict, but it failed to gain any traction with the Arabs, not just in Palestine but in the rest of the region as well.

As the time of decision neared, the atmosphere was inflamed, and American public opinion aroused on the side of the refugee Jews, by the *Exodus* affair. As the State Department's Evan Wilson recounted it in his detailed book about the Palestine deliberations, "The already tense situation was made worse by the incident of the S.S. *Exodus*, a former Chesapeake Bay excursion steamer which, greatly overloaded, took off at this time from a port in France with a shipload of illegal immigrants [that is, Jews who were outside the narrow immigration quotas set by Britain] bound for Palestine. The ship was intercepted by the British and sent back to France, where the authorities were willing to allow the passengers to disembark, but they refused. Eventually the British forcibly transported the refugees to camps in Germany, an action which was almost universally condemned in world opinion."

On August 31, 1947, a United Nations Special Committee on Palestine (UNSCOP), assigned to devise a solution, issued its report, which was made public the next day. The members recommended unanimously that the British mandate be terminated and that an independent federal state of Palestine be created. A majority of eight members—Australia, Canada, Czechoslovakia, Guatemala, the Netherlands, Peru, Sweden, and Uruguay—recommended partition into Jewish and Arab sectors, politically separate entities to be joined in an economic union: "political division and economic unity," they called it, in which Jews and Arabs would live separately, each community ruling itself but joined economically because neither would be viable without the other. Jerusalem would be an international city, its Christian, Jewish and Muslim holy sites open to worshippers of all faiths. The other three UNSCOP members, Iran, Yugoslavia and India, recommended instead a unitary federated state.

In either case, the majority report said, "It cannot be contemplated that Palestine is to be considered in any sense as a means of solving the problem of world Jewry. In direct and effective opposition to any such suggestion are the twin factors of limited area and resources and vigorous and persistent opposition of the Arab people, who constitute the majority population of the country." Nevertheless, it was obvious that the politically sovereign Jewish entity to be created would be able to make its own decisions on this crucial matter.

At that point even Evan Wilson, who was one of the State Department's earliest and most forceful opponents of partition and creation of a Jewish state, threw in the towel. "We should, of course, make it clear to the Arabs that we fully understand their point of view," he wrote in a memo to colleagues. "But we should seek, not to make the Arabs think that we are backing both sides at once—which is impossible—but rather to explain the humanitarian reasons which impel us to give our support to Jewish aspirations and the advantages which in the long run can accrue to the people not only of Palestine but of the whole Near East, from the continuing development of the Jewish National Home."

Eddy did not give up so easily. On September 15 he sent to Loy Henderson his "comment on the UNSCOP report."

The crucial issue is not immigration as stated in the report," he wrote. "Palestine has admitted 600,000 Jews, a number which could be 400 or 800 thousand without decisive effect on the political future. The crucial issues are two:

1. Whether there shall be a theocratic, racial Zionist state.

2. Whether there shall be areas of self-determination, and an end to outside pressure and artificial economy.

   I. The Minority report is probably workable, if the principal Arab centers of population are included in the Arab province.

   II. The Majority report is impossible of fulfillment.

      (1.) The Zionist state would be incapable of self-defense. Its indefensible and unprotected frontiers have already been rejected by the revisionists.

      (2.) The Zionist state would not satisfy political Zionists and would not satisfy the humanitarian desire of those who seek a Palestine refuge for many hundreds of thousands of

displaced Jews. It would thus solve nothing and would only intensify support for Zionist expansion.

(3.) The Arab State would not be viable. A visit to the 'ports' of Acre and Gaza will illustrate the point.

III. The Majority report will damage U.S. interest and leadership.

(1.) It is contrary to the U.S. example of non-clerical political democracy, without prejudice to race or creed. It is an endorsement of a theocratic sovereign state characteristic of the Dark Ages.

(2.) It will alienate from the U.S. the goodwill of the Arab and Moslem world, with repercussions that would reach to India and Pakistan. In this respect, the issue is more crucial than Greece, whose neighbors are already hostile to the U.S.

(3.) The Arab League will promptly align itself with Russia for survival, as we found it expedient to do from 1942-45. This, I regard as a certain effect of our support of the minority report. We might, therefore, find ourselves involved in police measures, or military operations in a hostile area not now hostile to the U.S.

A few days later, Henderson incorporated Eddy's arguments in a memo to Secretary Marshall, adding that "We are under no obligation to the Jews to set up a Jewish state."

Like so many documents churned out by the Arabists at the State Department, Eddy's memo to Henderson—who already agreed with what Eddy was telling him—was a mixture of accurate assessment and baffling wrongheadedness. It would turn out to be true that partition of Palestine would be a source of trouble in the region for decades to come and stoke Arab anger at the United States. It was true that at least some Zionists would not be satisfied with the territory assigned to the Jews by the United Nations and would seek to create a "Greater Israel," as they do even today. It was true that the Soviet Union would seek influence among the Arabs by trying to capitalize on their anger at the United States, Britain and the United Nations. And it was true that creation of a "theocratic, racial Zionist state" would be contrary to American ideals and principles.

But Eddy and his colleagues, in writing such memos, exposed their ignorance of Jews and Zionism. Zionism was more a political movement than a religious one, and many of its most influential leaders were secular Jews who had no intention of creating a theocracy. Moreover, the Jews who were fighting in Palestine and the Jews who survived the Holocaust in Europe were transformed people. They were determined never again to be victims. They would fight ruthlessly in and for the Holy Land as the Jews of Europe had never fought against their oppressors. The idea that "the Zionist state would be incapable of self-defense" would have seemed risible to the Irgun. It was true, as Eddy said, that the new Jewish entity proposed by UNSCOP would not have "defensible borders." That very issue is still part of the argument about Israel and Palestine sixty years later. But Eddy and the other Arabists vastly overestimated the fighting qualities of the Arab armies. That tiny, ill-armed Israel would expose the Arabs' militant bombast as empty threats within a year after Israel was created seems never to have occurred to the Arabs' friends in Washington.

All these defects of American analysis and more appeared in one of the first major intelligence assessments to come out of the newly created CIA. Titled "The Consequences of the Partition of Palestine," this secret 17-page document was distributed in numbered copies to a small group of authorized recipients on November 28, 1947, the very eve of the decisive United Nations vote on the UNSCOP report. The authors were not named, but the report had Eddy's fingerprints all over it: a footnote said the report had been "coordinated with the intelligence organizations of the

Departments of State, Army, Navy and Air Force," and Eddy was the State Department's chief intelligence officer while it was being drafted.

It predicted, correctly, that "Armed hostilities between Jews and Arabs will break out if the UN General Assembly accepts the plan to partition Palestine into Jewish and Arab States as recommended by the UN Special Committee on Palestine." After that, however, the CIA report went astray in the same way as Eddy had in his memo to Henderson.

The Zionists, it said, "are determined to have a state in Palestine or, in the view of extreme elements, all of Palestine and Transjordan as well. Whatever the UN recommends, they will attempt to establish a Jewish state after the British withdrawal (now set by the British for August 1948). The Jews are expected to be able to mobilize some 200,000 fighters in Palestine, supplemented to a limited extent by volunteers and recruits from abroad. The Jewish armed groups in Palestine are well equipped and well trained in commando tactics. Initially, they will achieve marked success over the Arabs because of superior organization and equipment." Up to this point, the CIA had it right. However, the report then went on to say that "As the war of attrition develop . . . the Jewish economy (severely constrained by mobilization) will break down; furthermore, the Jews will be unable continuously to protect their extended supply lines and isolated settlements or to plant and cultivate their fields in the face of constant harassing, 'hit and run' Arab attacks. Without substantial outside aid in terms of manpower and material, they will be able to hold out no longer than two years." The projection, like all the projections emanating from the U.S. government's experts at the time, understimated the military prowess and economic ingenuity of the Jews, as well as their ability to obtain money and weapons from sources all over the world, and greatly overestimated the warfighting skill and staying power of the Arabs.

On the political front, the CIA reported that "The US, by supporting partition, has already lost much of its prestige in the Near East. In the event that partition is imposed on Palestine, the resulting conflict will seriously disturb the social, economic, and political stability of the Arab world, and US commercial and strategic interests will be dangerously jeopardized. While irresponsible tribesmen and fanatic Moslems are haphazardly blowing up parts of the oil pipelines and attacking occasional Americans, it is possible that responsible government will refuse to sign pipeline conventions, oil concessions, civil air agreements, and trade pacts."

The great irony of this projection is that while many of those negative consequences the CIA foresaw are occurring today, hardly any of them happened in the immediate aftermath of the creation of Israel, to a great extent because of Eddy's diligent, successful cultivation of King Abdul Aziz. The King, and even more Prince Faisal, hated the very idea of Israel and felt that Truman had misled them, but by 1948 they had set their country on the course of economic and political alignment with the United States and there was no going back. As the CIA noted, the Saudis as early as 1945 had taken the public position that ARAMCO, as a private company, should not be penalized for actions of the U.S. government.

The CIA's gloomy report had no effect on the outcome of the UN vote because it was secret and hardly anyone had read it by the time of the balloting. The day after its limited distribution, the United Nations General Assembly voted in favor of partition by 33 to 10, with 10 abstentions, including Britain. The British Mandate was to be terminated and the partition was to become effective the following summer. The Jewish zone was to consist of approximately 53 percent of the total area of the Palestine Mandate.

By the time of the vote Eddy was no longer at the State Department. His resignation was effective on October 1, 1947. In a letter to friends nine days later, he said he was leaving because of the reductions ordered by Congress in his intelligence bureau staff. "While I have enjoyed government service," he wrote, "the particular work in which I was engaged lost much of its interest last June when its budget was cut in half by Congress which refused the funds requested by the Secretary of State to operate the full program of research and intelligence inherited by the Department of State from the wartime Office of Strategic Services." His letter said nothing about Palestine, but members of his family have long believed, and some historians have written, that Truman's endorsement of partition was the real reason for Eddy's departure.

"He was too much of loyalist" to commit his objections to writing, said Eddy's nephew Ray Close. "It was the family's understanding that it was because of Palestine," even if he made no public statement to that effect; going public would not have been his style, Close said.

"There was a guy at the White House named David Niles, who blocked every single memo that Dad wrote to Truman," recalled Eddy's daughter, Mary Furman. "He wasn't going to let any Arab point of view come across. Dad wasn't having any effect. He left because he was having absolutely no impact. When he took the job he hoped to have some kind of influence, and he was having absolutely no impact because David Niles was blocking all his memos to the president." She said her father was "just spinnng his wheels. Of course, Truman was right that he didn't have any Arab voters."

Having worked at the State Department herself, Mary Furman must have known that executive branch officials of Eddy's rank—assistant secretary—do not write memos directly to the president. They write to undersecretaries of state, who may or may not forward their comments to the secretary, who in turn may or may not forward them to the White House. And even if the secretary does send comments to the White House, those memos are transmitted over the secretary's signature, not that of some lesser official. Nevertheless, historians such as Philip Baram have accepted it as true that Eddy resigned not over budget matters but because of the Palestine issue.

The same motivation, of course, had been offered as the reason for his abrupt departure from his post in Saudi Arabia. In this case as in that one, the documentary record does not support it. But if Eddy did in fact quit over the Palestine issue, he was one of only two prominent officials to do so. The other was William Yale, who had been a member of the Interdivisional Area Committee on Arab Studies that the Department set up during the war. Loy Henderson went off to newly independent India as ambassador. Secretary Marshall is reputed to have told Truman he would not vote for him in 1948 but believed it was his soldier's duty not to resign. The rest of the Arabists swallowed hard and went on with their work—trying, as they saw it, to minimize the damage.

At about the time of Eddy's resignation, Clark Clifford sent Truman a memo noting that in all the presidential elections since 1876, only Woodrow Wilson in 1916 had won the presidency without carrying New York. In 1948 Truman—despite his decison on Palestine—would become the second. He failed to carry New York, Pennsylvania, New Jersey, Connecticut or Maryland, all states in which the Jewish vote was thought to be crucial. His strength in Texas and the west, where the Jewish population was much smaller, carried him to victory.

Chapter 9

BEIRUT

*I*n late February 1948, ARAMCO officials gave extensive interviews to Robert Miller, a correspondent of the United Press news service who was visiting Dhahran. This was in the frantic period after the United Nations General Assembly voted to partition Palestine into Arab and Jewish sectors, but before the partition actually took place. The Truman administration had engineered the UN vote, but now the White House was waffling again. Palestine was in turmoil. ARAMCO and its allies in Washington were making a final effort to stave off partition and prevent the creation of a Jewish state in the Arab heartland.

The article Miller wrote said that ARAMCO's parent companies—Chevron, Standard Oil of New Jersey (Exxon), Texaco and Mobil—were planning to spend $500 million to expand operations in Saudi Arabia.

"Despite increasing anti-U.S. sentiment throughout the Middle East because of the U.S. stand on Palestine partition," Miller wrote, "King Ibn Saud of Saudi Arabia has quietly assured ARAMCO that it will not be ousted, [company] officials said. . . . In return for Ibn Saud's continued friendship, the officials added, ARAMCO has redoubled its lobbying efforts in Washington to convince the government that support of partition might force abandonment of this project, potentially the greatest American investment in any foreign country.

"Col. William Eddy, former Middle Eastern expert in the State Department, has been retained by the company to present its case and the public relations budget has been increased, they said."

The story went on to say that more than two thousand Americans already worked in the Saudi oil fields and more were arriving every day as the company increased production and found new fields. "Company officials are confident they are capable of making the area the richest oil-producing zone in the world if the Saudi Arabians don't expropriate the properties and oust the company in revenge for the U.S. pro-Zionist position," the article concluded.

The information that ARAMCO gave Miller was transparently self-serving, conveying as it did the supposed threat to the Saudi Arabia concession posed by the Palestine issue, but the information about the expanded investment was news nevertheless and many newspapers in the United States printed the article. None gave it more prominent display than *PM*, a left-wing New York daily, which put it at the top of its front page under the headline "Oil Investments vs. Human Lives in Palestine." It was accompanied by a reference line asking readers to look at an editorial on the subject on the paper's opinion page.

> ARAMCO has redoubled its efforts . . . to convince Washington that support of partition might force abandonment of the company's projected half-billion dollar pipeline and oil development plan for Saudi Arabia and the Middle East.
>
> The ARAMCO officials [cited in the United Press article] introduce their candidate for the unofficial American Secretary

of State, designer of American foreign policy: their own Col. William Eddy, appointed to convince Washington that a half-billion dollar investment is worth more than [the] UN, worth more than five million dead Jews, worth more than any number of live ones.

The ARAMCO officials advanced their suggestion for America's unofficial Capitol: oil company headquarters at Dhahran in Saudi Arabia, where experts weigh the world's welfare in terms of profits per barrel and dole out policy in gallons.

Col. Eddy is finding—or if he's not there yet will find—the Washington climate salubrious.

Like him, and the Standard people and the Texaco people he represents, Washington, too, is interested in brimming wells, golden wells, wells deep and black and inexhaustible, richer than Fort Knox, even more marketable than Treasury notes. They are not wells of compassion.

Eddy found this commentary distasteful, and not only because of the content; he detested publicity and as far as the documentary file shows never gave an on-the-record press interview. At one point he even used his CIA connections to quash a profile of him that *Time* magazine was planning. "I have just been shown the attack on me in *PM* of February 27," Eddy wrote home from Beirut on March 3. "The story on oil mentions me but the editorial is a real attack. I am sorry as I had hoped to succeed in keeping my name out of print, but I have nothing to be ashamed of." Mary Eddy acknowledged that the *PM* editorial stung her husband, but said it was no more than one would expect from a pro-Zionist tabloid. As for the United Press news article, everything it reported was true.

The United Nations General Assembly voted to partition Palestine on November 29, 1947, but it had been apparent for some months that such would be the outcome unless the anti-partition forces could fend it off. Those forces of course included the oil companies doing business with the Arabs, which hired people who had good connections to government policymakers and were able to work to influence official policy. There was nothing sinister or illegal about this; it was how Washington worked then and how it works today. Corporations, like other organizations, do what they can to influence government policy along lines favorable to them. In this case, the foes of partition did not have much time: the General Assembly resolution specified that partition was to occur no later than August 1, 1948, but the British wanted to be out by spring.

As the historian Michael J. Cohen put it, "Eddy was arguably the most prominent of a small circle of American officials who went straight from government service into lucrative senior positions with ARAMCO. . . . In contrast to the high-profile, media-oriented Zionist lobby, former government officials such as Eddy, with all the right social credentials and entrees, served as a discreet, behind-the-scenes, yet no less powerful oil lobby. Unlike the Zionists, they enjoyed direct, easy access to the very highest power echelons in Washington." That is to say, Eddy and his colleagues and their allies in the State Department and the CIA had social ties from their days at Princeton, Dartmouth and Yale, while the Zionists were guys from Brooklyn College and CCNY who were not members of fancy country clubs but excelled at political street fighting. At the time it would have been unnecessary, as well as rude, to specify that most of the former were mainstream establishment Protestants and most of the latter were Jews from immigrant families. The oil companies' field hands may have been Texas roughnecks, but their Washington agents and allies were bluebloods.

If *PM*'s editorial writer had made a few phone calls, he could have ascertained that Eddy was already working in Washington; indeed, he had never left. Almost immediately upon resigning from the State Department, he began his new life as a "consultant" to ARAMCO, living in the house on Carvel Road but traveling frequently to the Middle East. He was dispatched to the region in October, where he met with the leaders of Syria, Lebanon and Saudi Arabia. Naturally he had long conversations with King Abdul Aziz, which he described in a letter to Mary written from the King's palace in Riyadh on October 27, 1947, a month before the U.N. vote.

"He asked right away about both you and Carmen and hoped you are both in good health," he reported. "I was really not prepared to find him so very friendly. I think he takes my leaving the

State Department and returning with ARAMCO as a proof of my real attachment to his land and race, as indeed it is. He was much more informal and confidential with me than he had ever been while I was minister." The king told him that in the absence of Prince Faisal, who was away, "I trust you as one of my own sons."

Two days later, Eddy reported on his talks with the King in a "personal and confidential" memo to his ARAMCO bosses. On behalf of James Terry Duce, ARAMCO's senior representative in Washington, Eddy gave Abdul Aziz a bound book of press clippings about the recent U.S. visit of Crown Prince Saud, complete with Arabic translations. Then, Eddy reported, this exchange ensued:

> Question from the King: Do you bring any news from ARAMCO?
>
> Answer: No, I just joined the company and this is a personal visit to pay my respects.
>
> Question: Do you have any government role? Are you a channel by which I can reach U.S. officials?
>
> Answer: No. I have no government role. [I told him] he should communicate with the U.S. government through diplomats now accredited to Saudi Arabia.

This may have been literally true in the sense that Eddy was on the payroll of ARAMCO, not the U.S. government, but it was not the whole truth, because throughout his years with ARAMCO he reported regularly to the CIA, where he had been present at the creation and was a trusted informant, about Arab politics and personalities. One reason he shunned publicity, his daughter Mary recalled, was that "even when he was with ARAMCO, the minute he got back to the country he reported to the CIA. And I think he didn't want anything to jeopardize the anonymity of what he did with the CIA."

David Dodge, a prominent descendant of missionary pioneers who knew the Eddys well, said, "I don't think there was any kind of formal relationship with the CIA, not to my knowledge. He had informal relationships." And according to Eddy's nephew Ray Close, a longtime CIA station chief in Saudi Arabia, "He never spent five minutes in Washington as a member of the staff of the agency. He was a friend of [CIA director] Allen Dulles's on a personal basis."

As those comments indicate, it is not clear whether Eddy's relationship with the CIA in this post-State Department period ever went beyond the informal. The biographical sketch posted with the information about his papers at Princeton's library says that after the Yemen mission, "he served in the OSS and CIA for the remainder of his life, and was also a full-time consultant for the Arabian-American Oil Company." It certainly was not unusual in that era for the agency to dispatch full-time operatives into the field disguised as businessmen or diplomats, but it was also common for these CIA agents and their superiors in Washington to cultivate unofficial networks of well-informed individuals who were not government employees but shared information with the CIA for reasons of their own, including a sense of patriotic duty. Eddy appears to have been in the latter category, but there were occasions during his post-government career when he took on more of an operational role, as will be seen from his part in a notorious episode involving the Greek shipping magnate Aristotle Onassis.

GETTING IT WRONG

After that initial Middle East tour as an employee of ARAMCO, in late October and early November 1947, Eddy returned to Washington to report his findings, not only to ARAMCO but to his contacts in the Truman administration. Not surprisingly, his assessment of what would happen in the event of partition was, to put it mildly, pessimistic. That is not to say that he distorted or misrepresented the information he received; he faithfully relayed to Washington what his many Arab interlocutors told him. But virtually everyone in the government's foreign policy, national security and intelligence organizations already knew what the

Arabs thought, and most of these officials agreed with the Arab point of view. It would have been shocking to them if Eddy had reported anything different.

On December 10, Eddy met with Major General Alfred G. Gruenther, chairman of the Joint Chiefs of Staff, Rear Admiral Cato D. Glover and other senior officers of the Joint Strategic Survey Committee to brief them on his tour of Arab capitals. A detailed record of that conversation has been preserved in the National Archives.

On his trip, Eddy told the officers, "I saw many persons of the middle class, a number of government officials and all of the top men, including the King of Arabia, the President of Syria, etc." This was precisely why he had been hired: through his own connections in the State Department and the Marine Corps, and through his extensive network of friends in the diplomatic corps, he had access to everyone the oil companies wanted to reach (except, of course, President Truman.)

"In my opinion," Eddy said, "the consequences of United Nations and United States actions in Palestine can be grouped into: (a) the damage already done and (b) the damage which still may be done."

In the former category were the disappointment in, and mistrust of, the United States that had developed in the Arab world over the Palestine issue. In the latter category were much more serious potential consequences that he foresaw, many of which had been reflected in the CIA's analytical paper on this subject: an outbreak of war in the region, heavy damage to American economic interests (i.e. oil), a rise of Soviet influence in the Middle East and more suffering for the Jews because, Eddy said, if there was war between the Jews and the Arabs, the Arabs would win. The minutes record this exchange:

> Colonel Eddy: When partition comes, the Arabs will throw the Jews out.
>
> Admiral Davis: How will they do it?
>
> Colonel Eddy: They'll have no difficulty at all.

Eddy told the officers that the Arabs would have many advantages in this contest: some 18,000 Arab members of the Palestine police force who would lose their jobs when the British left would take up arms against the Jews, already knowing "where the Jew depots and cells are." Arab armies and guerrillas in neighboring countries would enter the contest, with logistical support from their governments. Exposed Jewish settlements surrounded by Arab communities would be overrun. And a fledgling Jewish state would be strangled economically by the Arab countries encirling it.

In this line of argument, the creation of a Jewish state would augment rather than alleviate the suffering of the world's Jews, because the hopes of surviving European Jews for refuge in Palestine would be dashed, and the many Jews already living peaceably in Arab countries would now face persecution.

In the light of six decades of history this analysis may seem preposterous, but at the time Eddy's views were widely shared in Washington. Indeed, the Central Intelligence Agency said pretty much the same things in "The Consequences of the Partition of Palestine," its secret report to the White House on the eve of the United Nations vote.

How could Eddy and these other experts have been so wrong?

This was an early case in which the intelligence analysts were unable to discern the difference between the pieces of a puzzle and the whole picture. Many of the analysts and their like-minded colleagues in the State Department, including Eddy, were influenced by long association with Arabs whom they liked and admired. They made the mistake of believing what the Arabs told them about their collective determination to prevent the creation of a Jewish state in their midst—this gap between rhetoric and reality is a feature of Arab politics even today—and they grossly underestimated the determination and skill of the Jews. They failed to take into account the corruption of Arab governments and the disorganization and incompetence of the Arab armies other than Jordan's Arab Legion. They believed the Arabs were truly committed to a long, hard fight against the Zionists and would perform creditably, despite their well-known military and organizational deficiencies. As early as 1945, the State Department had interpreted the creation of the Arab League as a collective commitment to "take up arms" for a "common defense of Arab Palestine." King Abdul Aziz had told the Americans directly that the Arabs would fight to the last man to prevent the establishment of the Jewish state, and given his martial personal history, there seemed little reason to doubt him. Certainly Bill Eddy, who considered Abdul Aziz "one of the great men of the twentieth century," was not about to discount what his friend the warrior king told him.

Even after the first Arab-Israel war started in 1948 and it became apparent that the Jews would not be run out of Palestine so easily as Eddy had predicted to the generals and admirals in Washington, he shared the Arabs' wishful thinking about the outcome. "The only bright spot in the news," he wrote to Mary on June 4, 1948, "is the slow but sure success of the Arab troops which are really hemming the Zionists into their coastal strip."

Perhaps Eddy had to believe that was what was happening—it was what the CIA had predicted would happen in the "Consequences" report to which he was a major contributor, and some limited Arab successes in the first weeks of the war were validating what he believed—but pro-Arab Americans were in for a rude awakening in the late spring and summer of 1948. In quick sucession, partition took effect, the British withdrew, and the Jews declared the creation of the independent Jewish state of Israel—which Truman recognized immediately—and opened its doors to all Jews worldwide. When war broke out Jews, after some setbacks, won because of their well-developed mlitary prowess and the largely ineffective performance of the Arab armies and the fecklessness and corruption of Arab political leaders. The Jewish zone of what had been Palestinian territory increased in size. Thousands of Palestinian Arabs became refugees, to live thenceforth in sullen exile in neighboring countries, nurturing futile dreams of return, as they do even today.

These were bitter pills to swallow for the Arabs and their friends in the United States, and the fact that the Arabs have never reconciled themselves to the outcome of the 1948 conflict has been the cause of decades of violence and upheaval throughout the region.

Partly in response to the disaster in Palestine, the nascent nationalism of the Arab people burst to the surface, sparking coups and revolutions over the succeeding decade or so in Egypt, Iraq, Syria, Yemen,
Algeria, and Libya and political violence on a lesser scale in Lebanon
and Jordan. All the new regimes were opposed to the existence of
Israel and resented the U.S. role in bringing about its creation.

And yet the strongest blow that any Arab leader could have
delivered against the United States—revocation of the oil concession in Saudi Arabia—never fell, despite everything King Abdul
Aziz and his most prominent sons had said about Palestine and
Truman. Why not?

The King was not a sentimentalist. He thought highly of Bill
Eddy and of many of the American executives at ARAMCO, and
he was mostly pleased with the way the oil company conducted its
business. But his primary objectives always were the perpetuation of
the dynasty he had established and the modernization of the country he had created. These goals, coupled with his disdain for some
other Arab political leaders, stayed his hand as he contemplated how
to respond to the catastrophe in Palestine. He would do nothing to
jeopardize his oil revenue or the march of progress across his realm.

Eddy's account of his long colloquy with the King during his
October 1947 tour of Arab capitals reveals the thinking of both men,
with little need for elaboration. Eddy's die-hard anti-Zionism was gratifying to Abdul Aziz, but the King also surveyed a larger horizon.

The King said he wanted Eddy's personal views, as one who had
lived in both worlds and spoke both languages, on the disagreement between the Arabs and the United States over Palestine. "If
the U.S. government, under its political system, reflects the majority will of the people, then the majority of Americans favor Zionist
aggression against the Arabs," Abdul Aziz said. "Is this because they
misconstrue the real facts about Palestine, or is it because they wish
deliberately to alienate the Arabs?" The King said it was "important
for him to know the forces that motivate Americans with respect to
Palestine in determining his own decisions," Eddy reported in his
memo to Terry Duce.

Eddy repeated that U.S. government policy should be discussed through official channels; and he tried to explain to the

King that ordinary Americans were not hostile to Arabs, just ignorant about them. He told the King that their attitude "is almost
wholly uninformed about Palestine itself and about the Arab population. It is made up of (1) a general sympathy for the plight of
the Jewish race, homeless, persecuted by the recent enemies of the
USA, slaughtered in great numbers and driven from their homes
in Europe. (2) a legacy from Sunday school days and home reading of the Old Testament in which Palestine is Judea, the home
of the Jews from which they have been repeatedly exiled, eventually to return to their 'Promised Land.' (3) a vague notion that
there is another side to the story, namely that there are Arabs who
have lived in Palestine for a thousand years, but have not done
much to develop the country; (4) the idea that Palestine when
industrialized can assimilate many more hundreds of thousands
of Jewish immigrants without crowding the Arabs and with economic benefits to the Arabs; (5) the idea that, since both Jews and
Arabs have good historic claims to the land, it should be divided
between them, the judgment that Solomon gave to the two mothers [which would of course have killed the baby if carried out]; (6)
the hope that Palestine might be the solution for Jews clamoring
for a homeland, the further away from USA the better." He said
these are "superficial" notions but "there is no evidence at all of
anti-Arab motivation."

He told the King that all this described the American man in
the street, not the aggressive, active Zionists who were anti-Arab
and "anti-USA." Most Americans, he said, "have no opinion and
no information about Palestine one way or the other."

Eddy said he then "reminded the King of what he knows
quite well, that pro-Zionism has so many US sympathizers only
because of the ruthless Zionist propaganda machine," which he
said is "ready to sacrifice all principle to achieve a Zionist state."
Eddy estimated that only 200,000 of the six million Jews in the
U.S. were Zionists, but said their influence was disproportionately
great because they were desperate, committed and unscrupulous.

This analysis of American sentiment about the Arab-Israeli
conflict would be familiar to anyone who has ventured into these
turbulent waters for the past half century. Even today it fairly well

encapsulates the views of the relatively small number of American diplomats and scholars willing to distance themselves from Israel and see merit in cultivating ties with the Arabs.

The King said he understood the professional Zionists, but was curious about Eddy's remarks about the rest of the United States. If freedom-loving Americans supported Lebanon and Syria against French oppression and defended Greece and Turkey against intimidation by neighbors to the north, well, then, why didn't they hold similar sentiments about the Arabs of Palestine?

Since there was no satisfactory answer to this, the King turned to another subject. He "stated his conviction that the sharifians (Hashemites) together with a small group of politicians led by [Iraqi prime minister] Nuri Pasha, are endeavoring actively to embroil him with the Americans. They know," Abdul Aziz said, "that my cooperation and common interests with Americans are greater than those of any other Arab country; they are jealous of those bonds and, at the instigation of a well-known Great Power [i.e. Great Britain], they would like to terminate my cooperation with Americans."

The King told Eddy that the Iraqis were urging Syrian leader Shukri al-Quwatli to "use his influence with me to break the oil concession of ARAMCO. Shukry is my friend and told me of their plot."

Here Abdul Aziz revealed his deepest concern. He believed that the Hashemites, his old rivals for control of Arabia who had been installed on the thrones of Iraq and Transjordan by the British, were plotting against him in hopes of reclaiming their Arabian dominion. The King wanted American protection against this threat and feared losing that protection if he broke with the United States over the Palestine question. He said that the Iraqis, under the Hashemite King Feisal, had told al-Quwatli to tell him that they, the Hashemites, were taking steps against the Americans, the implication being that he should do so as well to show that he was a true Arab patriot. Iraq turned away a congressional delegation, and the Hashemite King Abdullah of Transjordan was not letting Americans in.

The King had no way of knowing that it was Faisal's throne in Iraq, not his own, that was doomed to be washed away by the Arab nationalist tidal wave of the 1950s.

He told Eddy that his response to these other Arabs was, "those moves cost you nothing. You have no cooperation with Americans to sacrifice. When you have cancelled the British oil concession in Iraq, and have driven them from the administration of your railroads and ports, then you would have a better right to make suggestions to me, not before." He said the Hashemites were using the Palestine issue "to eliminate America from its favored position with the Arabs," but "I am not fooled by these tactics, and I hope that Americans are not deceived. I know that the active cooperation of Americans with me and my country is in our mutual interest, and I hope that Americans believe that too."

This inter-Arab argument went on for some years after Israel became an established fact; Saudi Arabia's persistence in cooperating with the United States despite differences over Israel would become a heavy rhetorical weapon in Egyptian president Gamal Abdel Nasser's campaign to undermine the al-Saud dynasty in the 1950s and 1960s. In February 1952, Eddy reported in an internal ARAMCO memo, the King said the following to an important visitor, Adib Shishakly, then the embattled ruler of Syria:

My son Adib, I love Syria and the Syrian people. Sit here near me and let us talk frankly about our condition.

The Arabs wanted me and still urge that I cancel the ARAMCO oil concession and send the Americans scurrying home. My son, I am a man of war and will fight when I find it necessary. But in 70-odd years of my life I have learnt that I have to think first and act later. Now let us see what is the likely consequence if I were to accede to such urgings.

As a result of the oil operations I get a considerable revenue every year. We are improving the condition of our people in the field of roads and communications, health, education, agriculture, etc. The oil is here. They need it and have invested vast sums in the facilities to find it and produce it. If I were to cancel the concession, apart from going back on my word, the likelihood is that the [big] Powers will fight for it. They will beat me. Myself and my children will be ousted. Someone else may be installed in my place and he may accept less than I am getting and may do less for the people.

What would you do, my son?

This was a rhetorical question but it had a real answer: the American oil concession in Saudi Arabia would not be revoked, despite the King's bitterness about Palestine. Abdul Aziz had too much at stake to undertake such a course, and he was not an impetuous political actor, nor could he be overpowered by the arguments of those he considered lesser men. The King committed himself anew to the relationship with the United States in a message to President Truman that he transmitted through J. Rives Childs, Eddy's successor in Jeddah, in December 1947, right after the U.N. vote on partition. The U.S. decision to support partition was "most distasteful for the Arab world," he said, but it was water under the bridge. He did not wish a complete rupture with Washington over this one issue because on all others his views and those of the United States were in harmony.

THE EXTREMIST THREAT

If Eddy was wrong about the Arabs' military prospects against Israel, he was brilliantly prescient throughout this period and the next decade in foreseeing the rise of Islamic militancy as a threat to Western interests in the Middle East. Most strategic analysis in that era focused on the threat from Soviet-backed communism. Eddy recognized that threat and used it as often as anyone else to reinforce whatever points he had to make about American policy; but he also saw another, indigenous force that would have to be reckoned with—the force that Americans came to know as "Islamic fundamentalism" and, much later, as *jihad.*

Americans tended to assume, he noted in 1947, that newly independent Muslim countries would adopt the Turkish model of secular government. "We have had some reason to believe recently, however, that this dormant force which is very powerful, the force of Islam, the brotherhood of the Moslem, may become extremely serious, may be a very powerful cement in the years that lie ahead," he said.

Under Eddy's influence, the CIA included this threat in "The Consequences of the Partition of Palestine," the secret paper that it circulated on the eve of the U.N. General Assembly vote.

"The Arabs are capable of a religious fanaticism which when coupled with political aspirations is an extremely powerful force," the CIA paper said. "Whether or not the Arab governments are capable of guiding this force is difficult to judge. It is very possible that certain religious organizations will take the initiative in organizing Arab resistance in Palestine. The Ikhwan al Muslimin (Muslim Brotherhood), with headquarters in Egypt, is an organization of young Moslems founded for the purpose of orienting Arab society in accordance with Islamic ideologies. Branches of the Ikhwan have been formed in Syria and Lebanon, and one of the most active branches is in Palestine. The Ikhwan regards Westernization as a dangerous threat to Islam and would oppose any political encroachment of Zionism on Palestine with religious fanaticism. Should a 'Jihad' or Holy War be declared, the Ikhwan would be the spearhead of any 'crusade.' The Grand Mufti, as head of the Moslem Supreme Council, can count on the unanimous support of all members of the Ikhwan, who are assured of entrance into Paradise if they die on the field of battle."

Apart from the unfortunate use of the word "crusade" to describe a campaign by Muslims, this brief section is valuable for its insight even now. The CIA was well ahead of the curve in recognizing the mystical appeal to some zealous Muslims of death on behalf of the faith. At the time, most policy memos in Washington and dispatches from diplomats in the field based their anti-Zionist arguments on political and economic points, not on religion. Despite the rise of the Muslim Brotherhood in Egypt, most U.S. officials assumed that as the Arabs gained independence and modernized their societies, religion would diminish as a determinative force. The voluminous documentary record of the Truman administration's deliberations on the Palestine issue contains few if any other papers in which the potential for armed Muslim extremism and the force of anti-Western sentiment are raised as long-term threats. On the contrary, key officials such as Evan Wilson, the longtime Palestine desk officer at State, saw religion as a motivating factor more on the Jewish side, as Jews argued for fulfillment of their "biblical destiny."

Yet Eddy clung to the hope that Truman's decision about Palestine and U.S. support for Israel would somehow not result in a permanent breach between America and the Muslim peoples of the world. The situation could somehow be rectified, he believed. In a 1953 speech at the Naval War College in Rhode Island, Eddy said that "three hundred million Muslims, not yet militarized, offer to the U.S.A. a potent friend or a dangerous enemy. The choice is still ours on April 1, 1953. If we choose wrong, then may God have mercy on our souls."

Throughout the 1950s, in correspondence and public appearances separate from his ARAMCO duties, he would press this theme: the United States, as a Christian nation, had an opportunity to forge a "moral alliance" with Islam. To support instead what Arabs saw as the expansionist, usurper state created by the Zionists in Palestine would bring down upon America the relentless rage of militant Islam. In this he was the Cassandra of the Middle East.

HOME TO LEBANON

Declassified State Department records from 1951 show that in late October ARAMCO was the subject of an extensive meeting at the State Department. The company was represented by Floyd Ohliger, vice president for government liason; James Terry Duce, its principal lobbyist in Washington; and Bill Eddy, a "special consultant." They were talking to George McGhee and Richard Funkhouser, senior officials of the State Department's Near East bureau.

The topic was ARAMCO's relations with the government of Saudi Arabia and the rising sentiment there for at least some Saudi ownership of the consortium—sentiment that had been encouraged by nationalization of the oil fields in Iran.

The company's immediate problem, according to State Department files, was "the growing interest among Saudi Arabs of purchasing stock in ARAMCO. This was true not only of wealthy merchants but also some of the Royal family including the Crown Prince [Saud], who wished to invest money for his sons so that they could be financially independent of Government revenues in the future. The company had suggested, Mr. Ohliger said, that they might invest in the parent companies [whose stock was publicly traded] but this was not acceptable to the Saudi Arabs, first because they had less interest in investing abroad than in putting their money in Saudi Arabia, and second because investment in the parent companies would subject them to payment of a thirty percent income tax in the United States."

When McGhee asked Ohliger what would be wrong with opening ARAMCO to stock purchase by some Saudis, "Mr. Ohliger replied that the sale of stock would offer the possibility of some of it getting into the hands of Jewish investors, which would be objectionable to the SAG [Saudi Arabian government]. . . . The real reason, it developed, for ARAMCO objections to sale of stock was that there was only $11,000,000 of stock outstanding, while the value of the firm exclusive of the oil reserves was substantially in excess of this amount. Consequently, any change in its stock position might require revaluation and subject the company to a very heavy capital gains tax."

This memo is intriguing not only for what it says about Saudi sentiment toward the oil company but also for what it reveals about Eddy's role. With the establishment of Israel and the King's commitment to maintain the oil concession in spite of it, the importance of Eddy's job in Washington had diminished. The issues between ARAMCO and the U.S. government now concerned such matters as the tax status of the company's royalty payments and the valuation of its stock, on which Eddy's expertise in the Middle East was of little value. He was much more interested in the internal dynamic of Saudi Arabia and the implications of Crown Prince Saud's request, for it was clear that Saud would soon be king. Eddy had told ARAMCO that he did not wish to live abroad, but now he was restless because he had less to do in Washington and the immediacy of his contacts in the Arab world was fading. And so in the winter of 1951-52, Bill and Mary Eddy moved to Beirut.

ARAMCO in those days was virtually a state within a state in Saudi Arabia, and Eddy could be thought of as its ambassador to Syria, Iraq, Lebanon, Jordan and Egypt. In that capacity, it was logical for him to be based in the Lebanese capital.

Before it was torn apart by the civil war that began in 1975, Beirut was one of the world's most cosmopolitan and intriguing cities. Its hilly streets rose from inviting Mediterranean beaches toward nearby mountains where Lebanese could ski in the winter and rich Arabs from the Gulf could find relief from their 130-degree summers. With superb restaurants, beautiful women, and a heterogeneous population of Muslim Arabs, Christian Arabs, Armenians, Greeks, Cypriots, Lebanese Druze, Palestinians and other Arabs, as well as a substanial Western community, it offered a quality of life that no other Arab city could match. Lebanon was the business, banking and information center of the entire Arab world. The capitals of Syria and Jordan were easily reachable by car; Cairo was a short plane ride away. And on Lebanon's southern border was the land that had been Palestine and was now Israel.

To some extent the population of Beirut was reminiscent of the Tangier Eddy had known a decade earlier, a human stew of legitimate business people and diplomats, plotters and opportunists, spies and journalists, refugees and other transients. Eddy's job was to know as many of these people as possible and to keep his employer (and the CIA) informed about what they were up to. He also used Beirut as a base for information-gathering travel to other Arab capitals. With his contacts from his sojourns in Egypt, North Africa, Yemen and Saudi Arabia, his connections in the U.S. diplomatic corps and his family ties in Lebanon itself, he was a perfect fit.

The Eddys knew everyone. His professional and family correspondence of the early Beirut years shows that he was forever having lunch with this or that ambassador, prime minister or political party leader throughout the Middle East, cultivating the personal contacts that lubricate all business in the Arab world.

In Tunisia, Mary told the children, Eddy "was included in a stag lunch with [President Habib] Bourguiba, along with our Ambassador and Mr. Winthrop Aldrich [a prominent banker]. Bill had met Bourguiba twice before, the last time in Washington in 1946 when B. was still a refugee [from the ruling French]. In giving a lunch with all the Tunisian special dishes, Bourguiba was living up to his radical reform to free Moslems from the obligation to fast during the month of Ramadan, which he considers a waste of a month of the year."

The letters from those days are replete with such comments as, "We were guests for lunch of Musa Bey Alami, a good friend, formerly director of the Arab Offices of Information in the USA and the UK," or "I also ran into one of my favorite pupils of Cairo days, whom I had not seen since 1927, Bahaeddine al Bakri, formerly of the diplomatic service of Syria before he and his colleagues were booted out by [Syrian president] Husni Zaim who made a clean sweep of the service when he seized power a year ago. Baha is married to a daughter of a former Prime Minister of Iraq. . . ."

This social chitchat was not an end in itself. One of Eddy's tasks at ARAMCO was to help the company choose recipients of the charitable donations it distributed annually around the region, and his contacts informed this process. And like a good journalist, Eddy used what he learned from his contacts to construct detailed analyses of political events and trends in the region. Virtually all such information was important to ARAMCO because the era of nationalization was beginning in the oil fields of the Middle East, and events in any regional capital could influence the thinking of the King of Saudi Arabia. And it was important to the managers of the Trans-Arabian Pipeline, or Tapline, the oil pipeline that connected the Saudi Arabian oil fields to an export terminal on the Mediterranean. Tapline ran for more than a thousand miles across four Arab countries—Saudi Arabia, Jordan, Syria and Lebanon—and thus political developments in any of them could affect the oil industry. The original planned Mediterranean destination for the line was Haifa, then in Palestine; but partition put Haifa inside Israel, so the terminal was moved northward to Sidon, Lebanon, the city of Eddy's birth.

Tapline was nominally a separate business from ARAMCO, but its sole function was to transport ARAMCO output, and Eddy was a consultant to both corporations. He received his mail at Tapline's Beirut office and wrote letters on Tapline stationery. His casual reference to Husni Zaim's seizure of power in Syria—an event that made Tapline possible—masked a dramatic tale of deep and dubious American involvement in the internal affairs of an independent Arab country, Syria.

The Syrian government of Shukri al-Quwatli signed an agreement with the pipeline's developers in February 1949 to permit construction of the Syrian portion. At the time Eddy was working for ARAMCO and for the company it created to build the pipeline, but he was still living in Washington. The agreement required ratification in the Syrian Chamber of Deputies, or parliament, and there it encountered stiff resistance from nationalists who regarded it as an expansion of Western imperialism. Without the Syrian mileage, the rest of the pipeline, already under construction in Saudi Arabia, would be useless. Without Tapline, Saudi Arabian oil bound for Europe would continue to be shipped in tankers all the way around the Arabian peninsula and through the Suez Canal, a journey that vastly increased the time and cost of delivery.

On March 30, the Quwatli government was overthrown in a military coup led by the army chief of staff, Colonel Husni Zaim. The new ruler promised the Americans that if they extended recognition to his new regime he would authorize the pipeline—no need to worry about any messy objections from a parliament. The State Department advised President Truman to recognize the military government. He did so, and a few weeks later Zaim kept his word about the pipeline.

In his well-regarded history *The Struggle for Syria*, the journalist Patrick Seale described Zaim as "a heavy, thickly-built man with broad cheeks, a fierce eye, and the florid face of a Latin American dictator." According to Seale, Zaim was "an adventurer with few ideals . . . emotionally somewhat unstable and easily inflamed" and brave to the point of being foolhardy, but his policies—which included a willingness to negotiate with Israel—were welcome in Washington.

Seale quoted a letter from Khalid al-Azm, a prominent Syrian financier and politician, saying that "the United States believed, rightly or wrongly, that there was little chance of securing parliamentary ratification" under Quwatli. "They may therefore have looked with sympathy on anyone who promised to remove this obstacle. The facts speak for themselves: Shortly after Husni Zaim came to power he ratified" the Tapline agreement.

Seale said that as far as he was able to determine the American and British intelligence services knew of the coup in advance but were not involved in organizing or promoting it. But it came to light years later that Zaim was recruited and his coup was masterminded by the CIA—one of the first known examples of covert "regime change" action by the agency Bill Eddy helped to create.

Most Americans learned of the CIA's role only when Miles Copeland's *The Game of Nations* was published in 1969. Copeland, who was himself a CIA operative in Damascus at the time of the coup, said it was the work of "the famous Major Stephen Meade," nominally a military attaché in the U.S. Embassy.

According to Copeland, the chief U.S. diplomat in Syria, James M. Keeley, came reluctantly to the conclusion that Quwatli had to go; either he would be overthrown by radical nationalists who would be pro-Soviet, or he would be overthrown by army, which would keep order and would be anti-Soviet. Better the latter course, Keeley decided.

Once Keeley was on board, according to Copeland, "A 'political action team' under Major Meade systematically developed a friendship with Zaim, then chief of staff of the Syrian army, suggested to him the idea of a coup d'etat, advised him how to go about it, and guided him through the intricate preparations in laying the groundwork for it—a degree of participation which was only suspected by Syria's leading politicians. . . ."

As Copeland noted, many Americans found it hard to believe this tale when he revealed it, but documents unearthed later by the historian Douglas Little confirmed it. So closely was Meade associated with Zaim that he became an intimate adviser, offering suggestions as to who should be Syria's new ambassador to Britain and even as to what food the ousted Quwatli should be given in prison so as not to aggravate his ulcer.

By Copeland's account, Zaim was cooperative and malleable during the weeks he was awaiting U.S. recognition. Once it was extended, however, he became vainglorious and trucululent. He did go through with the Tapline agreement, as he had promised, but he otherwise seems to have infuriated everyone, American and Syrian alike.

"Zaim demonstrated, to all who would study this case," Copeland wrote, "that being a stooge of the most powerful government on earth was not enough to ensure tenure," at least not in

Syria, which is notoriously difficult to govern. Zaim was ousted in another military coup only a few months later, on August 14, and summarily executed. The American "stooge" was gone, but his successors honored the Tapline agreement and the pipeline was constructed as planned.

Several coups later, Quwatli returned to Syria in 1955 as its elected president. By that time, Tapline was carrying more than 300,000 barrels a day of ARAMCO oil to the terminal at Sidon.

Bill Eddy was on the ARAMCO payroll at the time of the Zaim coup, when gaining approval for Tapline was perhaps the company's most urgent task, and he traveled frequently to Arab capitals as a senior member of the team trying to get the pipeline in place. But he was still based in Washington, and his fingerprints do not appear on the events in Damascus. Given his contacts in the CIA and his relationships with everyone who mattered at ARAMCO and in Beirut and Damascus, it is unlikely that he was surprised when Quwatli was toppled; if he had any role in the coup, or any scruples about it, his famous discretion prevented him from saying so in his correspondence.

ANXIETY IN THE OIL PATCH

The nationalization of Iran's oil industry in 1951 stirred the anxiety of every American and European oil executive in the Middle East. Iran's action marked the beginning of the end of foreign control of the region's oil fields, but the inexorability of this trend was not yet fully apparent and the oil companies and their allies sought to forestall it. King Abdul Aziz was still alive at the time, and thus ARAMCO appeared safe for the moment, but who knew what would happen when Prince Saud succeeded him. In May, Eddy went to Iraq—where Abdul Aziz's old rivals, the Hashemites, still ruled, in the person of King Feisal—to assess the situation there. The reports he sent to Terry Duce in New York and to ARAMCO's center in Dhahran are illustrative of his work in this period. However wrong he may have been about Israel, and however much his inability to come to grips with the reality of the Jewish state may have clouded his judgment on other matters, he showed in his political reporting a remarkable ability, which any foreign correspondent would have envied, to discern trends and foresee trouble. Assuming he was sharing these analyses with the CIA, the agency could have had no better informed source of information about Arab politics and personalities.

In a week in Baghdad, Eddy saw members of Prime Minister Nuri as-Said's cabinet, prominent members of parliament, military officers, American and other foreign diplomats, and well-placed friends such as Bahaeddine Bakri, whom Eddy had known for twenty-five years. This is not much different from what a good journalist would have tried to do if sent on a reporting trip to Iraq, except that these sources were much more likely to be candid in private conversations with an ARAMCO-Tapline representative than they would with someone who would be writing for public consumption.

Eddy found the Iraqis eager to restructure their oil contracts to keep a larger share of the money for themselves, but they were also willing to negotiate rather than confront. "Unlike the hopped-up hotheads in Teheran," he wrote, "the leaders of the government, of parliament and of the opposition in Iraq all want a really business solution [sic] which will provide finances for the program of national development. Nobody wants chaos and national suicide, both of which seem to be courted ardently in Iran." By "hopped-up hotheads" Eddy was referring to Iranian Prime Minister Mohammed Mossadegh, architect of nationalization, and his radical supporters. Two years later, the United States would orchestrate a coup d'état to get rid of Mossadegh, a critical event in the unhappy modern history of U.S.-Iran relations.

Even though the Iraqis wanted to avoid "chaos and national suicide," and "in spite of a considerable amount of goodwill on both sides," Eddy wrote, "the negotiations are not easy." He said the Iraqis were waiting to see whether Mossadegh's defiance of the British would stand up before deciding how to proceed, but in any case would not settle for the even revenue split to which ARAMCO and the Saudis had recently agreed.

As usual, Eddy was perceptive and farsighted on all regional matters other than Palestine; he spotted tendencies in Iraqi thinking that foretold dramatic events of later decades. For example, he noted that while the extensive southern fields around Basra were not being developed at that time by the British-controlled Iraq Petroleum Company, "the oil of Basra is no doubt being syphoned off by the operations of the nearby Kuwait Oil Company, which is working the same pool!" This belief that Kuwait was stealing oil from Iraq's southern fields was one of the main reasons Saddam Hussein decided to invade Kuwait in 1990. Eddy also observed that the Iraqis wanted the oil revenue distributed for the benefit of all Iraqis, not just the people in those parts of the country where the oil reserves lay, an issue that would arise again in the debates over Iraq's new constitution after the U.S. ouster of Saddam Hussein in 2003.

Iraq, Eddy noted, was "envious of Saudi Arabia for its more profitable oil operations, and bitter against [the Saudi government] for its failure to sacrifice or contribute heavily to the Arab disasters in Palestine. If the oil discussions in Iraq should go sour, and the demand to throw out the foreign concessions prevail, we may expect Iraq to lead an Arab propaganda [campaign] against [Saudi Arabia] and its oil partner, ARAMCO." (Such a campaign did come about, but its instigator and leader was Egypt's Nasser, who had no oil at all, not the Iraqis. Iraq joined the radical Arab camp only after the upheaval of 1958, which would also affect Lebanon.)

In a separate memo on Iraq's domestic political situation, Eddy reported that Prime Minister Nuri as-Said, a "hardy, pro-British perennial" was "firmly in the saddle," but that in part because of communist agitation Iraq was drifting toward the Cold War neutrality advocated by such third-world statesmen as Jawaharlal Nehru of India.

"A hostile 'neutralism' against the USA is fanned by the continual repercussions of Israeli aggression for which the USA is held chiefly responsible," he wrote. "It is a mistake to think, as I used to do, that the resentment against Israel is hottest in Syria and Egypt, which suffered the chief military humiliation and defeats. It is as hot, if not hotter, in Iraq for the very real reason, among others, that Iraq's pocketbook suffered most by the denial of oil to the Haifa terminal. [An export pipeline from Iraq's northern fields to the same Haifa terminal originally selected for Tapline was mothballed in 1948.] Having impoverished themselves to hurt the economy of Israel, Iraqis are implacable in their hate and their desire to see the fruits of their financial sacrifice." He said the Iraqis were baffled and infuriated by the United Nations' refusal to take any action against Israel for its repeated cease-fire violations and seizures of additional Arab territory, and blamed the United States for this situation.

According to Eddy, when Israeli Prime Minister David Ben Gurion is "invited to the White House for a chummy birthday party" while "no Arab diplomat ever enjoys that privilege," the result is a "loss of hope of fair dealing by the USA in Palestine," a sentiment he said was "shared by leaders of all parties in Iraq."

Eddy included in this political report a commentary on the departure from Iraq of the country's substantial Jewish population.

"The exodus of Iraqi Jews to Israel (which is the subject of many tear-jerking advertisements and articles in the American newspapers and magazines) is proceeding apace," he reported. He said that 104,000 Jews had been authorized to leave, of whom 75,000 had already departed. "About 20,000 Jews, mostly the prosperous city type, have elected to remain in Iraq with full rights as citizens. . . . The abrupt departure of so many trained accountants and clerks has stripped many of the banks and foreign commercial houses of a large portion of their staffs, and has temporarily affected their efficiency."

He said the Iraqis had made up their minds to encourage Jewish emigration despite negative news coverage in the West of the Jews' departure, coverage that Eddy attributed to news accounts in "the mendacious Israeli press." The Iraqis figured that their standing in the West could not be worse anyway. "Iraqis are convinced now that nothing they do will give them a good name and they prefer to see every last Jew leave the country," Eddy reported.

Here again he picked up on an issue that would reappear years later. In the mid-1970s, the Iraqis decided it had been a mistake to encourage the Jews to leave because their departure deprived Iraq of productive talent and supplied useful manpower to what the Iraqis called "the Zionist entity." Baghdad instituted a campaign to persuade the Iraqi Jews to return, which for obvious reasons met with little success.

Eddy was similarly perspicacious in an assessment of the Cairo riots of January 1952, which presaged the revolution that would put an end to the monarchy six months later.

In the months leading up to the riots, he found, Egypt was in political turmoil as opposition to the government rose from two camps. One wanted a final break with Britain and an end to British domination of Egypt. The other wanted an end to the conspicuous corruption and nepotism that were enriching the privileged classes while the masses lived in abject conditions. When these two lines began to converge, trouble became inevitable, as the brewing "revolt aganst the rich and privileged" and the "revolt against 'Western imperialism'" were stoked by communist agitators. In both revolts, Eddy said, "the United States was linked with Britain as preservers of a policy of domination, enslavement and preparation for war."

Student demonstrations and labor actions broke out around the country. Armed skirmishes erupted between local police and British troops. On January 25, 1952, Eddy reported, forty-three Egyptian police officers and auxiliaries were killed and eighty wounded in the British-controlled Suez Canal Zone at Ismailia. That was the spark for the riots of the next day.

On January 26, students camped in front of parliament demanding that Egypt sever diplomatic relations with Britain and forge a security partnership with the Soviet Union. "The students had not contemplated more than squatting before Parliament until Parliament met to press these resolutions," Eddy reported, "but other groups were alert to an unusual opportunity."

In an outbreak of violence that must have been planned, Eddy wrote, all the resentments of the Egyptian masses—against the British, the rich, the Jews, and "foreigners in general"—boiled over. All across Cairo, fires were set at well-known landmarks identified with the West: Shepheard's Hotel, Barclay's Bank, Groppi's café, movie theaters, auto dealerships, night clubs, foreign-owned department stores.

"By the time the army had been called in to intervene, great damage was done and many people had been killed or burnt,"

Eddy said. "In less than 6 hours Cairo had suffered as much damage as would have been inflicted by an air raid of considerable strength." He said these events came as a "profound shock" to the government, which was in the aftermath trying to reinforce security, reassure foreigners, come to terms with the British and deal with the real issues raised by the riots, including the disparity of wealth. This shift might presage a "real opportunity" to open "new horizons of friendship . . . not only between the West on the one hand and Egypt on the other but between the West and the Arab world as an area."

It was too late. Eddy had written to Terry Duce in June 1951 that "It would appear that the King of Egypt can no longer be sure of the loyalty even of the officers of his Army," and once again he was right. In July 1952, the "Free Officers" led by Nasser overthrew the monarchy and seized power, determined to set Egypt on a new course in domestic and international affairs. When Nasser nationalized the Suez Canal four years later, after Iran had nationalized its oil fields, the handwriting was on the wall for western ownership of the great resources that Americans and Europeans had developed in Arab lands, including, eventually, ARAMCO.

ARAMCO'S TROUBLES

From time to time during the 1950s, Eddy left his comfortable perch in Beirut to work directly for ARAMCO at its offices in Saudi Arabia and Washington. By the mid-1950s, he told family members, he was eager to take on such stationary assignments because a heart ailment made it difficult to travel around the region as much as he liked.

This was a time when the company was dogged by two big concerns: the rise of nationalist and anti-colonial sentiment throughout the region, which the company rightly saw as a threat to its Saudi concession, and discontent among its Arab workforce, which raised the anger of King Abdul Aziz and then of Saud, who succeeded his father in 1953. The company boasted of all it had done for its local workers, the schools and clinics it had built for them and their families, the training given to workers with no skills, the roads and electricity that improved their lives. The workers, however, saw a different picture: they saw the Americans and their wives and children living in comfortable air-conditioned communities with swimming pools, while the lower-paid Arab laborers lived apart from their families in huts known as "barastis," and were routinely denied promotion into managerial and supervisory positions. When workers went on strike in 1945 and 1953, the government backed ARAMCO, jailing and deporting the ringleaders, but also pressed the company to respond to the workers' demands.

During one of the periodic flare-ups of these issues, in August 1951, Eddy was working in ARAMCO's Washington office when the company got caught in the middle of a looming power struggle within the House of Saud as King Abdul Aziz, ill and in decline, neared the end of his long reign. Eddy was not a direct participant is this episode, but his observations on it offer a fascinating glimpse of this piece of history.

"Telegrams from Dhahran indicate a very serious situation," Eddy wrote to his wife. "Trying to destroy the influence of the Crown Prince (Saud) and to get finances and power wholly in his hands, Abdullah Sulaiman (who is again drinking heavily) told the King a pack of lies and the King told [U.S. Ambassador] Ray Hare that ARAMCO has been insulting him, deceiving him, cheating the Saudi Gov't, and that 'all those with whom he has been dealing recently in the company must leave Saudi Arabia'. . . . The row is a frightful one, not only because of what the king has said and the difficulty of getting him to retract, but because the king is no longer a rational person; the last one to poison his ear is all he can remember, and we may have crisis after crisis like this . . ." He noted that Iran and Iraq were demanding that citizens of those countries receive seats on the boards of directors of the foreign-controlled oil companies there, and he predicted that "Saudi Arabia is sure to demand that right away," as indeed it soon did.

The original oil concession agreement signed by Standard Oil of California in 1933 required the company to employ, train and promote as many Arab citizens of Saudi Arabia as possible. This made obvious sense from the perspective of the King, who wanted to raise the living standards of the people and to replace non-Muslim foreign workers as quickly as possible. But it was a challenging assignment for the oil men, whose first objective was profit, not societal improvement, and who were in no hurry to work themselves out of lucrative jobs. Many of the Americans were field hands from segregated states such as Texas who knew little about Arabs, looked down on them, and referred to them as "coolies."

By the summer of 1955, labor tension was so high that Bill and Mary Eddy moved temporarily to Dhahran so he could be available to the company's executives full time. ARAMCO had a staff of Arabic-speaking scholars, but their expertise was more academic than practical.

The company's local workers were almost all illiterate, unskilled, and unfamiliar with basic tools when hired. They learned quickly, but even after training that ought to have qualified them for some advancement, the company found that promoting them to supervisory positions only stirred more resentment among the rank-and-file Arab workforce. Collectively, they demanded the promotion of Arabs; but when an individual was actually chosen for elevation, his colleagues objected, and often tried to block the promotion. ARAMCO executives were baffled by this phenomenon and asked Eddy to explain it. He responded in a letter to company executives on the subject of "Saudi Arabs as Supervisors."

"We believe this letter states very succinctly the problem which we have encountered in the past and will encounter in the future," said a company memo attached to Eddy's letter as it was distributed.

"Reference is made," Eddy's letter said, "to the problem confronting the Company in advancing Arab employees to supervisor positions: 'Invariably, when an Arab was made supervisor, his jealous subordinates would file trumped-up charges against him with the police and the court.' This problem is to my mind a symptom of a general attitude among Saudi Arabs which may require a considerable education to overcome.

In the first place, Saudi Arabs of the working class have been accustomed to obey the authority only of the King as expressed through his local representatives, in addition of course to the patriarchal duty of obeying elders in the family or tribe. The Saudi Arabs have no experience with the promotion of a man from the ranks to authority over his fellows. [This same problem would resurface two decades later when American officers began training the Saudi Arabian National Guard, most of whose members were bedouin who could not understand why they had to take orders from fellow bedouin who were not their superiors in life.]

In Saudi Arabia, there have been no Magna Cartas or Industrial Revolutions, and it is, therefore, even more true that a man does not expect to rise out of his class, and when he is promoted out of his class by ARAMCO, his fellows who think they are as good as he is are outraged. True, even in our own country we also often feel that the mayor or the chief of police is no better a man than we are and we may even despise him, but we have accustomed ourselves to popular elections and we, therefore, resign ourselves to recognizing the authority of an elected or appointed officer whether or not we consider him worthy to occupy this position. There will be no easy solution to this problem.

Secondly, the people of Saudi Arabia have been accustomed to obeying only representatives of the King and not representatives of private groups. The Government of Saudi Arabia is monolithic, or rather a pyramid in form, with power descending from the King to every locality where there is a 'Kingsman.' Even a soldier who accompanies foreigners crossing the country in an automobile derives his authority with the Bedou or with potential robbers not from his rifle but from the fact that he represents the King. I remember quite well that in Jeddah an attempt by some young effendis [gentlemen] to form a soccer team came to nothing, not only because the organization of a team was frowned upon [by authorities suspicious of any organized group not under royal control] but because the group proposed to elect a captain; whereupon the Kaimakam [district chief] informed them that he would have to be captain. This was several years ago and it might be that community groups are now allowed to organize and elect their own officers, but it is easy for me to understand that a Saudi employee in ARAMCO resents the promotion of a fellow worker to authority over him and prefers to run to the local government representative with complaints, true or false. This is not unlike the difficulty which the US Army had when it first commmissioned Negroes in Negro regiments instead of having white officers throughout. At a stevedore camp in Bordeaux, France, in 1917, I remember seeing a young Negro lieutenant attempting to reprimand a Negro soldier who had decided to lie down in the shade under a tree instead of carrying heavy boxes. The sleepy soldier merely looked up and said to the Negro lieutenant: "What do you think you is, Nigger? A West Pointah?"

It is inconceivable that anyone working for an American corporation would write such a memo today, but except for the final anecdote about the black soldier—probably a reflection of white American attitudes in the 1950s, not a manifestation of racism on the part of Eddy as an individual—the memo stands up to scrutiny and it is doubtful that Eddy would repudiate it. For decades Americans and Saudis groped for accommodation across a vast chasm of social, educational, religious and behavioral differences; that they succeeded in bridging those chasms to form successful binational enterprises such as ARAMCO, and common policies on regional and strategic issues, is at least in part attributable to the work of the few Americans such as Eddy who understood both sides. Over time, ARAMCO found multiple ways to overcome the problem described in Eddy's letter, to the extent that by the end of the twentieth century virtually all senior executives of the company, now a smoothly-run state-owned enterprise, were Saudi Arabs.

THE ONASSIS CAPER

For all the money and effort that ARAMCO invested in protecting its position in Saudi Arabia, the company was blindsided when the first major challenge to its exclusive arrangement came from an unexpected, and non-Arab, source: Artistotle Onassis, the Greek shipping tycoon and celebrity womanizer.

In January 1954 Onassis signed an agreement to create a fleet
of oil tankers that would fly the Saudi flag and to train Saudi crews
to operate them in exchange for the right to transport a guaranteed share of Saudi crude oil to world markets—a share that would
increase as the existing tankers operated by ARAMCO and its sub-
contractors aged and were retired from service. Onassis would
gain a huge and lucrative new market; Saudi Arabia would gain a
merchant fleet and the outside expertise to run it, much as it was
gaining an airline with help from TWA. King Saud ibn Abdul Aziz,
three months on the throne, would demonstrate that he was his
own man and did not take orders from the Americans. The obvious big loser would be ARAMCO, which under the 1933 concession agreement had the exclusive right for 60 years to "explore,
prospect, drill for, extract, treat, manufacture, transport, deal
with, carry away and export petroleum and other hydrocarbons"
by whatever means it saw fit.

ARAMCO's great ally in opposition to the deal, in addition to
the U.S. government, would be Onassis's hated brother-in-law and
greatest rival for shipping supremacy, Stavros Niarchos.

The murky story of the Onassis deal would have been high
comedy if the stakes had not been so large. It involved several
of the world's richest men, half a dozen unscrupulous intriguers
and Riviera playboys, the governments of three or four countries,
the CIA and, ultimately, Bill Eddy. Even today some of the details
remain unknown.

ARAMCO officials at first believed that the deal was the brain-
child of Abdullah Tariki, a politically outspoken Arab nationalist
who was Saudi Arabia's oil director at the time and later a founder
of the Organization of Petroleum Exporting Countries (OPEC).
Tariki's undisguised agenda was to break the grip of Western companies on Middle Eastern oil resources, and he saw opportunity in
King Saud's desire to prove himself as a leader.

It later developed, however, that the tanker agreement was
based less on politics than on money, pure and simple. The key
figure in the Saudi government was not Tariki but Abdullah Sulaiman, the crafty old finance minister, now diminished in capacity
by age and alcohol but still powerful and well connected.

The tanker agreement apparently originated at a meeting at a resort on the French Riviera in the summer of 1953 between Onassis and the brothers Muhammad and Ali Alireza, sons of the governor of Jeddah and prominent members of one of the Kingdom's wealthiest merchant families. (Muhammad Alireza later became minister of commerce; Ali Alireza was ambassador to the United States.) The meeting was arranged by an Onassis agent named Spyrion Catapodis, described by Robert Lacey as "a loud-mouthed Monte Carlo playboy" and by the *Sunday Times of London* as "the quintessence of the Riviera demimonde."

A concise account of what followed is provided in Nathan Citino's book about U.S.-Saudi relations in the 1950s: Onassis "offered to provide the Saudi government with a national tanker fleet in exchange for a guaranteed share in the transportation of Saudi oil. Abdullah Sulayman, the experienced Saudi finance minister, negotiated a draft agreement with Onassis's hired consultant and Hitler's former adviser Dr. Hjalmar Schacht." Onassis apparently brought in Schacht as a potential replacement for the odious Catapodis, whom he did not trust and who would eventually break with Onassis over the magnate's refusal to pay the seven-figure fee he believed he was owed for setting up the original Riviera meeting.

"By December 1953," according to Citino, "the agreement was complete, and Onassis traveled to Jidda to meet with Saud. Ali Rida's [Alireza's] demands for bribes totaling hundreds of thousands of pounds and a cut of the profits delayed implementation of the deal, at least according to Catapodis, and it was not until January 1954 that Onassis and Saud finally signed a contract sealing the agreement."

The Alireza brothers stood to gain a down payment of $1 million and guaranteed fees of at least $168,000 a year. Muhammad Alireza would become Onassis's agent in the Kingdom. According to Catapodis, Abdullah Sulaiman, whose role was to persuade the King to approve the arrangement, was paid off as well. The King, according to Robert Lacey's account of this episode, seemed unconcerned that Sulaiman was being paid to promote the deal, nor was he put off by Muhammad Alireza's role—he appointed him minister of commerce.

Onassis celebrated his new alliance with Saud and the start of this new venture by naming a tanker under construction in Germany the *King Saud I*. Catapodis said Onassis told him he was going to use the tanker agreement to move in on the Saudi oil industry in some larger way to make himself the world's richest man.

Now it was the opposition's turn to mobilize.

The U.S. government did not want to see so valuable a commodity as Saudi Arabia's oil under the control of an international freebooter such as Onassis, who was under indictment in U.S. courts at the time. The Defense Department was concerned about the 27 to 30 tanker loads of oil received from Saudi Arabia each month by the Navy. Those tankers were operated by the Navy's Military Sea Transportation Service.

At first the government in Washington tried to negotiate some compromise with Onassis. Spyros Skouras, the Greek-born Hollywood movie mogul who was head of 20th Century Fox studios, arranged for State Department officials to meet with Onassis, who wanted a way to "appease the oil companies without laying him open to a charge of breaking faith with the Saudi government," according to a State Department memo. But nothing came of these efforts, and over the next several months the U.S. position hardened: the entire deal had to be scrapped.

A White House policy document called for "all appropriate measures to bring about cancellation of the agreement between the Saudi Arabian government and Onassis for the transport of Saudi-Arabia-produced oil." The U.S. ambassador in Saudi Arabia, George Wadsworth—the same man who had been the spokesman when he, Eddy and their diplomatic colleagues met with President Truman about Palestine in 1945—was instructed to explain to King Saud what might happen if ARAMCO stopped producing for a while and his revenue was cut off. The Onassis deal was not in conformity with legally binding ARAMCO concession agreements and would set a "pernicious precedent" if allowed to stand, the State Department's memo to Wadsworth said.

ARAMCO, which believed with good reason that it was in an unassailable legal position—especially because the concession agreement required the parties to keep each other fully informed—refused to deal with Onassis and said his ships would be turned away if they arrived at the company's Ras Tanura terminal. (The company informed the U.S. government about this defiant step by passing the information to Deputy Undersecretary of State Robert Murphy, Eddy's former partner in the North Africa campaign. This was a small world.) These opponents of the deal were supported by the operators of independent tanker fleets who were under contract to ARAMCO to transport Saudi crude.

Meanwhile Catapodis—who had been regaling crowds at Riviera watering holes with tales of the rich coup he and Onassis had pulled off but was now bitter as he saw his big payday evaporating—gave documents and testimony to the British consul in Nice alleging that Onassis obtained the contract by bribing Muhammad Alireza and other Saudi officials. He said Onassis had told him that his real purpose was to use the deal as a lever to pry loose a huge payment from ARAMCO for him to go away. Niarchos, who cared nothing about Saudi Arabia or ARAMCO but wanted to torpedo Onassis, purchased copies of the Catapodis documents and used them as the basis for a campaign against the tanker agreement.

At this point the story becomes even murkier and more complicated. What follows is compiled from the accounts of Citino, Lacey, Anthony Cave Brown, Nicholas Fraser and the *London Sunday Times* team, news articles of the period, State Department and White House documents in the diplomatic record, and an interview with Ray Close, the longtime CIA agent who was Eddy's nephew.

Niarchos enlisted as his agent an American private investigator and part-time CIA contact named Robert Maheu, who put the Catapodis documents to good use.

On September 24, 1954, Maheu sent an associate, Paul Gerrity, to meet with John Jernigan of the State Department's Near East bureau. Gerrity delivered a set of the Catapodis papers, Jernigan reported in his memorandum of the conversation, including photostats of documents listing the terms of Onassis's agreement with Alireza.

"Mr. Gerrity said that his firm considered that these papers should be gotten into the hands of King Saud," Jernigan wrote, "and that this should be done quickly before there was any publicity about bribery in conncection with the Onassis agreement since such publicity would embarrass the King and make future relations more difficult." When Jernigan said the CIA would have to be consulted about any such plan, Gerrity said he had already briefed the agency.

The result was that at Gerrity's suggestion the CIA recruited none other than Karl Twitchell, the engineer who had first suggested the possibility of finding oil in the Kingdom to King Abdul Aziz twenty years before, to deliver the papers to King Saud. Maheu, who later became known to the public as the manager of Howard Hughes's Nevada casino empire, also leaked the Catapodis material to European newspapers, including one in Italy secretly owned by the CIA. (Hughes of course had his own Saudi Arabia connection: it was his airline, Transcontinental and Western, or TWA, that had the long-term contract to develop the country's national airline and train its pilots and mechanics.)

Ray Close at the time was a relatively junior CIA agent based in Beirut. Close said that on orders from CIA Director Allen Dulles, he went to Eddy's apartment in Beirut and picked up an ARAMCO check for $2 million, which he delivered to the Saudis through Maheu.

"I can remember going to Uncle Bill's apartment and picking up the check, and I handed it over in one of those restaurants in Pigeon Rocks," a Beirut neighborhood, Close said. "The person to whom I delivered the check was Robert Maheu. The instructions on what to do came right from Allen Dulles. I guess he picked me because he knew I was related to Bill Eddy."

Close described this payment as "a bribe to the Saudis," but said he did not know exactly which Saudis; presumably, he said, the money went to Abdullah Sulaiman or one of the Alirezas. Yet the outcome of all the intrigue was clear-cut: King Saud backed down and ARAMCO prevailed. The King fired Abdullah Sulaiman and agreed to submit the tanker issue to arbitration. That was satisfactory to ARAMCO, which believed with good reason that such a process would end with a favorable ruling, as indeed it did. Onassis was shut out of Saudi Arabia.

Not a word about any of this can be found in Eddy's papers. As with the Tapline coup in Syria, he left no fingerprints.

THE MORAL CRUSADE

All during the ARAMCO years of the 1950s, Eddy on his own time threw his considerable energy and knowledge into the pursuit of his own interests, including writing—he turned out topical essays, voluminous letters, commentaries on issues of the day, and draft chapters for a possible memoir. Despite health problems that began with his first heart attack in 1952, he and Mary were living what was for them an idyllic life, socializing with their innumerable diplomatic and Arab friends, traveling, visiting their children here and there, and splitting time between their Beirut apartment and a villa in the Lebanese hills at Ainab. Eddy joked in letters that he liked to listen to music in the evenings, his favorites being "Tchaikovsky's Fifth, Beethoven's Fifth, and I.W. Harper's Fifth."

He and Mary never reconciled themselves to the existence of Israel—if anything Mary was even more outspoken than he, accusing Israel in public forums of violating United Nations resolutions, encouraging communism and undermining American interests— and much of Eddy's non-ARAMCO activity of that period reflects their hope that America would yet come to its senses on this subject. As his biographical file at ARAMCO said, "He was an ardent friend of the Arabs and an unrelenting foe of political Zionism." In a letter to Beirut's French-language newspaper, Eddy said he was *"un citoyen conscient du Monde Arabe."*

It is apparent from Eddy's correspondence that he truly believed, or convinced himself, that Israel was not a tiny underdog defending itself against powerful enemies but an expansionist power bent on taking over much of the Middle East, and that these supposed Zionist intentions were dangerous to American interests. Eddy believed that Israel was taking advantage of the unlimited Jewish immigration that followed the end of British rule to argue that it needed more land, and that additional land, once acquired, created a demand for more immigrants to occupy and cultivate it. This cycle, according to Eddy, would continue indefinitely, always at the expense of Israel's Arab neighbors.

On May 29, 1951, he sent to Princeton University president Harold W. Dodds an unsigned four-page, single-spaced memo entitled "The Empire of Israel." Eddy told Dodds that "the author has been well known to me for the greater part of my life. I can vouch for the honesty with which he has personally excavated and compiled the facts which he has set down. . . . Together with Iran, the events in Palestine this spring constitute the twin threats to the U.S. strategic position in the Near East today." There is little doubt that the paper's author was Eddy himself; in a letter to Terry Duce he referred to it as "my memorandum."

"Israel," this memo said, "has passed from the consolidation of its territory to expansion of its frontiers. The unlimited immigration of Jews uprooted from their age-old homes in the countries of the Near East and northern Africa, as well as from Europe, has been a deliberate policy of the Israel government to produce the present need for '*lebensraum*,'" an intentionally inflammatory word in this context because of its centrality to Hitler's policies.

The paper said that Israel, deliberately creating a need for territory and equipped with a lot of money, had developed a three-part strategy:

1. Forcible evacuation of Arab villages and Bedouin living in the UN demilitarized zones and in the oases of the Negeb [sic]. This evacuation will produce a vacancy of arable land, which Israel argues should not be allowed to go to waste when Israel's pressure of population can occupy and civilize the "deserted" fields and marshes. This phase is already almost completed.

2. Control of all the waters on or near Israel's borders, including both shores of the Jordan and Yarmuk Rivers, Lake Houle, the Sea of Galilee, and the Dead Sea.

3. Finally, the small but strong, modernized, motorized, fanatical Israeli army is currently being advertised as the only efficient striking force in the Near East available to the Western democracies to oppose Russia." Israel's real purpose, the paper said, is to foment trouble in neighboring countries through infiltration by "Arabic-speaking

communists [who] are being trained in Haifa. . . . When
and if this disorder reaches alarming proportions, Israel will
offer to march to the troubled area to police it—and then
remain to occupy and finally annex the area in question.

The paper identified Israel's supposed targets as parts of Jordan, East Jerusalem, southern Lebanon and Damascus.

Whether or not Eddy was reading Israeli intentions correctly, the events of 1967 would later make it appear to the Arabs that such indeed was the Zionist master plan; it mattered little that the 1967 war was provoked by Egypt and Syria, not by Israel. Eddy's assessment reflected the thinking of many Arabs then and now, and helps to explain why it is so difficult even today for them to accept the legitimacy of Israel as a neighbor state.

Even President Anwar Sadat of Egypt, in defending his 1979 peace treaty with Israel against Arab criticism, argued that the treaty marked the first and only time that an expansionist Israel had accepted permanent limits on its territorial ambitions by returning the Sinai Peninsula to Egypt and recognizing the border.

Eddy kept writing to officials in Washington to try to bring them around to the Arab side. Israel, he told them, was looking for provocations from the Arabs so it would have an excuse to expand its territory at Arab expense, further stoking Arab anger at the United States—a view that he certainly would have believed validated by the outcome of the 1967 war, had he lived to see it. He was indignant about expressions of sympathy for "poor little Israel" from prominent people such as Clare Boothe Luce and Eleanor Roosevelt whom, he said, "a just God will, I am sure, in his own good time consign to the fires of Hell." He could not comprehend that in America this train had left the station and he was pretty much wasting his time.

In 1952, he sent a letter to Major General Robert A. McClure of the U.S. Army, who was director of "Psychological Warfare" at the Pentagon.

"Though I am living in the Near East, and was long ago retired from active duty with the Marine Corps, I have not retired as an American citizen," he wrote. "I am taking the liberty to write an open letter to you, as a general under whom I served on active duty, about the wrecking of the strategic interests of the US in the Near East which is being accomplished steadily by Israel and her political stooges in the USA." As he often did, he pointed out that Israel was buying arms from Soviet satellite countries, refused to contribute any troops to the U.N. war effort in Korea, and declined to permit American troops to be based on its territory.

"Is it known in the USA," he asked, "that of all the Near East countries, Israel is the only one which has not outlawed the Communist party and the only one which seats Communists in its parliament?"

In a similar vein he wrote to the prominent American diplomat George C. McGhee to complain about speeches by U.S. government officials hailing Israel as "an oasis of liberty in a desert of despotism," as Vice President Alben Barkley had put it. In a private letter to another person, he called Barkley a "Zionist stooge," but he usually kept such crude language out of his official correspondence and public remarks, and thus retained his credibility in Washington as an expert on regional issues.

He was asked, for example, to meet with a committee appointed by President Truman to propose development projects that would foster peace. The committee, which included such prominent people as Nelson Rockefeller and Ralph Bunche, was thinking big, and asked Eddy's opinion of a proposed Jordan Valley Authority, modeled on the Tennessee Valley Authority, which would develop dams and hydropower facilities on the Litani and Jordan rivers. The idea was that such a venture would effectively make Lebanon and Jordan partners of Israel instead of enemies.

"My answer to their question was a flat 'no,'" Eddy reported to Terry Duce. "I told them that any such proposals would fail at the present time and would result only in further alienation of the Arab countries, who would be convinced that any such proposal was only a thinly disguised stratagem to establish Israeli economic control of the water and land resources fed by these two important rivers. I further stated that in my opinion no Point IV [economic aid] program can now be devised which will require joint action by Arabs and Israelis." The Arabs, he said, would accept only projects that would aid them exclusively, not Israel, which was already getting plenty of help.

To counter the influence of the "Zionists," and to harness the potentially damaging surge of religious sentiment among Muslims that he perceived long before most professional analysts, Eddy promoted the idea of a "moral alliance" between Christianity and Islam, which he broached in a speech in Washington in 1950.

"It's always seemed to me," he said, "that not enough was made of the common ground between these great religions. We have not only the belief in one God—it was the need for monotheism which came first to Mohammed, born into an idolatrous world. We also share with Islam many of our prophets and much of our Scripture; the Muslims revere Jesus as a prophet, and we hold Mohammed in very high respect. We share the beliefs in reverence, humility, charity, the brotherhood of mankind, and the family as the sacred unit in society."

It is questionable whether the Christian world did in fact have "very high respect" for the Prophet of Islam, but Eddy forged ahead, seeking support for the project he called "A Crusade for Three Faiths" because, as he said in a letter to a friend, "from the point of view of psychological warfare alone, we need desperately some common ground to which we welcome the Muslims and the Arabs as respected and valued friends."

The specific objective of this "crusade" was to make Jerusalem an international city under United Nations control, as the U.N. had envisioned at the time of partition, rather than the capital of a Zionist state under Jewish control, as Israel had declared it to be.

Eddy believed that his Arab friends and contacts saw value in this scheme. In a 1951 letter to his friend Dorothy Thompson, the prominent journalist, he said he had "new proof that such a moral alliance would be welcomed by Muslim leaders who would, I think, come more than half-way in responding to a friendly overture from the Christian West." It is a measure of how deeply his antipathy to Israel clouded his judgment that he listed among these supportive "Muslim leaders" Al-haj Amin al-Husseini, the former Grand Mufti of Jerusalem.

That gentleman, a notorious hater of Jews, had been purged from office by the British because of his radical activism. During World War II he took refuge in Germany, where he actively supported the

Nazis, and in 1951 he was unrepentant. In a meeting with Eddy, he "insisted that we were on the wrong side in the last war and should have been allied with Germany against Russia," Eddy told Dorothy Thompson. Nevertheless, Eddy said, "no matter how low his political fortunes may have fallen, [he] is still a great influence in Islamic religious circles." Eddy seems to have had no sense of the political and moral unacceptability of making common cause with such a man, or of how damaging it was to his pro-Muslim campaign to suggest that Muslims found al-Husseini to be an important religious influence.

In January 1953, he distributed to friends and contacts a paper outlining his vision for the proposed crusade. "The hour has struck," it said, "for a Crusade to rescue Greater Jerusalem from the political passions and area ambitions of the princes of this world. We Americans do well to stay out of most of the territorial controversies of the Near East, where colonist and nationalist clash. Greater Jerusalem, however, need not be regarded as a province either of pan-Arabia or of pan-Israel; it belongs to the three faiths, Christendom, Islam and Judaism—all of whom would be served if the area were removed completely from the police power of any one nation or sect." The failure of the United Nations to act when David Ben Gurion declared Jerusalem to be the capital of Israel had reduced the world organization's prestige among the Arabs to "its all-time nadir."

Eddy's paper said that the United States, "which is known to be capable of resisting aggression elsewhere against the U.N. and freedom [as in Korea] is on final trial before the Faithful of the world who are waiting to see whether American principles apply to the Near East."

He kept at this for two or three years, undeterred by the tepid responses of his correspondents. He wrote about this "Ninth and Last Crusade" to his old friend Pete Hart, by then director of Near East affairs at the State Department, and to George Wadsworth, now ambassador to Saudi Arabia; to publishing tycoon Henry Luce, husband of the same Clare Boothe Luce whom Eddy so reviled; to the editor of Reader's Digest; to Dorothy Thompson and other well-placed journalists; and to scholars and academics in several institutions.

Most of those who responded said the problem was accurately described, and praised Eddy for taking it on, but predictably declined to get involved for one reason or another. Professor Millar Burrows of Yale, for example, questioned the appropriateness of the term "Crusade," the Crusades having been wars of Christianity against Islam. Wilton Wynn, a journalist with extensive experience in the region, said the Arabs would see the project as "only a scheme to take away from the Arabs that bit of Jerusalem which they now hold." When Eddy tried to persuade the Ford Foundation to move its regional office from Beirut to Jerusalem to support the idea of internationalization, he got a blunt brush-off from Kenneth R. Iverson, the foundation's assistant director of international programs. Such a move would cause enormous logistical difficulties for Ford's staff and its grant recipients, Iverson said, and besides, "having very recently reread the history of the Crusades, as written by [Steven] Runciman, the first thought that popped into my head was that no Crusade had ever been successful."

It appears from the files in Eddy's papers that he finally abandoned this quixotic effort after the Suez War of 1956, the first and only regional conflict in which the United States took a position that could be construed as anti-Israel and pro-Arab. (Eddy in a family letter described Israel's objective in that war as "the hatching of a Zionist empire, which, in time, will be a greater threat to all of us than Russia ever has been.") The only change in the status of Jerusalem came about in the war of 1967, after Eddy's death, when Israel captured from Jordan that part of Jerusalem it did not already control, and annexed it.

Family members and people who knew Eddy say that none of his campaigning against Israel and Zionism was inspired by aversion to Jews as Jews. As a product of the clubby Protestant, Ivy League background common to America's privileged classes in that era, he told ethnic jokes like all his peers, and belonged to clubs where Jews were not welcome. In one letter he wrote disparagingly about a woman who had married "a Hebrew." He was relentless in his criticism of Israel as a country, but did not think ill of Jews as individuals or of the Jewish religion. The same could have been said of some of his State Department and CIA colleagues.

"He would no more accept intellectually the concept of anti-semitism than fly to the moon," as Ray Close put it, but "one has to remember that was a different generation."

Indeed, throughout the period of his "Moral Crusade," Eddy supported his friend Rabbi Elmer Berger, executive vice-president of the American Council for Judaism, a group of prominent American Jews who were, like Eddy, anti-Zionist and opposed to the creation of a Jewish state. Even today, the ACJ says on its web site that "We interpret Judaism as a universal religious faith, rather than an ethnic or nationalist identity." As American Jews, the ACJ said in the 1940s and says today, "Israel is not our 'homeland.' We believe that America alone is our homeland." That was why Bill Eddy rowed in the same boat as Rabbi Berger.

WELCOME, MARINES

The Middle East upheavals of 1958 brought the Marines back into the Eddys' lives in a big way.

In the spring of that year, Lebanon was gripped by a political crisis as opponents of President Camille Chamoun tried to fend off what they feared would be an attempt to gain a second term. This was a time of turmoil and transition throughout the region. Nasser's nationalization of the Suez Canal after the U.S. withdrew funding for the Aswan High Dam ignited the war of 1956, which finally put an end to the era of French and British dominance. With India now independent, the canal mattered less to Britain anyway, and there was less reason for London to keep control of the Gulf statelets that flanked Saudi Arabia. The Middle East was now the arena for a different great power struggle, between the United States and the Soviet Union.

On one level Lebanon was a two-bit country of no strategic importance to the United States except perhaps as the Mediterranean terminus of Tapline. But in early 1957 President Eisenhower pledged that the United States would safeguard the political independence of any country in the region threatened by any other country controlled by "international communism," a description that in Washington's view now included Nasser's Egypt. When the uprising against Chamoun, a right-wing Christian, erupted into violence, Chamoun accused Egypt and its ally Syria of fomenting trouble and smuggling arms to the rebels. Lebanon's "confessional" system of government, which allocated political offices on the basis of religion, seemed about to unravel. Chamoun, the only regional leader to endorse what came to be known as the Eisenhower Doctrine, asked for American help. The 1958 crisis in Lebanon presaged the all-out civil war that would erupt there in 1975 and devastate the country for fifteen years.

Even under the Eisenhower Doctrine, the United States might have stayed out of the 1958 Lebanese crisis had it not been for that summer's coup d'état in Iraq. On July 14, leftist army officers led by Brigadier General Abdul Karim al-Kassim seized power in Baghdad, declared a republic, and executed King Feisal, the crown prince, and Prime Minister Nuri as-Said. From the perspective of Saudi Arabia, this might have been seen as a positive development because it eliminated one of the remaining Hashemite claimants to Arab leadership, but in the West the Iraqi coup was seen as a Soviet grab for influence in the oil fields of Arabia, a Cold War triumph for Moscow. Rumors swept the region that a similar plot was being developed against Jordan's pro-Western Hashemite King Hussein, and the United States feared that the new regime in Iraq would try to take over Kuwait—as Iraq indeed would do, under a different ruler, in 1990.

It was too late to do much about Iraq, but Eisenhower decided the United States had to intervene in the region to prevent further damage. He ordered a massive deployment of Marines and Army troops to Lebanon. On July 15, just a day after the coup in Baghdad, a landing team from the 2d Battalion, 2d Marine Regiment, out of Camp Lejeune, N.C., landed on the beach near Beirut's airport. A second battalion arrived the next day. Overall, the United States force deployed to the Middle East comprised 75 ships and about 45,000 men, of whom 5,000 were Marines.

Army troops and Marines took up positions on the ground in Lebanon, though only the Marines staged amphibious landings. In less than a week, there were 7,200 U.S. combat troops in the Beirut area, including three battalions of Marines. Within a month, the deployment in Lebanon grew to 14,000 troops.

As many historians and military analysts have noted, there were comic-opera aspects to this American intervention. The United States was not at war with Lebanon or any of its many factions, or with any neighboring country. The American forces never fired a shot, nor did any Lebanese troops shoot at the invading Americans, although it required considerable diplomatic arm-twisting to persuade Lebanon's chief of staff, General Fuad Chehab, to keep his troops in barracks. Chehab opposed the American intervention as an infringement on Lebanese sovereignty, and had to be talked out of armed resistance.

As Arthur Goldschmidt put it in his history of the region, "The American Marines in Lebanon confronted more Coke vendors than communists." Wilbur Crane Eveland, a veteran CIA operative who was there at the time, wrote in *Ropes of Sand* that "Pepsi and 7-Up umbrellas on the beaches sheltered vendors who prayed that fresh waves of Marines would land." Miles Copeland, another CIA operative and a rival of Eveland's, wrote that "the fleet arrived in less than twenty-four hours, to unload wave after wave of grim-faced Marines, rifles poised for action, to be greeted by startled bathers sunning themselves on Beirut's beautiful beaches and hordes of little boys selling chewing gum."

The reality of life in Beirut that summer was less amusing. Commerce and social life came to a halt. An overnight curfew was imposed. Construction projects were abandoned, tourists vanished, hotels stood empty. Roof tiles were blown off the Eddys' hillside villa in Ainab when shooting erupted during the turmoil surrounding the Iraq coup, but they escaped injury because they were on the road again.

On the day of the coup in Baghdad, Bill and Mary Eddy were in neighboring Syria, where Eddy was working his network on behalf of Tapline. In Damascus, they stayed with the U.S. Consul General, none other than Parker T. "Pete" Hart, who was the young consul in Dhahran while Eddy was running the U.S. Legation in Jeddah. Syria celebrated the news from Baghdad, but the excitement in the streets did not appear menacing so the Eddys went ahead with a plan to drive up to Syria's second city, Aleppo, near the Turkish border, which is where they were when the first Marines hit the beach in Beirut.

In Aleppo, they were guests of the U.S. consul there, Alfred L. "Roy" Atherton and his wife, Betty. (Atherton would later be ambassador to Egypt and chief of the State Department's Near East bureau.) When word of the landings reached Aleppo, Mary Eddy wrote, "We were told to pack and be ready to leave (for Turkey) at an hour's notice. I certainly admired Betty Atherton the way she calmly went ahead and packed emergency food rations, medicines and essential clothes for herself and three children. At the same time she invited all the staff to come for dinner and spend the evening. We listed to radio reports and waited for the reactions from the town. In case of unfriendly rioting, we were to leave. However the reactions were of stunned surprise and the town remained quiet. The next morning we were relieved to hear that the Beirut [airport] had reopened for civilian air traffic, so we boarded our Air Liban plane at noon and arrived in Beirut an hour later to look down on the spectacular scene of 14 ships of the 6th Fleet. Marines were all around the airport, and we passed men marching, tanks, land-rovers as we went into town."

It is almost impossible to sort out the many networks of competing, conflicting and conspiring interests and divided loyalties in the diplomatic, intelligence, and financial communities centered in Beirut at the time. The Eddys had friends and relatives in all the diplomatic posts and CIA missions in Lebanon and Syria. (James Moose, Eddy's predecessor in Saudi Arabia, was U.S. ambassador in Damascus, and thus the boss of Roy Atherton and Pete Hart.) Even Kim Philby, the notorious British turncoat and son of Harry St. John Philby, the longtime confidant of King Abdul Aziz, was lurking in Beirut's shadows, emerging to shock everyone by conducting a very public affair with the wife of the *New York Times* correspondent. Everyone knew everyone else, of course, and everyone had multiple agendas—even within the U.S. embassy, where rival CIA factions competed for influence and the ambassador, Robert McClintock, opposed the military intervention ordered by Eisenhower.

Miles Copeland—who had been on the CIA team that engi-neered the 1949 Husni Zaim coup in Syria—had now in 1958 gone to Cairo in an effort to broker an agreement between Nasser's supporters in Lebanon and the Chamoun loyalists. He described the Beirut intrigue in his notoriously cynical classic *The Game of Nations.* In his view, the fact that the Marines and Army troops were successfully deployed without encountering opposition from Che-hab's Lebanese forces was "a brilliant feat" of Ambassador McClin-tock. But Washington, he wrote, was hearing a different story "from sources other than the Embassy [i.e. Wilbur Eveland]. Although many of these reports were based on only a partial understanding of the problems, some of them were extremely convincing, especially the ones which were written in practical, businesslike language, in contrast to the Ambassador's somewhat literary style. When some of the more influential journalists began to write stories which, like these reports, implied that the Ambassador was not entirely on top of his job, Secretary [of State John Foster] Dulles decided upon the standard solution: send out a Great White Father."

This august personal representative of the president was none other than Robert Murphy. He was, according to Copeland, "a man of such long-established reputation that, by the time he was sent to Lebanon, he had fallen into the habit of neglecting his home-work, and relying on his experience and sagacity to make the right decision with what is euphemistically described as a 'fresh look' at the situation."

The joke around Beirut, Copeland recalled, was that Murphy's assignment was to prevent a coup within the U.S. embassy. In truth, Murphy's assignment was extremely complex and difficult: find a political solution in which Chamoun would finish his presi-dential term but not seek another, broker an agreement among all factions on a presidential successor, and prevent Lebanon from drifting into the leftist-nationalist camp occupied by Egypt, Syria and now Iraq. To do this Murphy had to come to terms with leftist opponents of Chamoun who were reluctant even to talk to him. The conduit by which he reached them was Bill Eddy.

On July 24, Murphy reported to the State Department that he had met with several key figures in the Lebanese standoff, including "opposition leaders Abdullah Yafi and Hassan Oueini. Through intermediary of former State Department officer, Colonel William Eddy, who speaks fluent Arabic, I met these two 'moderate' leaders of opposition at a neutral house. They were fervent in professing friendship for the west and the US but insisted their quarrel was only against Chamoun . . . their hatred of Chamoun appeared intense."

This meeting with two allies of former premier Saeb Salaam, a popular and influential figure, was crucial in persuading Murphy that the uprising against Chamoun was largely an internal Lebanese affair, not an anti-Western communist plot.

"After hours of conversation," Murphy wrote in his memoirs, "Saeb Salaam's henchmen seemed reassured that the United States was seeking only to protect the independence of Lebanon, and they finally said that they were not unfriendly to Americans. This gave me an opportunity to refer to the safety of the American forces in Beirut. . . . Could not Saeb Salaam's associates end their indiscriminate shooting in the city, which might lead to very grave sanctions? My talk evidently had some effect, because the shooting died away the following day and except for occasional outbursts, life became quieter in Beirut. I have always been grateful to Bill Eddy for arranging that meeting because it seemed to mark a turn in events . . ."

In September, General Chehab was elected to succeed Chamoun. Beirut calmed down quickly after that, and the transition was peaceful. The regional crisis receded after the new government in Iraq promised not to interfere with oil operations, and Washington relaxed. The American troops were withdrawn from Lebanon in October.

Lebanon—corrupt, hedonistic, faction-riven Lebanon—returned to business as usual. Social life, disrupted for months by a curfew, resumed with the usual suspects. The Eddys attended a cocktail party with "British friends," including Kim Philby. But the outcome of the U.S. intervention was not an unalloyed triumph for American policy, and it did nothing to solve the underlying problems.

According to a "Special National Intelligence Estimate" prepared by the CIA and other agencies, "The presence of US and [British] troops in Lebanon and Jordan slowed down the trend in both countries toward seizure of control by local forces sympathetic to the UAR [the United Arab Republic, Nasser's short-lived union of Egypt and Syria]. The landing of these forces has not, however, changed basic trends in the area and developments in both countries will continue in the direction of neutralism and accommodations with pan-Arab nationalism . . . the struggle between the Christian and Moslem elements [in Lebanon] is likely to continue for some time and to involve occasional resort to force, but we believe that large-scale outbreaks in the near future are not likely." In this, at least, the analysts were correct: full-scale civil war did not break out until seventeen years later.

The ever-cynical Miles Copeland offered an even dimmer assessment. The intervention looked like a success for enforcement of the Eisenhower Doctrine, he wrote, but "the outcome was exactly what Gamal Abdel Nasser was seeking. It was as though the Marines had been brought in to achieve Nasser's objectives for him." The new president, Chehab, and prime minister, Rashid Karami, were just the two men Nasser wanted, Copeland wrote. Worse, the opposition's tactics, which included kidnapping and random shelling, had established terrorism as an effective and even respectable weapon. And in reality, "the Eisenhower doctrine was dead" because of the events in Iraq, where the ouster of the pro-Western prime minister Nuri as-Said had been Nasser's primary objective.

On the other hand, the military intervention made clear that the United States was willing and able to take forceful action in the Middle East to protect its global interests. In just twenty years since President Roosevelt received his first letter from King Abdul Aziz, the United States had become the preeminent outside power in the region.

In the Eddys' 1958 Christmas letter to family and friends, Bill Eddy wrote that the summer's events showed that "Every cloud has a silver lining: the troubles in Lebanon brought to our Marine Corps home more Marines than we would ever see elsewhere, dozens of officers to enjoy Mary's hospitality and our terrace with its view unsurpassed in Beirut. Lieutenant General Pollock and Colonel Jenkins served with Bill Jr. and remembered him very well. Several officers demanded to know how I worked the racket to retire in such a charming spot. The conduct of the Marines in Lebanon was superb; not one incident to mar their personal record. They made friends with all, from the grimiest Arab bootblack to the Prime Minister. Lebanon saw only the open, friendly hand, never the mailed fist."

Two years later, the Eddys were honored at a ball staged in a Beirut hotel to celebrate the 185th anniversary of the founding of the Corps. "The expense of the affair is all borne by the few Marines stationed here as guards of the embassy and a few officers studying Arabic," Mary wrote, "but they spared no expense to put on a nice party. The most important ceremony is the cake-cutting, and Dad was asked to cut the huge cake with a Marine Corps sword. The first piece goes to the youngest Marine present and the next to the oldest, which was Dad . . . Col. Mathews, the officer in charge of this area, introduced Dad, gave a résumé of his life, and gave him a fine tribute which got a big hand from the audience." Once a Marine, always a Marine.

THE WRITING LIFE

For years Bill Eddy the raconteur, Bill Eddy the jokester and teller of tall tales, had nurtured the idea of collecting an English-language volume of the tales of Goha, a mischievous character of Arab imagination who delighted in foiling the rich and powerful. Now in Beirut, Eddy found time for this project.

"For the Arabs," the journalist David Lamb once wrote, "Goha is the Walter Mitty of Arabia, the little man living out his fantasies, always triumphing over great odds. And for the Westerner, to understand Goha is to comprehend, to a small degree at least, the character of the Arab."

Goha the Arab Everyman was lazy, impudent, irreverent, and sometimes downright subversive. He sometimes appeared to be a buffoon, as in this brief tale recounted by the Iraqi writer Khalid Kishtainy: Goha "was asked which is more useful, the sun or the moon. 'The moon without any doubt,' he said. 'The sun comes out during the day when it's not needed.'"

Of course he never held a real job, but he was actually clever. Fueled by boundless optimism, he outwitted sultans and sheikhs time and again. His origins have been lost with the passage of centuries, but as Kishtainy noted, "No measure of his popularity could be better than the jealous contest between the Arabs, Turks, Iranians and Kurds to claim him as one of their compatriots." His personal copy of the stories, Kishtainy said, "is a tattered, second-hand copy which I found in a remote Moroccan village offered for sale by a street pedlar."

In one Goha tale that Lamb picked up in his travels around the Arab world, a pompous sultan wanted someone to teach his donkey to read and write. Goha volunteered for the job, telling the sultan it would take three years and would require that he live in a sumptuous villa during that period. The sultan agreed, and Goha moved into a mansion with the donkey. He lounged comfortably in the house while the donkey grazed happily in the gardens. Goha's friends of course warned that if he failed to produce a literate donkey in the time allotted, he would lose his head, but Goha was unperturbed. "After all," he said, "one of four things might happen. The sultan may die. I may die. The donkey may die. Or, who knows, the donkey may learn to read and write."

The scamp Goha appealed to Eddy's sense of humor, developed as a naughty boy on the streets of Sidon. "He had a very strong mischievous streak in him," his nephew Ray Close recalled. "When he was a boy in Sidon, he used to steal an orange from a local vendor; he was always getting himself into trouble, he was a mischief maker." Friends from his youth called him by his middle name, Alfred, because it sounds like the Arabic words meaning "a thousand monkeys."

Eddy compiled and translated fifty-one of the Goha tales into a volume called "*50 and One Jests of Goha*," whom he called "Goha Ibn Insha'Allah al Masri," or "Goha the Egyptian, son of 'if God wills it.'" Published in Beirut by Khayat's Book Cooperative, it listed the author as "Al Hajj Lemuel Gulliver, Jr.," a multiple joke derived from Eddy's background. Three samples suffice to convey the tone:

The stingy Mutsarrif (finance minister) of Tamerlane fell into the Tigris and was drowning. Bystanders on the bank shouted "Give us your hand," but he ignored their advice and was about to go down for the third time when Goha appeared and said, "Take my hand," which the Mutsarrif did and he was pulled ashore. Goha said to the crowd, "You didn't know how to talk to the poor miser; he never gives anything but will always accept." So Goha was made Mutsarrif in his place.

Goha, serving temporarily as the Imam of a mosque in Cairo, mounted the pulpit on a Friday to preach a sermon which he had neglected altogether to prepare. He announced the subject of his discourse and then asked the drowsy congregation, "Do you folk understand this subject?" With true Arab politeness, they all nodded, yes, whereupon Goha exclaimed, "Why should I trouble myself to expound what is already known?" and went off to take a nap. The following Friday he repeated his routine to the congregation which had doubled in number owing to the report of his eccentric conduct. This time when asked whether they understood the point in theology to be analyzed, the assembly to a man shook their heads, no. At that Goha, in a rage, cried, "Why should I trouble myself to teach ignoramuses who know nothing?" and he departed. The third Friday, the faithful plotted to fix him, and to the same inquiry, half the congregation said "no" and half said "yes." At that Goha said, "That is fine, those who know tell those who don't." He then betook himself to his rest.

At one time Goha was the Judge in his city, and he proceeded to prove that justice is a mockery. One day a robber set up a ladder at night to reach the upper window of the richest man in town, whom he wanted to rob of the jewels and money kept in his bedroom. The ladder was a little too short and in trying to scramble into the upper window the rotten wood of the window-sill came off in the robber's arms and he fell to the ground, breaking his leg. The next day he was brought on a litter to Goha to file a complaint against the householder for having a window-sill which endangered the lives of fellow citizens.

Goha summoned the householder and accused him of causing the broken leg. The householder said, "Oh, Goha, it is not my
fault. A week ago I engaged a carpenter to come and make a new
window-sill but he didn't do it. The carpenter is to blame." So much
for the householder.

So Goha summoned the carpenter and said, "You are responsible for the broken leg." The carpenter said, "Oh, Goha, it is not my
fault. I did indeed promise to mend the window-sill. I had the new
piece of wood cut and set with hammer and nails all ready when
looking out through the window I saw the most beautiful woman
Allah ever made going down the street. Who am I to resist the gifts
of Allah? I laid down my tools and followed the irresistible beauty.
She is to blame for the broken leg." So much for the carpenter.

Then said Goha, "We must hang the woman since she is to
blame. Bring her here." The young woman said, "Oh, Goha, I am not
to blame, Allah made my face and figure, summon Him! Many a time
have I walked down that street and no man left his work to follow
me, but I have saved money for many years and I took it to the best
tailor in the city and he made for me a beautiful scarlet dress such as
was never seen before. It was this dress which distracted the carpenter, not I, and the tailor is to blame," So much for the woman.

Then Goha said "All right then, we will hang the tailor." The
tailor was brought and accused of the crime and he said, "I admit it,
and I glory in my crime. I have succeeded, I have lived. I am ready
to die."

So Goha ordered the tailor to be taken to the usual place of
hanging, a gate of the city, to be hanged by the neck until he should
be dead. But unfortunately the gate of the city was low and the tailor was a very tall man, and whenever they tried to hang him his
feet touched the ground. So they hunted about until they found a
short tailor, and they hanged him instead.

Other than the Goha tales and a treatise on *Gulliver's Travels*
back in his academic years, Eddy never wrote a full-length book.
He was a prolific author of essays on religious and educational subjects that were published mostly in obscure specialized journals.
(At some point in adult life Eddy gave up the Presbyterian faith of

his ancestors and became an Episcopalian, but his essays on religious themes do not appear to reflect the specific teachings of any particular denomination.)

Several prominent publishers talked to Eddy about a possible memoir, but he was at best ambivalent about such a project because he never wanted a high public profile. In one letter to his children, he said many people had urged him to write such a book because "Everyone who retires writes a book." There were many reasons not to do it, including laziness, he joked, but "I have now hit on a scheme for writing a book that suits me down to the ground. Here is the outline of my forthcoming book: (1) List all my acquaintances who have money or social ambitions or both. (2) Dig out the details of one or more shameful skeletons in their closets, lapses from honesty, chastity or veracity. (3) Write to each one stating that I intend to include the episode in my book to make it readable and salable. (4) Then I pocket the money they send me NOT to print the story. In this way I will earn funds far in excess of ordinary royalties, without ever bothering to write a book or hunt for a publisher. I will get rich and at the same time have the merit in heaven of having protected many characters and families from disgrace."

In another letter, he complained that publishers wanted "a personalized autobiography written in the first person, the sort of 'From Missionary Son to Ambassador' bunk. I always refused." Among his papers is a letter from an unidentified correspondent to an editor at Frederick A. Praeger Inc. saying he had talked to Eddy about the book project and "he showed me a large stack of correspondence from publishing companies . . . it was clear from what they said that they wanted a first-person narrative from him dramatizing himself as a great and colorful figure. He finds this idea nauseating."

These discussions continued on and off for a decade, until July 1961, when Eddy signed a contract with Thomas Y. Crowell & Co., then an important New York publishing house, to write *Adventures in the Arab World, 1896–1961*. An outline showed chapters about Roosevelt and King Abdul Aziz, the Yemen journey, Jeddah in wartime, the OSS campaign, and Lebanon and President Chamoun. Parts of this material, such as the "Spies and Lies in

Tangier" narrative, have been preserved in Eddy's papers, but the book never appeared because he died before completing it.

Thus he is known today, to the extent that he is known to the American public at all, only for the slender volume *FDR Meets Ibn Saud*, the most-cited source of information about that celebrated encounter. It was published in 1954 by American Friends of the Middle East, a CIA-funded but nominally independent organization that promoted good relations between Americans and Arabs.

THE FINAL DAYS

By the time the Marines pulled out of Lebanon in the fall of 1958, Bill Eddy was in the last four years of his life, and it is probably just as well that he did not live much longer. The Arab world he knew and loved was changing, and not for the better. The era of intellectual growth and social progress that led the region into independence was being overpowered by new regimes based on force and run by thugs. For America the time of the pioneers, the idealistic missionaries and adventurous oil wildcatters who planted the Stars and Stripes on Arabian soil, had also passed. For better or worse, the United States was now the major external power in the Middle East. From the Arab perspective, the disaster of the 1967 war would permanently poison this landscape. The influence of the "old Middle East hands" in the U.S. government would diminish as the acceptability of Arabs diminished in the decade after Eddy's death, and the very letters "CIA" inspire loathing and demagoguery throughout the Middle East. All romance about the region has evaporated, all illusions have long since been shattered. Nobody has time for Goha.

Bill Eddy's diseased and damaged heart finally gave out on May 3, 1962. Feeling ill after breakfast, he told Mary he had decided not to go to the office and went instead to the bedroom to lie down. A couple of hours later, Mary went in to check on him and found him in a coma. He was taken to the hospital of the American University of Beirut—the institution to which his missionary ancestors and colleagues had contributed so much—where he was seen by a prominent American doctor who was in town for a convention. But his breathing had stopped as he was carried down the stairs of their apartment building. He never awakened.

The mourners at his funeral service more than filled All Saints Anglican Church on Beirut's lovely seafront. With Mary were Bill Jr. and other family members, diplomats and intelligence agents, representatives of ARAMCO, and Arab friends and colleagues. "A United States flag covered the casket," Bill Jr. wrote to his sisters and brother, "and four Marine captains stood by as honor guard in their handsome blue uniforms. These Marines are friends of Dad's and provided this at their own request. It was most fitting." On the day of the funeral, the American flag flew at half staff at the U.S. embassy in Jeddah and at Hobart College.

As he wished, Bill Eddy was buried in Sidon, near the church and school to which his parents and grandparents had devoted their lives. That this American who gave so much of his life to service of the American government, and later his wife, would wish to be buried in a small foreign country far from American shores reflects their deep ties of family and of attachment to the Arab land and people, which were manifest in a letter Eddy wrote to family members in 1950.

> During a call from one of the sons of Hassan Accawi (father's faithful cook who was with him and Clarence and me when father died in the Bussa camp) I had promised to visit Majdeluna, the village which father freed from the oppressing Turkish landlord in the 1890s. He bought the village, house by house, with personal funds, and let the villagers buy their homes from him on easy installments. It is one of the many villages where his name is still a talisman.
>
> The Church is one which he had built under his own supervision and he preached the first sermon in it. The Sidon pastor, Qassis Ibrahim, and his wife were the first couple married in the church, both of them being natives of the village. I did not know that until I called on them in the A.M. so I invited them to ride with Hilmi and me to Majdeluna in the afternoon.
>
> Ruth and Condit [Eddy] will remember the terrain. . . . At Majdeluna all the local Protestants (two-thirds of the village) turned out for a jamboree and a gathering in the Church where speeches were made, a poem recited in father's honor, and later

coffee and sweets served in Hassan's home by his widow, a very old lady nearly totally blind. I felt like a wolf in wolf's clothing, wholly unfit to represent the family, the earlier generations, and the elder members of which had done so much for these simple, grateful folk. One old codger, ninety years old, leaning on a stick, rose in the Church to say to me, "I was a lad here when your father came to preach one day. He said there was room in Gerard [School] for one boarding pupil from Majdeluna, and a dozen of us wanted to be the one. He chose me, he gave me the chance to get an education, for thirty years your father was my teacher and friend, without him I would have been nothing." I told him "You are luckier than I; you had him for thirty years, I had him only for ten."

I was wholly unprepared for these tributes to father, and had to do my best in improvised remarks in Arabic. I told them I had just come from the cemetery where I had again read the inscription on father's gravestone: "He rests from his labors but his work lives on." I told them that the same day I had the living proof of that statement, this church which he built; those present whom he had joined in marriage, whom he had baptized or taught or befriended, these were living monuments. Some of them upbraided me for not returning to carry on father's work, but I told them they were carrying it on as no other could do.

And so Bill Eddy was buried where he was happiest in life, among the Arabs. His grave is in a small, ill-tended cemetery next to a weedy citrus grove on a hill in Sidon, the city of his birth. Even today many residents of Sidon remember the family and were able to give me directions to the grave site. Beneath a canopy of cypress trees that Bill Eddy himself planted, four simple slabs of marble lying flat mark the final resting places of Eddy, his parents, and his wife. The inscription on his gravestone, in English and Arabic, reads, "William Alfred Eddy. Colonel, U.S.M.C. Born Sidon, March 9, 1896. Died Beirut, May 3, 1962." Other than the Eddys, all the people buried in that cemetery are Arabs.

NOTES ON SOURCES

The three principal sources of documentary information about the life and career of William A. Eddy are:

1. The William A. Eddy papers, in the Mudd Manuscript Library, Princeton University. The files contain personal, professional and family correspondence, manuscripts and memorabilia, and photographs. Cited here as EP, sorted by box and folder, as EP 8/11, for Eddy Papers, box 8, folder 11.

2. The National Archives of the United States, in Washington D.C. and College Park, Md. Cited as NA. The files are sorted by Records Group, or RG, as in RG 19, General Records of the Department of State.

3. *Foreign Relations of the United States,* a collection of declassified diplomatic and presidential documents compiled by the historian of the State Department. Cited as FRUS. The published series is sorted by year, usually with one volume per year devoted to Middle East material, as in FRUS 1945, Vol. VIII.

Additional material was found in the papers of Robert Murphy, Stanford University; the papers of Franklin D. Roosevelt, Roosevelt Library, Hyde Park, N.Y.; the William E. Mulligan Papers, Georgetown University; the Harold E. Dodds Papers, Princeton University; the archives of the U.S. Marine Corps Historical Center, Quantico, Va.; the Clarence E. McIntosh Papers, Georgetown University; and the papers of Harry S. Truman, Truman Library, Independence, Mo.

Where I have included materials or drawn ideas from books and other writings by others, these are listed in summary form in the notes to the individual chapters. Full publication details on books are in the bibliography.

Bill Eddy's daughter, Mary Furman Eddy, was interviewed on September 27, 2004, in Buckeystown, Md.

Ray Close and David Dodge were interviewed together on June 25, 2004, in Princeton, N.J.

Archivists and scholars in Saudi Arabia have only recently begun to track down and catalogue Arabic documents relating to the period when Bill Eddy lived there. Saudi photographs from those archives are available and some are reproduced in this book, but I have not seen records of internal Saudi correspondence and royal memoranda, if indeed they exist.

NOTES TO INTRODUCTION

Powell's account, "The Romance of the Missionary," appeared in *Everybody's Magazine,* vol. xxxi, no. 3 (September 1909).

NOTES TO CHAPTER 1, FRANCE

Eddy's military and medical records are in EP, Box 10, and NA, RG 125, box 333.

Eddy's notebook is in EP, 15/26.

Capt. John West's paper, "Belleau Wood," is in the Belleau Wood files of the Marine Corps Historical Center, Quantico, Va.

Maj. Edwin N. McClellan's paper, "The United States Marine Corps in the World War," is at www.au.af.mil/au/awc/awcgate/usmchist/war.txt.

Lt. Col. Ernest Otto's article, "The Battles for the Possession of Belleau woods, June, 1918," was published in *US Naval Institute Proceedings*, vol. 54, no. 11, (Nov. 1928), pp. 940ff.

See also Dick Camp Jr., "And a Few Marines: Colonel William A. Eddy," *Leatherneck* magazine, April 2004, pp. 46ff.

Books cited in this chapter:

Pierce and Hough, *The Compact History of the United States Marine Corps*

Strawn, *The First World War*

Keegan, *The First World War*

Asprey, *At Belleau Wood*

Jones, *A Brief History*

Clark, *Devil Dogs*

Liddell Hart, *A History of the First World War*

Miller, "At Belleau Wood" in *Twentieth Century Marines*

Antonius, *The Arab Awakening*

Kaplan, *The Arabists*

Issawi, *Economic History*

Farwell, *Over There*

Keegan, *The First World War*

Mead, *The Doughboys*

NOTES TO CHAPTER 2, NEW YORK

Eddy's military and medical records are in EP, Box 10, and NA, RG 125, box 333.

Eddy's PhD dissertation is in the Mudd Manuscript Library at Princeton, separate from his personal papers.

Eddy's obituary was published in the New York Times on May 5, 1962.

On basketball, see Mulligan Papers, 1/18.

Files on the Dartmouth and Hobart years are in several EP boxes. See also Dodds Papers, correspondence, box 105.

NOTES TO CHAPTER 3, CAIRO

Wallace Murray memo is in EP 11/6.

Eddy's Cairo correspondence is in EP 5.

The declassified OSS history is *Top Secret*, edited by Kermit Roosevelt.

NOTES TO CHAPTER 4, NORTH AFRICA

For a good military summary of Operation TORCH, see the U.S. Army's web site at http://www.army.mil/cmh-pg/brochures/algeria/algeria.htm. A more detailed and dramatic account is given in Atkinson, *An Army At Dawn*.

Eddy's correspondence with Murphy and related documents, and Eisenhower's detailed orders for the TORCH landings, are in Murphy Papers, boxes 44–47.

Eddy's letters to family about this period and related documents are in EP, esp. boxes 5, 10 and 13. His "Spies and Lies in Tangier" narrative is in EP 13/24.

C. Coon's narrative, "North Africa May 1942-May 1943. My Part in OSS Operations During That Period" and other OSS documents are in "TORCH Anthology," NA, RG 226, box 49.

Eddy address to Naval War College, 1953, text in Dodds Papers, 105/1.

Books cited in this chapter:

Alsop & Braden, *Sub Rosa*

Smith, *OSS: The Secret History*

Murphy, *Diplomat Among Warriors*

Funk, *The Politics of TORCH*

Persico, *Roosevelt's Secret War*

Roosevelt, *Top Secret*

Eddy, *FDR Meets Ibn Saud*

Hymoff, *The OSS in World War II*

NOTES TO CHAPTER 5, SAUDI ARABIA, PART I

The story of Roosevelt's meeting with the King is told principally in the accounts of three participants: a brief narrative by Eddy, *F.D.R. Meets ibn Saud*; "Mission to Mecca: The Cruise of the *Murphy*," a magazine article by U.S. Navy Captain John S. Keating, commander of Destroyer Squadron 17, published in U.S. Naval Institute Proceedings, January 1976; and *White House Sailor*, a memoir by Wiliam M. Rigdon, who was Roosevelt's naval aide at the time. See the bibliography.

Crane letter to Roosevelt, online at http://charlesrcrane-edu. info/_wsn/page5.html.

Eddy's reports to the State Department, Roosevelt's April letter about Palestine and the text of the joint statement in FRUS 1945 VIII; other declassified documents of this period in FRUS, 1942, 1943, 1944. Roosevelt letter to Wagner, FRUS 1944, appendix 1. Other State Department records in NA, RG 59.

State Department briefing papers about the King for President Roosevelt in NA, RG 59, lot file 57, D298, box 15. Murray memo on Hafiz Wahba in RG 59, lot file 57D 298, Office of NEA 1941–54, box 10.

Roosevelt's correspondence with Moffett and other memos to and from the president relating to Saudi Arabia in Roosevelt Library, President's Secretary's file (PSF), box 50, diplomatic correspondence, and OF (official file), 3500.

State department memo on Eddy's assignment in EP 11/7; Eddy letter to Jack in EP 3/4; comments on Prince Mohammed in EP 4/1.

BBC report on British documents, broadcast Nov. 23, 2006, is at http://www.bbc.co.uk/radio4/today/listenagain/.

On James Moose, see Kaplan, *The Arabists*.

On King Abdul Aziz, see William A. Eddy, "Ibn Saud: Our Faith and Your Iron," Middle East Journal, Summer 1963, 257ff.

For details on Jeddah in the mid-1940s, see the letters of Clarence J. McIntosh, McIntosh Papers, as well as EP, especially box 11.

Other books cited in this chapter

Holden and Johns, *The House of Saud*

Philby, *Saudi Arabia*

Cave Brown, *Oil, God and Gold.*

Bohlen, *Witness to History*

Lacey, *The Kingdom*

Kaplan, *The Arabists*

Hart, *Saudi Arabia and the United States*

NOTES TO CHAPTER 6, SAUDI ARABIA, PART 2

Key documents documents on the airfield and financial aid negotiations are in FRUS 1945, VIII. For a fuller discussion of the Dhahran airfield matter, see James. L. Gormly, "Keeping the Door Open in Saudi Arabia: The United States and the Dhahran Airfield, 1945–46," Diplomatic History, vol. 4, no. 2 (Spring 1980), pp. 189ff. See also documents in Mulligan Papers, 7/23.

Other relevant documents are in NA, RG 59, General Records of the Department of State, Lot file 57 D 298. Nils Lind's paper is in box 10; other documents, including the State Department briefing paper describing the King and memos on Mary Eddy's illness, are in box 15, folders 2 and 3. Some of Eddy's diplomatic dispatches not printed in FRUS are on microfilm at the National Archives, File LM 168, document list 890F, roll 1.

On King Abdul Aziz, see William A. Eddy, "Ibn Saud: Our Faith and Your Iron," Middle East Journal, Summer 1963, 257ff.

Books cited in this chapter:

Grafftey-Smith, *Bright Levant*

Holden and Johns, *The House of Saud*

Hart, *Saudi Arabia and the United States*

Philby, *Saudi Arabia*

Eveland, *Ropes of Sand*

Lacey, *The Kingdom*

NOTES TO CHAPTER 7, YEMEN

The State Department memo on U.S. role in the region is in NA, RG 59, lot file 57d298, box 10. Other State Department documents in box 15 and in FRUS 1945 VIII.

Eddy's account of the Yemen expedition is in EP 10/10. His notes on Imam Yahya are in EP 16/8.

Books cited in this chapter:

Sanger, *The Arabian Peninsula*

Copeland, *The Game of Nations*

Halliday, *Arabia Without Sultans*

NOTES TO CHAPTER 8, WASHINGTON

The principal documents concerning the creation of the CIA are in a special volume of the FRUS series, 1945–1950, Emergence

of the Intelligence Establishment, online at http://www.state.gov/
www/about_state/history/intel/index.html.

See also the historical studies by CIA intelligence historian
Sherman Kent at https://www.cia.gov./csi/kent, and country files
in FRUS series for 1945 to 1948.

Eddy's JCS briefing in NA, RG 218, Chairman's file, Box 10,
folder 56.

Eddy's comments on UNSCOP report in EP 6/2.

State Department memorandum of conversation on Truman
meeting with envoys in FRUS 1945 VIII pp. 3ff.

For details on McCormick Plan vs. Russell Plan, see http://
www.state.gov/www/about_state/history/intel/intro2.html.

Eddy's memo to Henderson in NA, RG 59, lot file 57, box 15.

Books cited in this chapter:

Miller, *Plain Speaking*

Alsop and Braden, *Sub Rosa*

Hymoff, *The OSS in WW II*

Troy, *Donovan and the CIA*, originally an in-house
study classified secret, later declassified.

Acheson, *Present at the Creation*

Baram, *The Department of State in the Middle East*

Cohen, *Truman and Israel*

Kolsky, *Jews Against Zionism*

Wilson, *Decision on Palestine*

Eddy, *F.D.R. Meets Ibn Saud*

NOTES TO CHAPTER 9, BEIRUT

On Palestine, see Michael J. Cohen, "William A. Eddy, the Oil
Lobby and the Palestine Problem," Middle Eastern Studies, January 1, 1994; and Thomas W. Lippman, "The View From 1947: The
CIA and the Partition of Palestine," Middle East Journal, vol. 61
no. 1, Winter 2007.

Eddy's conversation with the King in EP 6/2; memo on the 1951 crisis in EP 6/4; comments on Jordan Valley Authority in EP 11/9; Eddy's 1951 "Empire of Israel" memo in Dodds papers 105/1; Eddy correspondence with publishers in EP 1/1/; Eddy account of visit to Majdeluna in EP 6/3; memo on Arabs as supervisors, Mulligan papers 7/l; "Moral Crusade" materials in EP 8/7 and 10/4.

Eddy's JCS briefing in NA, RG 218, Chairman's file, box 10, folder 56.

On the Onassis deal, see Cave Brown, *Oil, God and Gold*; Fraser et al,, *Aristotle Onassis*; Lacey, *Saudi Arabia*; Citino, *From Arab Nationalism to OPEC*; Norman Kempster, "How the CIA Helped Torpedo an Onassis-Saudi Oil Deal," Washington Star, Dec. 18, 1975; and extensive documentation in FRUS 1952-54, vol. IX.

On military operations in Lebanon, see Mark A. Olinger, "Airlift Operations During the Lebanon Crisis," Army Logistician, May 1, 2005, and Micah L. Sifry, "America, Oil and Intervention," The Nation, March 11, 1991. Post-landings intelligence report on Lebanon in FRUS 1945 IX, pp. 1671ff.

On Zaim coup, see Douglas Little, "Cold War and Covert Action: The United States and Syria, 1945–1958," Middle East Journal, vol. 44 no. 1, Winter 1990.

Books cited in this chapter:

Eveland, *Ropes of Sand*

Murphy, *Diplomat Among Warriors*

Copeland, *The Game of Nations*

Goldschmidt, *A Concise History*

Gendzier, *Notes From the Minefield*

Kolsky, *Jews Against Zionism*

Wilson, *Decision on Palestine*

Lamb, *The Arabs*

Seale, *The Struggle for Syria*

Kishtainy, *Arab Political Humor*

BIBLIOGRAPHY

The published literature concerning some events in the life of William A. Eddy is skimpy, but on others, such as the battle of Belleau Wood and the creation of the Central Intelligence Agency, it is voluminous. This bibliography includes only those works cited in the text and a few others from which I have drawn ideas and perspective.

—THOMAS W. LIPPMAN

Acheson, Dean. *Present at the Creation.* New York, Norton, 1969.

Adler, Frank J. *Roots in a Moving Stream: the Centennial History of Congregation B'nai Jehudah of Kansas City, 1870–1970.* Kansas City, Mo., The Temple, Congregation B'nai Jehudah, 1972.

Alsop, Stewart, and Thomas Braden. *Sub Rosa: The O.S.S. and American Espionage.* New York, Reynal and Hitchcock, 1946.

Antonius, George. *The Arab Awakening: The Story of the Arab National Movement.* New York, Putnam, 1946.

Asprey, Robert B. *At Belleau Wood.* New York, Putnam, 1965.

Atkinson, Rick. *An Army At Dawn. The War in North Africa, 1942–1943.* New York, Henry Holt, 2002.

Baram, Philip J. *The Department of State in the Middle East, 1919–1945.* Philadelphia, University of Pennsylvania Press, 1978.

Bohlen, Charles E. *Witness to History, 1929–1969.* New York, Norton, 1973.

Brown, Anthony Cave. *Oil, God, and Gold: The Story of Aramco and the Saudi Kings.* Boston, Houghton Mifflin, 1999.

Citino, Nathan J. *From Arab Nationalism to OPEC: Eisenhower, King Saud, and the Making of U.S.-Saudi Relations.* Bloomington, Indiana University Press, 2002.

Clark, George B. *Devil Dogs: Fighting Marines of World War I.* Novato, Ca., Presidio Press, 1999.

Cohen, Michael J. *Truman and Israel.* Berkeley, University of California Press, 1990.

Copeland, Miles. *The Game of Nations.* London, Weidenfeld and Nicolson, 1969.

Eddy, William A. *F.D.R. Meets Ibn Saud.* New York, American Friends of the Middle East, 1954.

Eveland, Wilbur Crane. *Ropes of Sand: America's Failure in the Middle East.* New York, Norton, 1980.

Farwell, Byron. *Over There: The United States in the Great War, 1917–1918.* New York, Norton, 1999.

Finnie, David H. *Pioneers East: The Early American Experience in the Middle East.* Cambridge, Mass., Harvard University Press, 1967.

Fraser, Nicholas, et al., *Aristotle Onassis.* New York, Ballantine, 1978.

Funk, Arthur L. *The Politics of TORCH: The Allied Landings and the Algiers Putsch, 1942.* Lawrence, University Press of Kansas, 1974.

Gendzier, Irene L. *Notes From the Minefield: United States Intervention in Lebanon and the Middle East, 1945–1958.* New York, Columbia University Press, 1997.

Goldschmidt, Arthur Jr. *A Concise History of the Middle East.* Boulder, Co., Westview Press, 1979.

Grafftey-Smith, Laurence. *Bright Levant.* London, John Murray, 1970.

Grose, Peter. "The President Versus the Diplomats," in *The End of the Palestine Mandate,* W. R. Louis and R. W. Stookey, eds., Austin, University of Texas Press, 1986.

Hahn, Peter. *Caught in the Middle East: U.S. Policy Toward the Arab-Israeli Conflict, 1945–1961.* Chapel Hill, University of North Carolina Press, 2004.

Halliday, Fred. *Arabia Without Sultans.* London, Penguin Books, 1975.

Hart, Parker T. *Saudi Arabia and the United States: Birth of a Security Partnership.* Bloomington, Indiana University Press, 1998.

Holden, David, and Richard Johns. *The House of Saud: The Rise and Rule of the Most Powerful Dynasty in the Arab World.* New York, Holt, Rinehart and Winston, 1981.

Hymoff, Edward. *The OSS in World War II.* New York, Ballantine, 1972.

Issawi, Charles. *An Economic History of the Middle East and North Africa.* New York, Columbia University Press, 1982.

Kaplan, Robert. *The Arabists: The Romance of an American Elite.* New York, Free Press, 1993.

Keegan, John. *The First World War.* New York, Knopf, 1999.

Kishtainy, Khalid. *Arab Political Humor.* London, Quartet Books, 1985.

Kolsky, Thomas A. *Jews Against Zionism: The American Council for Judaism, 1942–1948.* Philadelphia, Temple University Press, 1990.

Lamb, David. *The Arabs.* New York, Random House, 1987.

Lacey, Robert. *The Kingdom: Arabia and the House of Saud.* New York, Harcourt Brace Jovanovich, 1981.

Liddell Hart, B. H. *History of The First World War.* London, Pan Books, 1972.

Lippman, Thomas W. *Inside the Mirage: America's Fragile Partnership With Saudi Arabia.* Boulder, Co., Westview Press, 2004.

Mansfield, Peter. *The Arabs.* (rev. ed.) New York, Penguin Books, 1985.

Mead, Gary. *The Doughboys: America and the First World War.* Woodstock, N.Y., Overlook Press, 2000.

Miller, Col. John G. "Belleau Wood, The Legend, the Reality and the Myth," in *Twentieth Century Marines: Three Touchstone Battles.* Quantico, Va., Marine Corps Association, 1997.

Miller, Merle. *Plain Speaking.* New York, Berkely, 1973.

Murphy, Robert. *Diplomat Among Warriors.* Garden City, N.Y., Doubleday, 1964.

Persico, Joseph E. *Roosevelt's Secret War: FDR and World War II Espionage.* New York, Random House, 2001.

Philby, H. St. John. *Saudi Arabia.* Beirut, Librairie du Liban, 1955.

Pierce, Philip N., and Frank O. Hough. *The Compact History of the United States Marine Corps.* New York, Hawthorn Books, 1960.

Rigdon, William M. *White House Sailor.* Garden City, N.Y., Doubleday, 1962.

Roosevelt, Kermit (ed.). *Top Secret: War Report of the OSS.* New York, Walker, 1976.

Sanger, Richard H. *The Arabian Peninsula.* Ithaca, N.Y., Cornell University Press, 1954.

Seale, Patrick. *The Struggle for Syria.* New Haven, Yale University Press, 1987 (2d. ed.).

Smith, R. Harris. *OSS: The Secret History of America's First Central Intelligence Agency.* Berkeley, University of California Press, 1972.

Strachan, Hew. *The First World War.* New York, Viking, 2004.

Troy, Thomas F. *Donovan and the CIA.* Frederick, Md., University Publications of America, 1981.

Truman, Margaret. *Harry S. Truman.* New York, William Morrow, 1973.

Wilson, Evan M. *Decision on Palestine: How the U.S. Came to Recognize Israel.* Stanford, Ca., Hoover Institution Press, 1979.

INDEX

Hamadan
Kom
Tekrit
Samarra
Khanaqin
Kermanshah
Kizil Ribat
Baquba
Hit
Qubaisa
Ramadi
BAGHDAD
Kashan
Karbala
Hillah
Babylon
Tigris
Isfahan
Dizful
MESOPOTAMIA
Nejef or Meshed Ali
Al Diwaniya
Samave
Lamlum
Jubeilen
Daffas
Shushtar
Yezd
(Stony Plain)
An Nasiriya
Al Qurna
Souk esh Shuyukh
Qasr Uthaimin
Sobeir
Basra
Mohammerah
Bandar-i-Shahpur
Dahman
BUBIAN I.
FELEJE I.
KARAGH I.
Kuwait
Bushire
Shiraz
Niris
Sabukah
KUWAIT
Firuzabad
Lar
JEBEL
KINGDOM
Jobbah
Hail
Kefar
SHAMMAR
Kefd
Zulfah
Mejmah
Maghris
BU ALI I.
Lingeh
Kowarah
Rass
Eyoon
OF
Aneizeh
Shakra
Hoolah
Sedus
Qatif
Manama
BAHREIN
Ras Tannurah
Ras Reccan
Wab
Meborraa
Hofuf
Doha
Bedaa
PERSIAN GULF
Medain Salih
Al-Ala
Surah
Khaibar
Sadiwa
MEDINA
Ghurab
Ghomeis
Shaarka
Riyadh
Dhalum
Shaabar
Manfunah
Naam
Hauta
Hajar
EAST INDIA COMPANY IS.
Abu Debi
Katan
SAUDI
Bedr Honem
Kerah
Sarsa
Kurfah
TRUCIAL
Suwerikiya
Tropic of Cancer
Dhool
Hatifa
Ozal
Kobo
Merkab
Amru
Laila
Kholeis
ARABIA
Hararah
Zaimeh
MECCA
Taif
Tarabah
Leileh
Farah
Mekhra
Raneih
Kaina
Meteleh
RUB' AL KHALI
(Great Sandy Desert)
Doga
Roheita
Tenunha
Qunfuda
Bel Asman
Halli
Debaba
Selayel
Ibl
Letan
Tabab
Derb Solman
Wakasha
Thoran
Sanian
Boghasen
Beled Barath
Dizan
Abu Arish
Saadeh
Kaiwan
Majil
FARASAN IS.
Morbat
Risut
Damqut
Kamar Bay
Sawa
Shibam
Tarim
Jaizer
Loheia
Khamir
Amran
Mareb
Marcha
Haura
Ras Furtak
Kishin
KAMARAN I. (Brit.)
San'a
YEMEN
Nissab
Reida
Saihut
Hodeida
Doran
Surajeh
Biedah
Hotah
Shihair
Misenat
Shuram
Dhamar
Beit el Fakih
Yerim
Habban
Hajar
Mukalla
HANISH IS.
Zebid
Reda
British Protectorate
Edd
Hais
Ibb
Haura
Mocha (Mokha)
Taeiz
Raha
Sheikh Hurba
Shukra
Sherm Magatim
GULF OF ADEN
Tamridah
PERIM I. (Brit.)
Bab el Mandeb
Birgheg
ADEN
ABD EL KURI
SOCOTRA (British)
FRENCH
Djibouti
SOMALI LAND
Zeilah
C. Guardaful
Las Guri
Meid
ITALIAN
ERITREA

Sarifa
Istabilat
Euphrates R.
Diala
Kizil Ribat
Hit
Baquba
Qubaisa
BAGHDAD
Ramadi
I R A Q
Karbala
Ruins of Babylon
Hillah
Kut al Imara
Tigris
(M E S O P O T A M I A)
Ezrak
Mukur
Nejef or Meshed Ali
EL HAMED
Al Diwaniya
Lamlum
(Stony Plain)
Samave
Jubeilen
Amara
Jadidat 'Ar'ar
Al Qurna
An Nasiriya
Souk esh Shuyukh
Bir al Mane'iyah
Qasr Uthaimin
Hedschasiya
Birkat al Jumaimah
Jauf
Bir Ansab
Hadsh
JEBEL
K I N G D O M
Jobbah
G R
Hail
Kefar
Lazafah
Taima
SHAMMAR
Medain Salih
Kefd
Zulfah
Al-Ala
Kowarah
Mejmah
Rass
Eyoon
El Tueim
Surah
O F
Aneizeh
Khaibar
Shakra
Hoolah
Sadiwa
Abar Othman
Sedus
MEDINA
Kabur
Ghurab
Ghomeis
Shaarka
Deroyeoyah
Riyadh
Wadan
Manfunah
S A U D I
Bedr Honem
Kerah
Sarsa
Kurfah
Suwerikiya
Tropic of Cancer
Dhool
Hatifa
Kobo
Rabagh
Ozal
Merkab
Amru
Kholeis
Hararah
A R A B I A
Soloomeh L.
Zaimeh
Leileh
MECCA
Taif
Tarabah
Warada L.
Engala
Farah
Mekhra
Raneib
Meteleh